Myths of the Plantation Society

Slavery in the American South and the West Indies

Nathalie Dessens

University Press of Florida
Gainesville · Tallahassee · Tampa · Boca Raton
Pensacola · Orlando · Miami · Jacksonville · Ft. Myers

08 07 06 05 04 03   6 5 4 3 2 1

Library of Congress Cataloging-in-Publication Data
Dessens, Nathalie, 1963-
Myths of the plantation society: slavery in the American South
and the West Indies / Nathalie Dessens.
p. cm.
Includes bibliographical references and index.
ISBN 0-8130-2682-2 (acid-free paper)
1. Slavery—Southern States—History. 2. Slaves—Southern States—
Social conditions. 3. African Americans—Southern States—Social conditions.
4. Plantation life—Southern States—History. 5. Southern States—Race
relations. 6. Slavery—West Indies—History. 7. Slaves—West Indies—Social
conditions. 8. Blacks—West Indies—Social conditions. 9. Plantation life—
West Indies—History. 10. West Indies—Race relations. I. Title.
E441.D43 2004
306.3'62'09729—dc22   2003057913

The University Press of Florida is the scholarly publishing agency
for the State University System of Florida, comprising Florida A&M
University, Florida Atlantic University, Florida Gulf Coast University,
Florida International University, Florida State University, University
of Central Florida, University of Florida, University of North Florida,
University of South Florida, and University of West Florida.

University Press of Florida
15 Northwest 15th Street
Gainesville, FL 32611-2079
http://www.upf.com

This book is dedicated to Marcienne Rocard, Professor Emeritus at the University of Toulouse, who led my first tentative steps along the path of research; to my family, who has supported me ever since I started exploring the field of American history; to Jim Bolner, Marvin Holdt, Sheryl Rahal, and Bertrand Van Ruymbeke, who spent long hours revising the manuscript; to Patrick for his love, computer technical help, and unswerving support throughout the long writing process.

Contents

Illustrations

Preface

The work presented here is the result of over ten years of research, and its genesis requires a few comments. My interest in slave societies dates back to 1986, when I set out to choose the topic of my Ph.D. dissertation. At the time, my focus was limited to the American South, and more precisely to the development of Southern ideology in the antebellum decades, as well as to the role of Southern novelists in this all-inclusive movement.

In 1992, my first position as an assistant professor led me to the University of the Antilles-Guyane and to the tropical skies of Martinique in the French West Indies. This was my first contact with a society of the Western Hemisphere originating in the French colonial past (I was not yet acquainted with Louisiana then). It shared with the American South a common history, being born from a slave society that ultimately suppressed the institution of slavery in the nineteenth century. Many features reminded me of the South; many others were blatantly different from those of the region that I had been studying for several years, and which had so attracted me by its charms and mysteries. Thus began my interest in the history of Martinique, and of the Caribbean in general. I started compiling historical material on the West Indies. The more I traveled in the Caribbean, the more obvious it became that there was much matter for research. The more I read about the history of the islands, the more I was sure that a comprehensive comparative study of the two regions was called for.

At the time, the work was already beginning to take shape in my mind, but the structure eluded me. My project would seem empty if it remained a mere comparison, so to speak for comparison's sake, but without an original approach. I thus went on working on the project, trying to absorb everything I found on the topic but not yet ready to write. In parallel, I pursued my research on the South, and more specifically on the mythologizing of the South after the defeat of the Confederacy in the Civil War. I knew precisely where the legend of a Southern Golden Age had originated—in the works of Simms, Kennedy, Tucker, and Caruthers—before the war. I went on studying the myth in late-nineteenth- and twentieth-century literature. At the time, all my publications bore upon this topic.

I started wondering if there was a similar trend in the West Indies. My incursions into Caribbean literature seemed to show that there was none, or at least that, if there was a mythologizing of the Caribbean societies, it took an altogether different form. Suddenly, the core of the comparison I had been seeking for so long materialized: why was there a Southern myth but no West Indian myth? This is how this work was born in its present form. The rest is but the story of an unplanned encounter with Meredith Morris-Babb (and thus the University Press of Florida) at the annual meeting of the Gulf Coast Historical Association at Pensacola in 1997. I thank her with all my heart for offering me the opportunity for such an enriching experience, and hope the result will be worthy of her trust and enthusiasm. My deep gratitude also goes to the anonymous readers who guided me with their constructive criticism and numerous precise suggestions that helped me improve my initial manuscript.

Introduction

For over a hundred years, historiography has dealt with the American South, its history, its ideology, and its myths. However, very few attempts have been made at examining the origins of the distinctive cultural features of this regional entity or at determining the various stages of the construction of a Southern identity. What makes this question still more fascinating is the absence of similar evolution in other plantation societies of the Western Hemisphere. A comparative study of the American South and other contemporaneous civilizations of the Americas might be very useful to highlight the existence of a Southern distinctiveness, as well as to account for its emergence.

Comparative history is a relatively complex approach, presenting numerous methodological difficulties due to abundant bibliographical material and to problems inherent in comparison itself: richness of the material compared, questions of comparability, and difficulty in organizing the conclusions of the comparison. It is, however, particularly revealing through the study of common features and divergences. Comparative history might indeed offer rich insights into different societies, especially if they have evolved concurrently through time, while ultimately displaying divergent social patterns. A monographic study of a given civilization may lead to erroneous or exaggerated conclusions. The comparative perspective, by highlighting conformity with the rule, might mitigate this risk. Concomitantly, it may evidence specific features and thus enable firmer conclusions.[1] The research presented here originates in the fact that while the European colonies of the Americas indeed experienced similar background conditions of creation and common phases of history, they nonetheless evolved differently—historically speaking—and gave birth to extremely diversified social patterns.

The societies considered in this research are those of the West Indies and of the American South, from their foundation (in the sixteenth and seventeenth centuries) to the abolition of slavery (between the 1830s for the British possessions and the 1880s for the Spanish colony of Cuba), although the consequences of abolition will also be shortly examined. Several reasons explain the choice of the geographical limitation of the present study, among which historical reasons predominate. All these societies directly or indirectly originated from Columbus' "discovery" of the continent in 1492. After a relatively slow early process of colonization, the settlement of the American continent (and of the islands of the Caribbean) accelerated in the seventeenth century. This settlement was the result of expansionist colonial policies of various European nations. The colonies thus experienced influxes of similar populations motivated by similar feelings: the spirit of adventure, the wish to expand the nation's wealth, a search for opportunities and riches. It is thus not surprising that similar colonial societies emerged from this European migration.

The decision to consider only the West Indies and the American South springs from the parallel evolutions of these colonial societies between the seventeenth and nineteenth centuries. The northern American colonies were excluded from the study because they relied on very different social and economic principles (at least from the eighteenth century onwards). Because of the climate and nature of the soils, they never relied on extensive agriculture and plantation organization. They very early opted for an economic organization that relied much more on a nascent manufacturing development and the birth of a market economy. Their need for manpower was thus diminished, all the more so since they benefited from a constant migratory influx from Europe. Although slavery legally existed for over a century in the Northern colonies, the latter remained "societies with slaves" until the emancipation movement of the late eighteenth century and never became "slave societies."[2]

The Southern colonies, on the contrary, like those of the West Indies, experienced a different expansion. It would have been legitimate to include the colonial societies of Latin America in the comparison. However, they will not be considered here, because such inclusion would so diversify the study as to make it barely manageable. Moreover, except for the Guyana settlements, the Latin American societies depended exclusively on Spain and Portugal and thus offer a much more restricted diversity.

The colonies of the American South and of the West Indies thus present many similarities and can be easily contrasted with the development of the northern American colonies. Their climate and soils favored the development of specific plantation societies. Relying almost exclusively on the cultivation of certain crops (despite many regional differences, the main products were cocoa, coffee, tobacco, cotton, indigo, and sugar), they gave birth to agricultural societies with little manufacturing activity. They soon relied almost exclusively on the exportation of their agricultural products and importation of most of their consumer goods.

Another common trait has to do with manpower. These agricultural economies obviously required extensive manpower. The Southern colonies, as well as those of the Antilles, experienced a permanent labor shortage. Immigration was much less developed there than in the Northern colonies, which made them rely first on the system of indentured servitude. When indentured servants were no longer sufficient, they all readily adopted the system of slavery, which subsequently underwent unprecedented development. The importation of slaves from Africa steadily developed in the late seventeenth and eighteenth centuries, inducing a progressive institutionalization of the practice, the enactment of rules, and the organization of a repressive system. Concomitantly, the Northern colonies abandoned this system, rendered useless by their divergent social and economic options. To conclude this overview of the obvious similarities between the West Indies and the South, all these societies witnessed the emergence of a debate on the legitimacy of the institution of slavery before experiencing its disappearance in the nineteenth century.

This short presentation of the various slave societies in itself legitimizes the interest of a comparison. The progressive appearance of differences between these societies is another justification. As time went by, specific features started coming to the fore in the slave societies. Some had to do with the mother country: the Catholicism of France and Spain, for instance, differentiated the two nations' American colonies from the Protestant possessions of England. Other differences emerged from the varying status of the territories: with the birth of the United States, its independence from the mother country and the development of a democratic process, the South started diverging from the colonies which still depended on the European monarchies. The troubles occasioned in the French Antilles by the revolution of the late eighteenth century also had tremendous impacts on those territories. Moreover, there were differences unrelated to the mother countries, which derived from the opposition between mainland and islands. The English colonies of the South differed in their organization from the English Caribbean colonies, as did French Louisiana from the French West Indies, or Florida from Cuba or Puerto Rico.

These similarities and differences justify a comparison between these societies, all the more so since there are few comparative works in the field. The history and civilization of the South have been extensively studied as the bibliography on the topic proves. The Caribbean has also been the subject of many studies by American, British, French, Spanish, and West Indian historians. Although the point is certainly not to synthesize these works, it is indispensable to rely on them to organize a global comparative study. Indeed the material is so profuse that it is impossible to rely solely on primary sources. To reach satisfactory conclusions, it is indispensable to borrow from the existing literature.

In the past decades, historians have directed their attention to comparative works, dealing with two societies or certain specific aspects of several societies.[3] Recently, broader works have been published, although they tend to focus on one society with comparative references to others.[4] A wider reflection may thus bring new insight into the field, legitimizing the project of studying the English, French and Spanish possessions of the South and of the Caribbean under various historical, social, economic, and cultural aspects.

The work of a comparative historian, however, requires a number of methodological reflections. The first task is to give a precise spatial and temporal definition of the research area. In the present work, the Continental possessions of the European powers in Latin America have been excluded, as has the American North. The emphasis is thus on the Spanish, English, and French possessions south of the Mason-Dixon Line and in the Caribbean. The Danish and Dutch colonies of the West Indies are mentioned, although more anecdotally, because of their relatively reduced number and size. Concerning the time frame, the period extending from the foundation of the colonies to the aftermath of the disappearance of slavery is the main focus. As for the question of comparability, all the colonies display sufficient similarities to legitimize the comparison, despite the diverse nationalities represented. At first sight, it may seem risky to compare Spanish islands with English mainland colonies, yet neither the South nor the West Indies were monolithic at the time. Both were shared among the major European powers, and in both regions, the nationalities of the colonies shifted, due to the expansionist race between the mother countries.

The main difficulty remains the demarcation between "constructive generalization" and abusive homogenization leading to incomplete or even erroneous conclusions. Throughout the comparison, it is essential to constantly delineate general features, while remaining attentive to minor

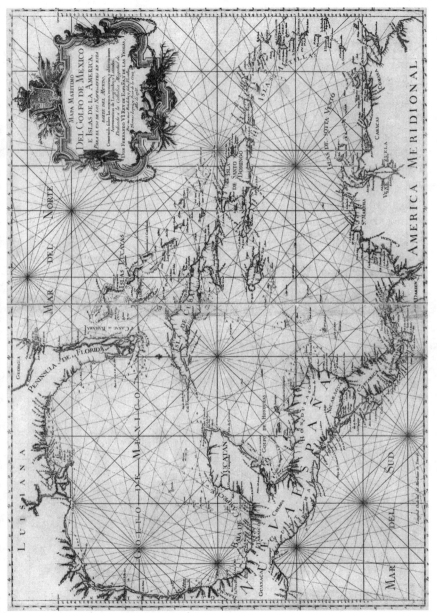

Map 1. Mapa maritimo del Golfo de Mexico e islas de la America. Map of the whole Caribbean Basin, including the American South, the West Indies, and part of Latin America. LC Maps of North America, 1750–1789, 1685. Library of Congress Geography and Map Division. 1755.

variations. The weakness and strength of comparative techniques lie in that constant navigation between the contradictory processes of unification and diversification. From this apparent dichotomy, however, springs the creativity of the comparative approach.

Finally, it is essential to define sources: extant comparative studies are of course used, as are many secondary works. A number of primary sources are also considered, since relying on direct testimonies is of key importance. Diaries and slave narratives are examined, although with the necessary caution required by any piece of writing that might be either biased or heavily romanticized. A last category of primary material has to be mentioned here, one of especially great interest: travel narratives. Travel literature was a very fashionable genre in the eighteenth and nineteenth centuries and is of great significance for comparison's sake. Indeed, sources include narratives written by American colonists visiting other colonies of the Western Hemisphere, thus drawing the attention of the reader to the differences among societies. They also include a wide variety of narratives written by Europeans visiting the American colonies, thus bringing to the fore a different vision of these societies and sometimes including comparison of the different colonies visited. Considering the specificity of the genre, the same caution as that mentioned for other personal narratives applies here. Even though most of these narratives are partly (or even largely) biased, the comparative technique helps steer clear of a naive reading of them as expressions of historical truth.

Now that the frame of the study is set and the interest and legitimacy of the comparison highlighted, the approach remains to be defined. The idea of the comparison sprang from many years spent studying the Southern myth in literature and popular culture. In its most basic form, which might be called "triumphant," this mythologizing trend turned the era of slavery into a Golden Age, lost to a North both mercantile and deprived of any ethical value.[5] In its elaborate avatars, it turned the South into a geography of the mind, based on a very complex reaction of both empathy and rejection on the part of the novelists toward its peculiar characteristics.[6] Whatever its form, the South's mythic origins may be traced back to the whole antebellum debate on slavery, North versus South, and the necessity to protect this "Peculiar Institution" as well as the society built on it. Southern fiction writers took part in the debate, bringing their voices to the defense of their threatened region.[7] From the first historical and plantation novels, written to the glory of Southern civilization, the legend of the Old South was born. The outcome of the Civil War, with the demise of the ancient order and subsequent feeling of a lost cause, marked the birth of the mythmaking trend. From the late nineteenth century to the present, the myth of the South, in its various manifestations, has pervaded literature—that of the South, first, but also contemporary world literature—to become a protean myth of the collective unconscious, both everlasting and international.

While the Southern myth developed and expanded, no parallel mythologizing of West Indian societies existed. The plantation societies were debunked rather than glorified. This Southern cultural distinctiveness leads the historian to contemplate the differences that may have triggered its development and to examine closely the various civilizations concerned to try to understand why the slave societies of the Americas ultimately evolved so differently.

The present comparison is not a mere thematic juxtaposition; it is aimed at determining the origin of Southern cultural difference. It relies on the similarities between the various societies, but mostly dwells on the differences that account for later cultural evolution. Because the comparison here is made not for comparison's sake but in the interest of the very specific question of Southern cultural distinctiveness, certain elements have been purposefully ignored.

Before examining the slave societies themselves, it is appropriate to devote a first chapter to the settlement of the American colonies, both in the Caribbean and in the American South. The social and economic organization of the plantation system and of the slave societies at large will be studied in chapter two, before moving on in chapter three to an examination of the institution of slavery, its codification and daily organization. The next chapter will be devoted to the development and various manifestations of conflicting ideologies: abolitionist attacks and pro-slavery responses will be examined here, before the different abolition processes themselves are addressed in chapter five. This will lead to discussion of the aftermath of these processes and subsequent development of the Southern myth and its manifestations in chapter six, eventually inscribing the cultural distinctiveness of the American South in history.

"Discovery" and Settlement

The discovery and early settlement of the American continent by European nations has been the subject of many accounts. It is important, however, to recall them here in a comparative perspective, to highlight the similarities of the migration, but also the first differences that began to appear between the colonies of the Caribbean and those of the American South.

Common Early Developmental Stages

The first obvious common feature among all the colonies of the Americas is their founding by the Western European nations which, in the sixteenth and seventeenth centuries, had clear expansionist drives. Be it the Caribbean islands or the American continent (both north and south), all the settlements of the Americas had the same origins: Christopher Columbus' "discovery." All of them had the same reasons for emerging: the European wish to expand. Despite their being established at different times, they can all be inscribed within the same movement.

All the European nations that became involved in the colonization movement had similar reasons for doing so. The initial reason was the commercial necessity of finding a quicker and safer route to the Indies that led Christopher Columbus to set foot in America. The process is, however, much more complex.

The fifth centennial of the discovery prompted a large production of research by historians, especially in the West Indies. They interpreted the first colonizing impulse along several lines. For many historians, the reasons for the expansion must be traced to a wide-ranging movement that spread throughout Europe in the fifteenth century: the Renaissance.[1] It can be contended that Europe contained about seventy million inhabitants, who, at the time, were better fed than any population ever, who had managed to become immunized against the main pandemics, and had been stimulated both materially and spiritually.[2] The Renaissance also spurred changes in the political concept of the state, considered, from then on, in its Machiavellian sense, as a sovereign body politic ruled by a government exerting definite power over the people. With the political evolution that curtailed previous centuries' bipolar struggle between empire and papacy, nations emerged, and this emergence induced rivalries and a struggle for power. The Renaissance gave the European nations a certain optimism, boosted by scientific progress and combining passion with curiosity. It also gave them a definite practical spirit, granting preponderance to the individual. There was a clear creative dynamism, based on the sense of risk and a spirit of adventure.[3]

Moreover, the main Christian nations were intent on preserving Christianity and protecting themselves from the expansion of Islam. Spain and Portugal, the two nations that came first in the expansionist surge, were, by the end of the fifteenth century, accustomed to both conquest and evangelization. The presence of Muslims on the Iberian Peninsula and the constant struggle either to be rid of or convert them to Christianity had given the two Iberian nations a thirst for conquest and a real missionary spirit. The best proof of this is that the Spanish crown's acceptance of Columbus' proposal corresponded to the last stages of Muslim resistance on the Peninsula and to the end of the *Reconquista* with the fall of Granada. It is this twofold movement—the confluence of the thirst for conquest and the desire to work for the expansion of Christianity—that led these nations to sea, first to the coasts of Africa, then beyond the Ocean.

Among the push factors, the economic and commercial one traditionally set forth should not be neglected. The European nations indeed needed "exotic" products—spices, medicinal plants, perfumes, silk, indigo, sugar, and cod. They were also actively seeking gold and precious stones. This was the starting point of expansionist dynamism, fueled by acknowledgement of the many opportunities the Mediterranean basin had already offered. The necessity of finding an easier and safer route to the Indies was also important. The land route was not convenient: it was risky and allowed only the transportation of small quantities. Moreover, the Venetian merchants had a monopoly on trade with the Indies, and the Turks levied heavy duties and import taxes on everything that crossed their territory. A sea route definitely had to be found.

In short, the motives were manifold: economic, religious, and political.

They were the result of a real competition among European peoples, but also of a thirst for adventure. They were also favored by a number of inventions and by technical progress, including the discovery of the astrolabe, as well as techniques aimed at computing latitude and longitude. Astronomy made several steps forward in the fifteenth century. Several devices were perfected, making navigation more accurate, while progress was made in the construction of boats. In the thirteenth century, the invention of the sternpost rudder, as well as the habit of mixing square and triangular sails, had made sailing easier. The invention of the caravel by the Portuguese around 1440 was also a great step forward. Sailing became more precise, less risky, and cheaper.[4] Everything was then ready to lead Europeans to the American continent. They had both motives and means.

While the Portuguese were asserting their supremacy over Africa, diplomatic negotiations granted Spain a complete virtual exclusivity over the Americas. In 1493, Pope Alexander VI issued the *Inter Caetera*, giving the Spaniards the right to sail beyond a line situated a hundred leagues west of the Cape Verde Islands. This bull was subsequently confirmed by the Treaty of Tordesillas, signed by Portugal and Spain in 1494, which moved that line 270 leagues to the west to the advantage of Portugal, but maintained Spain's potential domination over the Western Hemisphere.

Columbus assured this domination in four expeditions. Although he was by no means the first European to reach the American continent (the Vikings had done so around 1000 A.D., as well as, probably, the Polynesians), he is considered the "discoverer," because his arrival there was followed by conquest and colonization within a deliberately expansionist policy on a worldwide scale.

In these four expeditions, Columbus explored most of the Caribbean islands, from the Bahamas in 1492 to Trinidad in 1498. The last expedition took him to the mainland, more precisely to Nicaragua, Costa Rica, and Panama. In a decade, European colonization in the Americas had started, although remaining clear of the Northern Hemisphere.

Although explorers other than Columbus first set foot on the North American continent, he is nonetheless considered the forerunner of its colonization. One of the reasons for this attribution is that the discovery of the continent in general dates back to his 1503 expedition, when he reached only its southern part. Moreover, the first settlement in North America originated in the Spanish colonization of the Caribbean, since Juan Ponce de Leon, the governor of Puerto Rico, explored Florida in 1513. Moreover, Lucas Vasquez de Ayllon left Hispaniola and discovered Chicora, situated in present-day South Carolina, which he attempted to colonize. Similarly, in 1528, Panfilo de Narvaez landed on the Florida coast and explored the inland, as well as the whole Gulf Coast and part of the future Texas. The accounts of that exploration led Hernando de Soto to leave the Florida coast with six hundred men and to explore, for four years, part of what was to become Florida, Georgia, the Carolinas, Alabama, Mississippi, Arkansas, Oklahoma, and Texas. Finally, Spaniards came from the Caribbean settlements to launch Florida ones and in 1565 founded the oldest town on the North American continent, St. Augustine, before settling forts and missions as far north as Georgia and the Carolinas.

The early Spanish colonization of the Americas (although it was more limited on the northern continent) thus originated from Columbus' discovery of this new hemisphere. The background conditions experienced by the European nations at that time spurred their desire for exploration but also for conquest, which accounts for the fact that Columbus' discovery was followed by settlement.

Spanish settlement first spread in the northern Caribbean: Hispaniola in the late 1490's, then Puerto Rico in 1505, Cuba in 1508, Jamaica in 1509, then the South American continent. Although colonization first experienced some difficulty (strong Indian resistance, material hardships, a painful climate little adapted to traditional agriculture), it went on steadily through the enslavement of the natives and progressive destruction of their civilization. Supposedly aimed at insuring their survival and instructing them in the Catholic faith in exchange for their work, the system of *repartimientos* was replaced in 1503 by that of *encomienda*, which consisted in a division among the colonial settlers of arable land as well as of the Indians as a work force.

The rapid expansion of the colonies was marked by the development of urban units by a mostly Castilian population of volunteers under exceptional conditions meant to be incentives to the colonization experiment.[5] Colonization was made possible by constant recourse to bonded labor, first the subjugated Indian populations, then, as their number decreased, imported slaves, first from the Iberian Peninsula, then directly from Africa. Although the search for gold had been the first motive for colonization, for lack of a real profusion of gold, the Spaniards rapidly turned to agriculture. They succeeded in growing rice, date palms, oranges, and olives, but also spices, such as pepper and cinnamon, and then cotton, and, of course, sugar cane. The sugar industry developed, and by 1546 the number of mills reached twenty-four in Hispaniola, about ten in Puerto Rico, and around

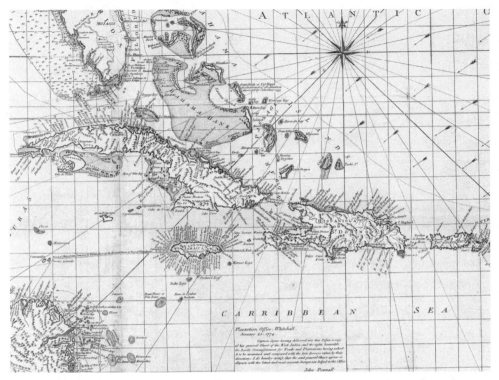

Map 2. Map of the Greater Antilles. Containing Cuba, Jamaica, Hispaniola, and Puerto Rico. Extracted from the chart inscribed by Thomas Bowen "To His Royal Highness. Georges Augustus Frederick. Prince of Wales." LC Maps of North America, 1750–1789, 1699. Library of Congress Geography and Map Division. 1774.

fifteen in Cuba.[6] The Spaniards imported cattle, goats, horses, and hogs, which quickly multiplied.[7]

The West Indian colonial expansion slowed down, however, and stopped altogether after 1550. After a brief period of prosperity in Hispaniola due to the development of the sugar industry between 1519 and 1530, and after a period of settlement expansion in the West Indies, the Spaniards turned toward other sources of interest. There were almost no Indians left; the only possibilities offered by the islands were agriculture and cattle raising; and gold had still not been found in large quantities. It was assumed that the precious metal was to be found elsewhere. The *Conquistadores* decided to go further and set off for the South American continent. By the mid-sixteenth century, the Spanish colonists had turned to horizons other than the West Indies, looking elsewhere for *Eldorado* and leaving behind them sparsely populated islands no longer of interest to the Spanish crown.

The same quest for gold led the *Conquistadores* to Florida, the Carolinas, Texas, and the Gulf Coast. Although settlement occurred later than in the Caribbean and was much slower and much more limited, it followed the same pattern as in the West Indies with the founding of urban centers, such as St. Augustine. If in the Caribbean colonization boomed before the Spaniards moved further west to the mainland, in Florida it remained sparse and never spread either north or west, at least not in the beginning. The result, however, was that in both cases, although for different reasons, Spanish colonization left room for other European nations to become involved in the colonization experience.

The sixteenth century marked the end of exclusive Spanish domination: settlement was decreasing in the Upper Antilles; had never started in the Lesser Antilles; and stagnated on the northern continent. The first non-Spanish European expansionist drive was diplomatic: François I contested *Inter Caetera* as well as the 1494 Treaty of Tordesillas. His position thus legitimated the competition that was later made easier by the progressive weakening of Spain. In the sixteenth century, Spain was entangled in many wars, and its three challengers—France, England, and Holland—entered the race. Warfare became still more widespread in seventeenth-century Europe; with the Thirty Years' War from 1618 on, the war against the United Provinces after 1621, and the war against France in 1635, Spain's three main contestants became bolder. Added to the weakening of their common adversary, many reasons drove other Europeans into the contest: religious dissent in England, poverty and population increase in France, desire to found commercial bases in Holland. Non-Spanish colonization of the Americas was ready to start.

Throughout the Caribbean and whatever the nationality of the challenger, the principle was the same: in the sixteenth century, corsairs (officially commissioned by European governments) and freebooters (freelance adventurers) carried out the challenge to Spanish domination. In a second stage, these adventurers started launching attacks against Spanish settlements. (The French, for instance, attacked Hispaniola and Puerto Rico in 1554 and took Havana in 1555; the English, under the lead of the famous corsair Sir Francis Drake, attacked Hispaniola and St. Augustine in 1585). While the sixteenth century was marked by isolated attacks without any real progress on the part of Spain's competitors, the seventeenth century was more favorable to the challengers, inaugurating non-Spanish colonization and witnessing the progressive settlement of non-Spanish European nations in the West Indies. Following a decrease in Spanish resistance and fueled by a stronger desire for competition, other Europeans launched a real policy of colonization and settlement.

Progressively, the corsairs and freebooters started settling on the unoccupied islands to repair or career their ships, store their booty, and find food. This is how non-Spanish colonization really started, with former sea rovers become hunters (the buccaneers). The first European challengers to Spanish colonization of the West Indies were thus mere adventurers, hunters or sailors, either freelance or by official appointment of their governments.

The prevailing principle was that whenever seamen of a given nationality settled on an island, it was afterwards thought to belong to the nation from which they came. The settlement of the islands was progressive, and throughout the seventeenth century almost all the islands of the Caribbean were thus colonized by European nations. England colonized St. Christopher (now St. Kitts) in 1624, then Nevis, Antigua, and Montserrat. They took Barbados in 1625 and seized Jamaica in 1655.

Meanwhile, the French started to settle St. Christopher in 1624 (a joint occupancy was agreed upon by the English and French corsairs, Warner and Belain d'Esnambuc), and around 1635, they settled Guadeloupe and Martinique, followed by Grenada, St. Lucia, St. Bartholomé (now St. Barthélemy), St. Martin, and Tortuga, a tiny island off the northern coast of Hispaniola. From there, France colonized the western part of Hispaniola (now Haiti), which had been vacated by the Spaniards. The island became the realm of buccaneers who hunted the cattle and herds of pigs run wild after the departure of the Spaniards. They sold smoked meat and skins to the Dutch in exchange for guns, gunpowder, clothes, canvass, and other supplies from Europe and provided the corsairs and freebooters with food. Adventurers turned to buccaneering and thus became sedentary. They started employing indentured servants (generally under three-year contracts), because the Amerindians who had survived the slaughters were not sufficient and because the African slaves used by the Spaniards were much too expensive.[8] The colonization was officially acknowledged by Spain in the Treaty of Ryswick in 1697, and the French part of Hispaniola became St. Domingue.

At the same time, Holland, freed from Spanish tutelage, also entered into the West Indian colonizing race. The Dutch traded from island to island and soon dominated trade (by 1650, out of the 25,000 vessels trading in the Caribbean, 15,000 were Dutch).[9] They also created the Dutch West India Company, in search of a stable form of colonization. They set foot on St. Eustatius as early as 1600, settled in Guyana around 1621, then Curaçao, Aruba, Bonaire, and Tobago. In 1648, they shared St. Martin with France (St. Marteen), a joint possession that has lasted to this day.

In the meantime, Spain's European contestants had started colonizing the northern continent. The French were first; between 1524 and 1535, they explored the northern coast and founded Quebec; between 1562 and 1565, they also unsuccessfully attempted to challenge the Spanish claims to Florida. The second half of the sixteenth century was also the period of English exploration and attempted settlement of the northern continent as the various failed attempts at colonizing Roanoke Island prove.

The Dutch left their imprint on the territory as well, in 1624 founding New Netherlands, which they later exchanged with England for Surinam. Two failed attempts at North American colonization also deserve mention here: the Swedes' attempt to found New Sweden in 1638 and the Danes' attempt to found New Denmark soon thereafter. In fact, the first really successful North American colonization experiment was that of Virginia in 1607 at Jamestown. English colonization spread from there, while the French were also leaving their imprint on the South, more precisely on the Mississippi region, in a relatively similar way, although later. In 1682, Robert Cavelier de la Salle sailed down the Mississippi River from Canada, claimed the territory he had crossed for France, and called it "Louisiana." In 1699, Pierre Le Moyne d'Iberville founded the first French fort at Biloxi and started exploring Louisiana up to Baton Rouge. From then on, the colony progressed regularly, with the founding of Natchez in 1716 and New Orleans in 1718. The French and English colonization of the northern continent was very different from that of the Caribbean, probably because of the weakness of the Spanish presence. Although the continental settlers traded with the sea rovers, there were among them virtually no corsairs, no freebooters, no buccaneers—only plain colonists, who started building settlements and cultivating for survival.

To conclude, the early history of all the American colonies displays many common stages. They all originated in the same movement of European expansion, and they first experienced an era of total Spanish domination before becoming objects of a real contest with the same European nations that challenged that domination. Spain's three principal challengers for both the Caribbean and the North American continent were France, England, and, to a lesser extent, the Netherlands. Quite rapidly, however, these colonies were confronted with different local conditions, and the Caribbean colonies and their North American counterparts started displaying slightly different evolutionary patterns.

Toward a Continental Difference?

The first difference, which has already been delineated in the previous discussion, has to do with the fact that there was much more space to colonize on the northern continent along with a much less strongly established Spanish presence. This made the settlement of the various colonies somewhat easier and enabled both their steady development and a relatively peaceful coexistence.

The West Indian colonies were indeed the scene of many wars among European nations and shifted many times from one nation to another in the first two centuries of their existence. The struggles were permanent and unrelenting: some islands changed control more than ten times. The first wars were aimed at taking the islands from the Spaniards who retaliated, for example, by recapturing Tortuga for a short period in 1638. After a period of relatively isolated actions in the seventeenth century, the eighteenth century was more troubled; once the other European nations had confirmed their presence in the Caribbean, they started trying to wrest territories from one another. It was, of course, a question of political domination and economic power, but was largely fueled by the wars the Europeans were waging against each other in Europe. These European conflicts sparked naval battles in the Caribbean, which resulted in changes in nationality for the islands. The War of the Spanish Succession (1702–1713), the War of the Austrian Succession (1744–1748), and the Seven Years' War (1756–1762) all had repercussions in the West Indies. So did even the American Revolution, where the French alliance with the revolutionaries similarly fueled French/English opposition in the West Indies. With each European conflict, the warring nations—primarily France and England— seized their opponent's islands. Possession was sometimes confirmed by subsequent peace treaty (St. Kitts remained British after the 1713 Treaty of Utrecht), although most treaties simply restored the *status quo ante bellum* (Aix-la-Chapelle, for instance, in 1748).

In short, the fate of the islands was highly unsettled in the seventeenth and eighteenth centuries. Some islands changed hands many times: St. Lucia, for instance, changed control fourteen times in 150 years; Tobago, the great winner in the contest, changed thirty-one times. Some colonies remained stable (Barbados, for instance, remained English throughout, probably because of its geographical isolation.) In the late eighteenth century, things were finally settled. By then, England possessed Jamaica, some of the Virgin Islands, Anguilla, St. Kitts, Montserrat, Antigua, Barbuda, Dominica, St. Vincent, Grenada and the Grenadines, and Barbados. France had St. Domingue (the western part of Hispaniola), the northern part of St. Martin, Guadeloupe, Desirade, Marie Galante, the Saintes, Martinique, St. Lucia, and Tobago. St. Eustatius, Saba, and the southern part of St. Martin were Dutch. Some of the Virgin Islands were Danish (St. Thomas, St. John, and St. Croix); St. Barthélemy had become Swedish (as a temporary concession by France in exchange for trading facilities); and Spain retained the eastern part of Hispaniola (Santo Domingo), Cuba, Puerto Rico in the Greater Antilles, and Trinidad in the extreme southern part of the Caribbean.

Although the same European wars could have similarly affected the North American continent, local conditions reduced the consequences of warfare on the life of the colonies. Because of the relative initial vacancy of the territory and of the much greater space to colonize, the race for conquest was less bitter. Direct warfare was not as frequent; there was less violence; and being continental, the colonies hardly felt the weight of the European fleets. The northern continent was, at times, the theater of opposition between France and England (primarily in Canada), but the development of the colonies of the South was somewhat less problematic. There was enough space for every nation to enjoy a first century of expansion with very few direct economic or military confrontations, all the more so because the colonists were not sufficiently numerous to permit any direct warfare. The French colony was expanding along the Mississippi River between the Gulf Coast and Canada. The English settlement was established on the eastern coast. Spain concentrated on the southern part of the continent and did not fight to expand its Florida territory while it could expand unchecked north of the Rio Grande. As for the Dutch, they remained in New Amsterdam and never had any possessions in the South. The oppositions thus remained limited and sporadic (between the French and the Spaniards on both sides of the southern Louisiana Territory; between the English and the Spanish on the Carolina Coast; between the English and the French on the eastern bank of the Mississippi) and were often indirect. The European nations had allies among the Indian tribes and led the tribes to war to gain control of new territory. In the early eighteenth century, for instance, the English colonists encouraged the Chickasaw, the Creek, the

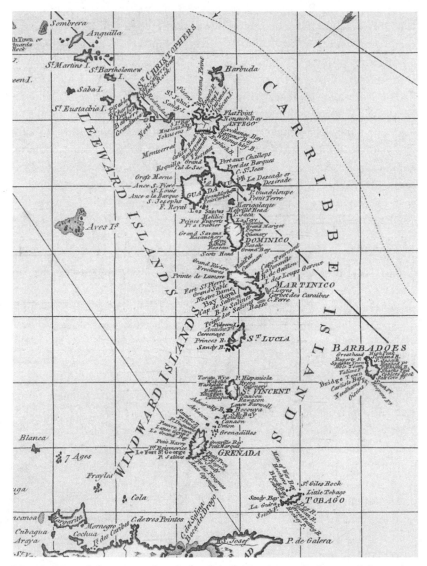

Map 3. Map of the Leeward and Windward Islands. General map of the Lesser Antilles. Extracted from the chart inscribed by Thomas Bowen "To His Royal Highness. Georges Augustus Frederick. Prince of Wales. LC Maps of North America, 1750–1789, 1699. Library of Congress Geography and Map Division. 1774.

Cherokee, and the Alabama to go to war against the Choctaw, who had allied with the French. The only direct fighting between European nations occurred, in fact, against Spanish Florida (in Pensacola, for instance, which the French coveted). For the first century, no real disturbance affected the northern continent.

The troubles and changes in nationalities involving European possessions came later (half of them occurring after the creation of the United States), and were the result not of wars, but of commercial operations. The exchange of New Netherlands for Surinam, involving England, has already been mentioned. Louisiana also underwent some changes, which were the result of transactions instead of confrontations. In 1763, after the Seven Years' War, France ceded the territory to Spain, which returned it secretly to the French in 1800. The nineteenth century, of course, saw the Americanization of the northern continent, including the South. In 1803, the United States purchased Louisiana from France, and, in 1819, Florida from Spain, leaving this part of the territory free from bloody wars between Europeans.

This essential difference, due to local conditions, explains important divergences in the historical development of the colonies of the American South and of the Caribbean in the eighteenth century. The ceaseless struggles in the Caribbean may account for some evolutionary peculiarities and the birth of different characteristics as compared with the northern continent, in particular, uncertainties in the political organization of the colonies. Constant shifts in the possession of the islands might also explain the apparent independence of the islanders from their mother countries, as well as the relative uniformity of West Indian societies; traces of early Spanish settlements may be discovered in the Greater Antilles, and common features may be found between the English and French islands, sometimes because they spent almost two hundred years occupied by both nations (St. Kitts and Tortuga, for instance, or the early settlements of St. Lucia), sometimes because they kept shifting from one nation to the other.

Little change was brought to the life of the occupants of the islands by the shifts in national control. The conquest of Guadeloupe by England in 1759 was an act of war rather than a real attempt at annexation and colonization. When the French surrendered to England, they did not really abandon the island, and the cession treaty contained clauses protecting the colonists' interests. The island remained officially neutral in the conflict between France and England, its inhabitants retained complete religious freedom, French law remained the rule, and children could still be educated in France. Colonists remained the sole owners of their slaves and had to be compensated if the occupying authorities used them. Last but not least, British subjects could not purchase land in Guadeloupe.[10] The result was that colonists generally had no hostility toward the invaders. They accepted their domination without changing their habits in any way. They became used to dealing with another nation, which, together with similar local conditions, explains the relative social, economic, and cultural uniformity of the islands (whatever their nationality) and the moral independence of the colonists from their mother country.

At times, the colonists even tried to obtain the protection of another nation. This was the case, for instance, during the French revolutionary period. As early as August 1789, the planters of all the French colonies (St. Domingue first, then St. Lucia and Tobago, and finally Martinique and Guadeloupe somewhat later) were ready to secede and proclaim their allegiance to England. The only loss to France was St. Domingue, and not for the benefit of either the planter class or another nation, since it was to become Haiti, the first black republic in the Americas, in 1804.

The conclusion to draw from this is that colonization in the American South was indeed influenced by the main three nations that ruled over the Caribbean. In the South, however, although there were a few rare skirmishes (for instance Anglo-American attacks against Spanish Florida in the 1740s), there was enough space in the first decades of colonization to avoid any significant overlapping between the European claims. The three settlements advanced simultaneously, unimpeded until the American Revolution. The fusion of the colonies came later and constituted a peaceful (and commercial) Americanization of the French and Spanish colonies. In the Caribbean, the situation was otherwise, because the nations constantly fought to retain their possessions or to capture others. The development patterns were different, a fact which was to have undeniable consequences on the later evolution of the societies.

As a result of these already emerging differences between the Caribbean and the American South, the colonization process in these two areas followed different patterns. The first process was slower and more progressive and evinced what might be called a shift "from pirating to cultivating." This applied essentially to the French and, to a slightly lesser extent, to the British West Indian colonies. The northern Caribbean was the realm of adventurers; first, corsairs and freebooters, who used islands as naval

bases between operations; then the slightly more sedentary groups of buccaneers. The adventurers slowly became *habitants* [residents], that is to
say cultivating colonists.[11] This was first the result of a thoughtful policy
organized by the governing authorities of the islands. For instance, in the
French settlements of Tortuga and St. Domingue, Governor Bertrand
d'Ogeron de la Bouère, appointed by the king in 1665, tried to turn his
adventurers into proper colonists. He twice asked the king in vain to import women into the colony and finally chartered boats carrying volunteers, who were sold to the freebooters. For him, it was a first means to
ensure the stability of the adventurers. He also granted loans to those who
wanted to settle down. Little by little, the French authorities managed to
replace freebooting with agriculture. The French also favored the development of trade by opening markets where freebooters and corsairs could sell
their booty and buccaneers their products.

The domestication of the adventurers was a slow process, at times involving the existence of a "mixed" society. In his famous account of his life
in the West Indies, Alexandre-Olivier Exquemelin, an indentured servant
who worked for the buccaneers of Tortuga in the late seventeenth century,
describes the population of the nascent colony, as well as the government
of d'Ogeron.[12] Interestingly, the subtitle of his book reads "Les colons-
marins du XVIIe siècle," associating in a neologism the two words "colonist" and "sailor" and thus insisting on their dual identity. He describes
d'Ogeron's attempts to develop the colony, the incentives he offered to
encourage adventurers to settle down; he explains how the governor commissioned the freebooters to attack Spanish vessels and mentions the importation of women and colonists to the island. Exquemelin first describes
the population of the island, composed of freebooters, buccaneers, and *habitants*. He mentions the gradual decrease in cattle and the fact that buccaneers had to shift from hunting to other activities. He also alludes to the
hardships of buccaneering and to the relative overpopulation of Tortuga,
thus explaining the migration of the buccaneers to St. Domingue, where
they became colonists.[13] The process of colonization and settlement was
slow and progressive, as Exquemelin's very vivid pages show. Colonists
generally started clearing the land before planting for their own needs and
building their *cases* [houses]. Next they planted market crops (tobacco in
Exquemelin's description) and hired indentured servants.[14]

The second process of colonization, that of direct and immediate settlement, had been inaugurated by Spain in the sixteenth century and later
adopted by the colonies of the American South. This was true for both

Spanish Florida and French Louisiana, as well as for English Virginia, where the 144 initial colonists who reached Jamestown in 1607 started the process, which was then pursued with the help of the additional colonists who came to Virginia in the years that followed. They started cultivating the land for survival, then for commercial purposes (relatively rapidly, since the first load of Virginian tobacco reached England in 1617). England purposefully took measures to help the expansion of the colony by offering favorable incentives to those who volunteered to settle (any volunteer was granted fifty acres of land if he paid for his own transportation), and sending shiploads of women encouraged the natural demographical development of the colony. New settlers thus reached the colony and devoted themselves to agriculture. Progressively, these colonies began to organize into settlement units, the settlers building towns and sowing the first seeds of "civilization."

To conclude, the colonies of the Caribbean and of the northern continent were born of the same European drive for expansion. They first experienced total Spanish domination, then became the stakes of a bitter European colonizing race, and finally started expanding as plantation colonies. They all started with a true pioneering stage, where settlers had to fight for survival. Then, after a time, production shifted from food to commercial products. Turning away from pioneering, these American colonies all eventually became plantation societies. Although the products they grew were slightly different from one colony to the next (according to the climate and the soil), there was relative uniformity. In spite of local specialties (like shipbuilding in Havana), the colonies mostly cultivated indigo, tobacco, coffee, cotton, cacao, and, in the West Indies, sugar cane, which quickly became the most lucrative product.

All these societies expanded with the arrival of new colonists, either volunteers or transported criminals (primarily in the French and English colonies). Although Spain ignored the system, France and England developed indentured servitude—both in the South and in their Antillean possessions—to overcome the increasing difficulty of recruiting volunteers in Europe. All the islands, following the Iberian model, gradually turned to the use of African slaves (initially a Portuguese practice, which the Spaniards had rapidly adopted). The practice spread to the French and English colonies—the first Africans reached the colony of Virginia in 1619, although their initial status was that of indentured servants—which thus progressively became plantation societies, based on slavery, on the development of a mercantile system, and on the expansion of the slave trade.

Those colonies, however, were rather early subjected to slightly different patterns of colonization, due to local conditions and to the different time periods in which they were created. Being born a century later than their Caribbean antecedents and offering a vast space to colonize, being continental (and thus less affected by the naval battles which were the principal means of warfare among European nations), the colonies of the northern continent underwent a different eighteenth-century evolution. Established at a different time, they matured at a different rate. They were, from the very start, exclusively settlement colonies, mostly unaffected by the pirating that reigned in the Caribbean. They were also much less directly affected by the violent struggles among European nations. Although they were not spared by warfare (the southeastern frontier areas, for instance, were characterized in the seventeenth and eighteenth centuries by nearly continual belligerence among Indian tribes spurred on by the European nations), these struggles never revolutionized the socioeconomic frame of the colonies and did not result in changes of government, let alone nationality. These continental colonies thus developed more steadily in relative peace.

These emerging differences are pertinent to the initial thesis of the present book: although they are not determining factors *per se,* they had consequences for the later evolution of the societies. It might be contended that the early stages of colonization cannot be considered as directly essential to the discussion of a Southern distinctiveness. They offered, however, favorable ground for later divergences, particularly in matters of demographic, economic, and social developments, which require closer examination.

Society, Societies

To better comprehend the origins of Southern distinctiveness, the development of all these colonies in terms of political, social, economic, and cultural organization requires close examination. In all these areas, the colonial societies of the West Indies and of the American South presented obvious similarities, but also important variations that have to be delineated. The task here is particularly difficult because of the numerous variables involved, the multiplicity of colonies, and the very broad time period which this research spans: about four centuries range between the foundation of the first colonies and the final abolition, a span which brought about many changes in the societies involved. This study also becomes, at times, relatively complex, due to the various changes in the political control of the Caribbean colonies. However, it remains possible to give an overall view of the slave societies of the Americas.

The first chapter has shown that, despite differences in settlement date, which, on the scale of global history, are insignificant, the colonies of the Americas were all the product of the same discovery/colonization movement. After the early all-Spanish period, they were mainly shared between three European nations. While the three nations had mostly equal shares of the Caribbean (with a discreet Dutch, Danish, and Swedish colonizing presence), in the American colonial South, the seventeenth century was largely under English influence, with a much weaker Spanish presence in Florida and a later French presence in Louisiana.

Although, in the early era of colonization, the differences existing between the various colonies were generally related to the European power in command, later evolution shows the emergence of a clear North American model, increasingly diverging from the Caribbean pattern. This was first true of the political organization of the various American colonies.

Political Organization

Until the eighteenth century, the differences in the political organization of the American colonies depended on the colonial policies of the European nations. Both in the Caribbean and on the northern continent, two different models theoretically ruled political organization: the Spanish model on the one hand and the French and English one on the other.

The Spanish colonies depended very closely on their home government. Except for the economic regulation managed by the House of Trade, all colonial affairs were settled at home by the king-appointed Council for the Indies, tasked to confirm all decisions made by colonial governments. The council nominated all the top-ranking officials of the four American Vice-Royalties, themselves subdivided into *audiencias* [appeals or district courts of justice] administered by a council of lawyers appointed from Spain. The *audiencias* represented the Viceroy, transmitted his decisions, and were responsible to him. They also acted as supreme courts. All of the Caribbean possessions, as well as the Florida colony, were under the authority of the *audiencia* of Santo Domingo. Although governors and local officials in the Spanish Caribbean were granted a relatively high discretionary power, very few appointments of Creoles (that is, people born in the colonies) were ever made in the Spanish possessions, with the exception of the *cabildos* [city councils], which were administered by the residents. As a consequence, the Spanish West Indies proved much less favorable to the emergence of a local hierarchy of offices than the Anglo-American colonies.

Despite this overall remarkable homogeneity, Spain regarded its northern continental colony somewhat differently than its West Indian islands. Florida never developed as a colony of settlement. It was rather a military and missionary colony with an essentially defensive strategic design, although the Spaniards take pride in having built St. Augustine, the first European town on the northern continent. Florida was founded with the aim of protecting the Bahamas channel, thus ensuring Spain an easy connection with its Caribbean sugar islands and Mexican colony. Spanish efforts on the continent focused rather on the southern continent and, from the late eighteenth century onwards, on the colonies of New Mexico and Upper California. In Florida, as one historian puts it, the Spanish "garrisoned rather than inhabited."[1] Apart from this military presence, there were only missionaries (especially Franciscans) hopeful of evangelizing the Indians.

After France ceded Louisiana to Spain, under the 1763 Treaty of Paris, the Spanish authorities expanded their political colonial model to the colony. They exerted close control from home, abolished the French Superior Council and replaced it by a Spanish bureaucratic superstructure. In the Spanish way, a *cabildo* was created in New Orleans, offering public offices to Louisiana settlers. The situation remained unchanged until the integration of the territory into the United States. Indeed, if the territory was secretly returned to France in 1800, it remained controlled by Spain until its purchase by the United States in 1803.

One preliminary conclusion can be drawn from this. Despite strategy-related differences (concerning Florida, in particular), the Caribbean islands and the northern continental colonies of Spain were closely connected and kept under close metropolitan control, which theoretically left limited space for colonial enterprise and self-government and worked against a hierarchy of offices among Creoles. This probably accounts for the remarkable uniformity of the Spanish possessions, as well as their longevity in their original form and the absence of demands for autonomy in their first centuries of expansion.

The other European governments worked differently and presented a relative homogeneity in their development. In British and French America, there was no single colonization model but rather three quite distinct types of colonial organization, which alternated throughout the colonization period. The first model, encountered on a large scale both in the northern continent and in the Caribbean, was colonization by a chartered company: Virginia, for instance, was founded in 1607 and developed under the responsibility of the Virginia Company of London until 1624. At times, this was also the case of Louisiana, which was administered by the *Compagnie des Indes Occidentales* [Company of the West Indies] between 1720 and 1731.

In the Caribbean, the creation of the colonies was placed under the responsibility of commercial companies, a trend that can be equated with the creation of trade monopolies. Except for the Spanish colonies, the metropolitan governments were, at first, not involved directly in the colonization process. The Dutch colonies, for instance, depended on the Dutch West Indies Company, which presided over the birth and development of Guyana as well as of the tiny territories of Curacao, Aruba, Bonaire, Tobago, and St. Eustatius. In a similar way, the creation and expansion of St. Thomas was left to the Danish Company of the West Indies. The French West Indies were also entrusted to chartered companies several times during their colonial existence.[2] Their foundation was the work of the *Compagnie de Saint-Christophe* [St. Kitts Company], created in 1626, while their further development was the responsibility of the *Compagnie des Isles de l'Amérique* [Company of the American Islands] from 1635 to 1650. After a period when the colonies were sold off to private owners, Colbert reestablished a single company in 1664, the *Compagnie des Indes Occidentales*, which spent the next ten years purchasing back the islands from their owners. In the French possessions, the role of the companies generally took on paramount importance, because the colonists were less numerous than in the rest of colonial America and very often had little personal wealth. The English colonies of the Caribbean had a closely parallel evolution, which was related, at least in the beginning, to England's administration of the colonies of the northern continent. The beginning of English West Indian colonization, for instance, was left to two competing companies: the Warner Company and the Courteen Company.

After colonization by chartered company, the second non-Spanish model, also common to the Caribbean and the northern continent, was the proprietary colony. This was the case, for instance, of the Carolinas, from 1663 to 1665 granted by Charles II to eight English noblemen, who bore the title of Lord Proprietors. In the same way, Georgia was created after George II gave a charter to twenty proprietors, named trustees, in 1732. Under this regime, the British North American colonies were organized on a quasi-feudal basis, the proprietors generally favoring immigration on a large scale, as well as a real settlement policy and the constitution of large plantation units; this was the case in the Carolinas under the precepts of Lord Shaftsbury's Fundamental Constitutions of Carolina. This pattern of colonial control was also often encountered in the rest of the French and English American colonies. During the war of 1712, for instance, and until 1717, the colony of Louisiana was leased to a wealthy commoner, Antoine Crozat. Similarly, from 1650 to 1664, the French Caribbean colonies became proprietary colonies: the *Compagnie des Isles d'Amérique* sold them, in general, to their former governors, who became *Seigneurs Propriétaires* [Lord Proprietors]. The British West Indies also underwent such a stage; in 1627, Charles II issued a patent to the Earl of Carlisle, who became the proprietor of the "Caribees Islands" situated between the tenth and twentieth northern parallels. Similarly, from 1629 onwards, the Bahamas were a proprietary colony, placed under the ownership of Sir Robert Heath.

The third model of colonization was the royal colony, implying a close control of the colonies by the crown. This was the case, for instance, of

Virginia after 1624 and of Georgia from 1755 on. In the second third of the seventeenth century, the British West Indies also became royal colonies; the monarch—who appointed the governor and the council composed of ten leading planters—then exerted close control. The French colony of Louisiana was a royal colony several times in its history: first at its birth and again when Crozat returned it to the crown in 1717. The superior council—which had some policy-making powers, but largely exercised judicial functions after the French manner of colonial administration—then ruled it under close supervision by the crown. As for the French West Indian possessions, they also became royal colonies from 1674 onwards and were placed under a strict monarchical regime. Jean-Charles de Baas, who had administered the *Compagnie des Indes Occidentales* until 1674, was left in command, and he was directly responsible to the monarch.

To conclude, in matters of colonial political organization, the French and British colonial policies were relatively close throughout the Americas. The only main difference is that, whatever the political status of the colony, a larger part of self-government was officially granted to the English colonists—on the mainland as well as in the Caribbean. As early as 1619, for instance, the Virginia colony was granted a general assembly composed of representatives chosen among the settlers and referred to as burgesses. In the British West Indies, the planters were very early granted a degree of self-government. Although the governor generally came from England, the judges and high officials were appointed from among the residents. The assembly, composed of local planters, had some legislative power and could pass legislative acts on condition that it followed the instructions of the governor and respected English laws and royal prerogatives. The assembly could also levy taxes. It did not have any control over the governor, although, in some cases, the assemblymen could pressure the king to obtain a new governor. When the islands were royal colonies, they had a house of assembly whose members were appointed in the early period of colonization, but later, between 1639 and 1663, were elected by the freeholders.

In the French colonies, the situation was quite different; the lieutenant general and the governors were still appointed by the king. In the eighteenth century, colonial assemblies were created, but the regime remained authoritarian in the French mode, with little room for self-government, as opposed to what occurred in the English colonies of North America. The king appointed the representatives, and there was no elected assembly. This may partly explain the outbreak of the autonomist movement launched by the planters in French St. Domingue, which ultimately led to the loss of the colony to slave rebellions. Conversely, it may also explain why the French managed to retain the other islands, by exerting tight control over their colonies.[3]

Despite this divergence between French and English concepts of local affairs, the political organization of the non-Spanish Caribbean colonies thus was very close to that of the colonies of North America until the late eighteenth century. The continental colonists were more independent from their governors, while smaller populations and absenteeism tended to weaken the West Indian legislatures. The main difference, however, came in the 1770s; the drastic change occurring in the form of government of the American South was, of course, the result of the American Revolution. The separate national existence of the ex-colonies brought about many changes in their structure and subsequent development. This is all the more interesting since these changes also affected, in the early nineteenth century, the former colonies of Spain (Florida) and France (Louisiana), which, together with the Southern states born of Independence, formed the American South as it is generally defined. Louisiana, for instance, experienced a short territorial phase, during which it was administered by a territorial legislature (New Orleans was placed under the responsibility of a municipal council), before obtaining statehood after a period of barely nine years.

Meanwhile, the Caribbean possessions remained colonies and, despite their different nationalities, underwent a parallel evolution enhanced by the numerous exchanges of territory that occurred between the various European powers. The American Revolution simply brought about the passage of some very explicit laws in the West Indian English colonies. In Jamaica, for instance, the Assembly added to its legislative system a clause stipulating that no law could be passed concerning a colony without its assent.[4] This acceptance of colonial status may be accounted for by the tendency of the Caribbean planters to be absentees. They left their property in control of overseers and spent most of their life in London, living off the revenue of their West Indian property. This led to the creation of a lobbying power, a "West Indian interest," in the London Parliament. This group ultimately gained a relatively strong influence in Parliament, receiving emissaries sent by the colonial assemblies, putting forward their requests in London, and thus obtaining favorable legislation.[5] As a result, they never lodged the North American complaint of "taxation without representation"; they did not have to submit to legislation imposed on them by a remote Parliament with which they had no contact. This permitted the maintenance of their colonial status well into the twentieth century, and, at any rate, until the end of the slave societies. The French authorities obtained similar results (that is, persisting colonial status) by exerting a very tight control over their Caribbean colonies.

In short, the early patterns of colonial government did not reveal any real difference between the administration of the Caribbean islands and that of the northern continental colonies. The main divergences had to do with various national patterns, although Spanish colonists had *de facto* more power than what was officially granted by the administrative organization. The slight tendency toward more independence observable in the American Southern colonies, along with more active pressure exerted on local representatives of European powers, is probably due to greater population and a lesser tendency to absenteeism, which made the colonists more active locally. The northern continental colonies started displaying distinct political features after the Revolutionary War and the acknowledgment of their independence. Within four decades, interestingly enough, this momentous event had erased the variations related to national colonial policies, once Louisiana and Florida were incorporated into the United States.

After this short presentation of the different forms of government, the social and national origins of the settlers should now be examined as we move toward an understanding of the later development of Southern distinctiveness.

Origins of the Settlers

In the national and social origins of the inhabitants of the American colonies, a number of common features must be noted. In the Caribbean colonies, the settlers—as distinct from the slaves—came essentially from the colonizing country. There was very little immigration from other countries. This was also partly true of the North American colonies, although much less exclusively so. French Louisiana, for instance, principally received populations of French origin: people from France first, then, later in the eighteenth century, Acadians of French descent and refugees from French St. Domingue after the slave rebellions. The Louisiana settlement was also later influenced by the fact that it became a Spanish territory in the second half of the eighteenth century. Although few settlers came directly from Spain, the colony received an influx of immigrants from the

Canaries. Moreover, even before being purchased by the United States in 1803, its gradual Americanization was accomplished by the arrival of settlers coming from the United States. As for Anglo-Saxon North America (although the figures vary tremendously from one colony, or later state, to the next and according to the period), a large majority of its population also came from the British Isles (60.9 percent from England, 8.3 percent from Scotland, 9.7 percent from Ireland).[6] Louisiana welcomed migrants from other European nations as well, primarily from Germany (8.7 percent), but also, in smaller numbers, from Northern Europe and from France (for instance, Huguenots who settled in several colonies, mainly in the refuge of South Carolina, or, later, French refugees from St. Domingue, who moved to various American cities: Boston, New York, Philadelphia, Charleston, and Savannah in particular).

This ethnic composition already establishes a slight difference between the Caribbean and the northern continent. The future United States received immigrants from diverse cultural backgrounds, which makes for its cultural heterogeneity and originality; this might also explain the revolutionary movement of the late eighteenth century, which although hesitantly begun, never encountered strong resistance. Moreover, this immigration promoted a steady growth of the continental population (as opposed to that of the Caribbean), definitely making the northern continent a land of colonization.

As for the social origins of the settlers, they were much the same in all the English and French colonies, but displayed some differences as compared to the Spanish colonies. Indeed, for one essential reason, the Spanish system neither resorted to the deportation of convicts nor relied on indentured servitude: immediate recourse to the institution of slavery, first through the enslavement of natives and later through the importation of African slaves.

In contrast, all the French and English colonies imported convicts, although in different proportions. The British North American colonies received convicts from English jails, the total amounting to around 50,000.[7] From the 1720s on, Louisiana underwent the same influx of prisoners. There were also "social deviants" recruited on the streets and "libertines," for example, children sent away by their parents for misdemeanors.[8] Both France and England thus sent the same types of settlers to their Caribbean colonies. In the English West Indies, this type of colonization started in the 1670s, when it became harder to recruit voluntary settlers and indentured servants. Cromwell's government had already deported a number of Irish political dissidents to Barbados. In the French colonies, such deportation lasted until the 1720s. To all these colonies the European powers also sent poor people recruited, sometimes even kidnapped, on the streets.[9]

In the non-Spanish colonies of the Americas, if the first inhabitants were free settlers, the next waves of settlers were likely to be indentured servants (*engagés* in the French colonies). Some historians go so far as to say that in the seventeenth-century North American British colonies, half the migrants from Europe, and maybe two-thirds of them, were indentured servants from England.[10] The French possessions, including Louisiana, revealed a similar pattern of settlement, with the number of indentured settlers peaking in the late seventeenth century.[11]

This system was encouraged by colonial policies, some islands offering a headright to anyone who indentured a new colonist from Europe by paying for his passage. The latter was virtually enslaved for a time, often under very harsh conditions, before being liberated and granted financial aid (called "freedom dues"). This financial aid was often used to settle, buy land, and sometimes bring over other indentured servants: a novel situation that turned the servant into a master. The principle was the same in all the colonies; only the terms of the contracts changed. The period of indenture was from four to seven years in the British North American colonies, three years in the French colonies, five years in the British Caribbean settlements, and seven years in the Dutch colonies. The financial help also varied from one colony to the next: from a piece of land in the North American colonies to a certain amount of tobacco (or, as crops changed, of sugar) in the English Caribbean. The result was that the definitive settlement of these workers was generally predictable in the North American colonies, while conditions for ex-indentured servants were more uncertain in the Caribbean; some of them turned to freebooting or buccaneering, others engaged in trade or became artisans, others simply returned to Europe once their contract was over. Here again, the policy of the northern continental colonies was definitely one of colonization through settlement, while the Caribbean islands did not necessarily encourage people to remain—probably not in conformity with any definite policy, but because land was less available there. This was all the more important for the population of the future United States, since the majority of indentured servants were men between the ages of fifteen and twenty-five and of good pioneering stock. Moreover, it is estimated that about seventy percent of them could read and write, which constituted a clear potential for the future United States.[12]

Throughout British and French America, the importation of indentured servants peaked in the late seventeenth century. The system disappeared or, at least, took a residual form in the eighteenth century when these colonies started following the Spanish model and importing African slaves on a large scale.

In all the colonies, it is possible to say that a substratum of lower social classes represented the majority of the population. The proportion of over two-thirds has already been mentioned for the continental colonies. In Louisiana, it may even have been larger.[13] The islands, whatever their nationality, followed the same pattern, including the Spanish islands where the influx resulted from direct voluntary migration.

Each of the societies had a population of middle-class origin (to be found among the small planters and in the professions) and a small group from the nobility, in general the lesser nobility (as in the French and Spanish colonies), or even the gentry (in the English ones). Although they were not proportionally numerous, these noblemen had a very great influence on the societies. Many of them participated in the foundation and development of all the settlements, and their descendants remained influential. For instance, the Virginia gentry played an essential part in the social, political, and economic life of the colony, as well as in the political organization of the American Revolution and of the new nation. The Lee, Carter, Byrd, and Randolph dynasties are often mentioned in American history. In the French Caribbean islands, there were fewer migrants of noble origin, and the ruling class was rather that of the wealthy mercantile bourgeoisie. The Spanish Caribbean colonial society was said to be "a cross-section of Spanish society,"[14] composed of peasants, soldiers, and a few gentlemen, in general sons of the lesser nobility, who could not really hope for much of a future in Spain. In the English West Indies, there were, among the planters, people from the nobility, "gentlemen of squirerarchical background,"[15] and members of the mercantile bourgeoisie. The vast majority of the planter class, however, originated in the yeomanry.

If the inhabitants of the colonies mostly came from similar social classes, they also shared the same will to succeed and make a fortune. In most of the American South as well as in the Caribbean colonies, there were very few idealists of the Mayflower type. The desire was not to build any "shining city upon a hill," but to make a personal fortune and eventually to work toward the increased wealth and power of their motherlands, although this was never the primary design. This, of course, changed when the South became involved in the national destiny of the United States.

Despite a relative homogeneity in social patterns, some minor differences have been detected. As in the field of government, most of the social features of early colonization rather depended on the colonizing nation, with, again, a rather close proximity between France and England and a slightly divergent Spanish model. However, a few North American differences may be noted. There was more diversity in the settlers' national origins, which favored a larger cultural blend; the conditions for indentured servants were far better, which tended to favor their settlement in the colonies, thus making for the pioneering future of the country. These differences may, to some extent, explain specific patterns of subsequent evolution in the South. An examination of specific demographic developments will clarify this hypothesis.

Demographic Evolution

In the field of demography, there was no real equality among the colonies, and the English colonies of the northern continent were clearly exceptional. The influx of population to the Caribbean colonies, to French Louisiana, and to Spanish Florida was never massive. As already noted, Florida was never a priority in Spanish settlement. The colonizing population of Louisiana did not grow significantly in the colonial period. If, between 1718 and 1721, for instance, 7,020 white people reached the colony (which is not an enormous number in the first place), after that date, French immigration to Louisiana never exceeded 1,000 people a year until the end of the French colonial period.[16]

The French Caribbean islands first experienced a much steadier immigration from France. The white population grew steadily until the mid-eighteenth century but, on the eve of the Revolution, it started declining.[17] The same pattern can be found in the English Caribbean, as well as in the Spanish colonies where the decline occurred much earlier and can be accounted for by the above-mentioned change incurred in the focus of colonization from the Caribbean to the Southern continent.

Among the reasons for this shortage was a great geographical mobility with constant flux and reflux of populations, as well as a high mortality rate (largely due to diseases such as yellow fever). The relative difficulty of recruiting volunteers for settlement created the necessity of importing African slaves, which, in turn, brought about a proportional reduction of the economic prospects offered to potential settlers. Moreover, the absence

Fig. 1. Habitation Clément, Domaine de l'Acajou, Le François, Martinique, French West Indies. Picture of the Clément Plantation House. Photo by Nathalie Dessens.

of foreign immigration to the Caribbean colonies reduced their demographic expansion.

In the North American English colonies, the demographic evolution was different. The existence of non-English immigration has already been noted. However, this is largely insufficient to account for the explosion of the population in the thirteen colonies. The beginnings were difficult. In Virginia, for instance, many settlers died or returned to England in the early decades of colonization. The figure of 1,000 settlers was not reached until the 1620s. Subsequent growth was slow: perhaps 3,000 in 1628; 2,500 or more in 1630; and almost 5,000 in 1643.[18] After these difficult decades, however, growth was both significant and rapid and did not display any reversal in trend. In the thirteen colonies (although with a slight advantage to the northern ones), the population multiplied tenfold between 1630 and 1720. At the time of the American Revolution and in the first years of the American nation, Benjamin Franklin contended that it doubled every twenty years. He was right. At the time of Independence, it was roughly two and a half million; the first official American census gave a population of four million in 1790.

The first original feature of the thirteen colonies was thus, in the seventeenth century, the rapid growth of their white population through immigration. This caused another significant increase in the eighteenth century, but this time mainly through natural growth. In the West Indian colonies, no such phenomenon occurred. Many reasons have been advanced to explain a very slow demographic evolution: a low birth rate partly due to the preponderance of males in the population; a high death rate tied to diseases favored by a climate the colonists were unaccustomed to; and also a trend of return to Europe. In the thirteen colonies on the other hand, the birth rate varied between 40 and 50 per mill, sometimes verging on the biological maximum of 55 per mill, which means that it was much higher even than in Europe. People married at a younger age; there was so much potential in the colonies that they acquired the resources necessary to settle down much earlier in life. The death rate, around 25 per mill, was much lower than in Europe (where it was around 35 to 40 per mill). All this gave the American colonies a growth rate of around 1.5 percent.[19] Although the topic will be discussed in detail below, it is important to note that the same pattern existed for the slave population of the thirteen colonies.

The last particularly patent demographic difference between most of the Caribbean colonies and the northern continental ones is the numerical importance of the slave population and subsequent ratio of whites to slaves. Bondsmen never represented a majority in the South. Only a few southern states (South Carolina and Mississippi for instance) had as many slaves as whites among the population, and this did not occur until the nineteenth century. In the Caribbean, only the Spanish colonies had similar proportions, with the white settlers largely exceeding the slaves in number. In Cuba, in 1774, among a population of 172,000 inhabitants, the proportion of slaves was only 26 percent after almost three centuries of slavery.[20] The institution started earlier there than elsewhere, but experienced a much slower development. The only exception to the rule was Trinidad, which reached a proportion of 53 percent of slaves in 1789, a high figure for a Spanish island but still much lower than its English and French counterparts. Only 10.9 percent of the Puerto Rican population consisted of slaves in 1787, and the figure in Santo Domingo was 19.7 percent. These figures are all the more striking since they are the result of a very long practice of the institution of slavery.

On the contrary, the French and British West Indian colonies experienced an inversion of this white-to-slave ratio very early. As will be seen later, the growth of the slave population was essentially due to the slave trade. In Martinique, for instance, the proportion reached 68,000 slaves for 12,000 whites on the eve of the Revolution. In 1807, the difference was still more obvious: 80,473 slaves for 10,377 whites.[21] This also happened at early stages in French Louisiana, with, for instance, the arrival of 4,112 slaves for only 1,629 whites in 1731.

The proportion was much the same in the British Caribbean colonies, although the numerical superiority of the slaves occurred slightly earlier than in the French West Indies, due to the enormous numbers of slaves imported in the seventeenth century: in 1700, the slave population of the British islands was four times that of the French ones.[22] In Barbados, the slaves constituted a majority as early as 1660, slightly earlier than in Guadeloupe and Martinique (1664).[23] The eighteenth century largely confirmed this trend: in Jamaica in 1791, there were 250,000 Africans for 30,000 whites; in Barbados, the proportion was 62,115 for 16,167. In the total population of all the English islands, the ratio at that time was 455,684 to 65,305, which means that about 85 percent of the population was of African origin.[24] All these figures represent only indications of the white-to-slave ratio. However, since growth toward these climactic values was steady throughout the colonization period, it seems more revealing to consider late-eighteenth-century statistics for comparison's sake so as to overcome the difficulty created by the broad time span across the birth of the various colonies. A more detailed study of these ratios would have required numerous figures, corresponding to various periods of the colonial era, without contributing much to the main thesis here: that of a North American difference. In this respect, the only relevant conclusion is the overall predominance of the white population in the American South as compared with the Caribbean colonies taken together.

As far as demography is concerned, a last interesting difference distinguishes the English colonies from the rest of the colonial possessions of the American continent: the proportion and status of free colored people. In the South (as in the British West Indies), there was always a very weak proportion of free colored people. It never represented much more than 5 percent of the population of African origin. In 1860, it reached 6 percent but was very unevenly distributed among the slave States: the highest figures were found in Maryland, an Upper Southern State (about 84,000 out of a total of 260,000), and Louisiana, which had had a different French and Spanish colonial background. In the French West Indies, it was not very high in the early period of colonization.[25] However, it grew significantly throughout the eighteenth century, especially in St. Domingue. Although

proportionately to the slaves, the ratio of free colored people was still relatively low (due to the huge slave population), on the eve of the revolution
in St. Domingue, the numbers of whites and free colored people were almost even.[26] The highest proportions were found in the Spanish islands,
where the slave population was never very numerous compared with the
total population, and where freedom was granted much more easily to the
slaves (in particular, thanks to the possibility of *coartación*, that is, self-
purchase).

The most important difference, however, lies in the status the free
people of color were granted. In the English colonies, racial prejudice was
very strong, and if free colored people could be found, although in smaller
proportions, their status was only slightly higher than that of the slaves.
Meanwhile, the Spanish and French possessions granted freemen an official status. The reasons for this large and visible free colored population are
manifold. Manumission was made easier by law; the whites were used to
freeing their mulatto children; freedom was obtainable through marriage,
and even, especially in the Spanish colonies, purchasable. Details will be
given in the next chapter, but it is important to note that this feature gave
birth to a distinctive organization of society in the French and Spanish
colonies, including Spanish Florida and French Louisiana.[27] The marked
difference was the existence of a three-tiered system, where the free colored people could partake in the social and economic life of the colony, and
even, to a certain extent, in the political life of the colonies (the beginning
of the slave rebellion that ended in France's loss of St. Domingue, for instance, was born of the agitation of the free colored people, who wanted to
take advantage of the French Revolution to obtain total equality of rights).

In short, there were, here again, a number of differences between the
French and Spanish colonies and the British ones, particularly where the
size and status of the group of free colored people is concerned. These differences might not seem totally relevant here, although *in fine* they had a
tremendous influence on the increasingly characteristic features of the
American South, which was largely influenced by this British pattern after
the War of Independence and the purchase of Louisiana and Florida by the
United States. Moreover, by contrast with the West Indies, the American
South was marked by a rapid and steady growth of its white population,
due to greater land availability, better climatic conditions, and stronger
government settlement policies.

The social organization of the various European possessions of the Caribbean and of the American South is another feature that requires exami-

nation when attempting to determine the existence of a Southern differ-ence.

Social Organization

The first obvious conclusion, when dealing with the slave colonies of the Americas, is that they all followed similar overall patterns in social organi-zation. The first common feature had to do with the predominance of the white class, and more precisely of the planter class. Numerically, this class generally represented a small minority of the white population. For in-stance, in the South (if the usual definition of the planter as the owner of more than twenty slaves is considered) this category represented only 3.5 to 4 percent of the heads of household and only 0.6 percent of the white population in 1860. As for the big planters (over fifty slaves), they repre-sented 1 percent of the heads of households among them and 2.5 percent in Louisiana.[28] In spite of their small numbers, they dominated the social, political, and economic life of the colonies, as exemplified by the Virginian "aristocracy" (a reproduction of the model set by the English landed aris-tocracy). In the late eighteenth century, the hundred wealthiest Virginians indeed belonged to a very small group of distinguished families (the Lees, the Washingtons, the Randolphs, among others). Louisiana, despite its French origins (slightly influenced by its Spanish period), displayed a similar organizational pattern. Although this is far from true in an overall perspective, the colony was very "American" in many ways, which prob-ably explains its relatively easy political integration into the United States in 1803, although the cultural "Americanization" process of the territory did not occur until the second half of the nineteenth century. In many respects, it would probably be more judicious to speak of a "continental" pattern, as opposed to an insular one, a terminology that would avoid the cultural connotations contained in "Americanization."

In the Caribbean islands, although the early development pattern of the various colonies were sometimes slightly different, the societies ended up being very similar. In the early days of the English period, the estates were generally small units. In 1645 in Barbados, for instance, 60,000 acres be-longed to 18,000 owners, including 11,000 plantation masters. An obvious concentration of property and wealth occurred in the following decades. Because some planters left, became merchants, or decided to colonize other territories, the same amount of land was held by only 745 persons by the late seventeenth century.[29] The Spanish and French colonies were simi-

Fig. 2. Le Moule, Guadeloupe, French West Indies. Plantation House at Le Moule, Guadeloupe. Photo by Nathalie Dessens.

larly organized, with a clear concentration of wealth, land, and power in the hands of a few. The planters dominated the legislatures of the northern mainland, and all the officials that were local appointees in the West Indies belonged to the planter class. These planters, who could be of noble origins, retained exclusive political power.[30]

All these colonies had a small intermediary middle class of small owners, traders, artisans (very often ex-indentured servants in the Caribbean societies), and people of the professions. The importance of the trading categories was especially manifest in the Caribbean colonies. Artisans were not very numerous in the Caribbean colonies, because the tendency to train slaves as skilled professionals on the plantations (much less developed in the American South) made the need for outside professionals less important.

Finally, in all the colonies of the Americas, the majority of the white population was composed of poor whites. Most of the time, in the Caribbean, they were former indentured servants who had had difficulty achieving economic integration. In the colonies of North America, the indentured servants mostly became squatters in the frontier areas, because the development of slavery left no room for them as salaried workers on the plantations. The practice of indentured servitude slowed down in the late seventeenth century and stopped altogether in the eighteenth century (except in Pennsylvania with the redemption system), when it was defini-tively replaced by slavery. The system was no longer profitable, unlike sla-very, despite the fact that the latter required a larger initial investment. Slavery meant lifetime servitude, the children born into slavery also be-longed to the master, and it guaranteed greater social stability. Indeed, the existence of too many liberated indentured servants might have threat-ened the balance of this highly inegalitarian society. Despite the disappear-ance of the system, its social repercussions remained visible long after-wards.

In the French and Spanish colonies, as already seen, in addition to slaves, there were also many free people of color, who were granted a spe-cial status within the society. They could hold certain positions, become property owners, and were likely to be educated if they were the offspring of mixed unions between masters and slaves. Instead of hiding or enslav-ing their mulatto children, the Spaniards and the French were likely to give them an education, a piece of land, and enable their inclusion within the society of the colony.

To complete the study of the hierarchy, at the bottom of the social order were the slaves, who were the numerical majority in the non-Spanish Car-ibbean colonies. Needless to say, slaves played no direct role whatsoever in the society, either on a social or political level. The economic stake they represented did not give them any direct weight either. Nevertheless, their paramount importance lies in their being the real laboring substratum of society, one of the factors that turned all these colonies into slave societies.

Finally, the last main common point among the societies, apart from their hierarchical organization, was the mobility and relative fluidity of their white component. First, strong geographical mobility was an essen-tial factor throughout the colonial period in all these colonies. In the Carib-bean, people went from one territory to the next should the prospects of-fered by one colony be insufficient. The Spanish colonists very often moved from one island to another or from the West Indies to the main-land. The same inter-isle movement was found among the French and En-glish Caribbean possessions. In the American South, the white population was also very mobile.[31] Poor whites tended to become squatters in the frontier areas, and even the planters, pushed by land exhaustion, tended to move westward with their slaves in search of more fertile land in the terri-tories added to the Union. This westward movement was accelerated by the rapid growth of the United States' territory after Independence. Fi-nally, there were transfers between the West Indies and the North American colonies. Many Barbadian planters settled in the Carolinas, while the American Revolution brought many loyalists to the Caribbean islands and the Bahamas. Similarly, the Haitian revolution drove thousands of people away to Santo Domingo, Jamaica, Cuba, North America, and, more particularly, to Louisiana (where 15,000 to 20,000 refugees landed).

Social mobility and fluidity was another essential factor in the white population. Small planters could marry into the higher planter class. In the American South (in the English colonies as well as in French Louisiana), some small independent farmers started at the bottom of the social ladder, clearing the ground of a small piece of property, and became large landowners. This upward mobility was promoted by the practice of granting a piece of land to indentured servants at the end of their contract and was reinforced by the existence of wide expanses of available land. It was also facilitated by the measures taken by the governments to encourage settlement and the expansion of the colonies: in Virginia, for instance, the system of headrights, which granted 50 acres of land to any settler who paid to bring an additional colonist over from England, was instituted and then expanded to other colonies such as the Carolinas. This social mobility could be noted throughout the American South. To give another example, at the turn of the nineteenth century, migrants from St. Domingue reached the Louisiana shores with close to nothing and climbed the social ladder very speedily.

Although the contracts of indentured servitude were less favorable in the Caribbean and although land availability was limited, the same social fluidity existed to a certain point. In the French islands, land was free and its tenure was based solely on an obligation to work it in order to prevent its reversion to the government or the company. In the English islands, land was purchased, which advantageously precluded the obligation of working it.

Everywhere, because of the relative absence of a social fabric in the very early days of colonization, it was easy even for obscure adventurers to reach the upper levels of society. According to Michael Craton, "West Indian plantations were a machine for creating wealth and aiding upward mobility" (59). The noblemen who arrived in the islands had many opportunities to become highly visible in a very short period and to launch dazzling political careers. This was also true, however, of people who came over with nothing, as self-made men flourished in these colonial societies where it was possible to come as an indentured servant and end up as a reasonably wealthy planter.[32] A relative, potential upward economic and

Fig. 3. Rue Case Nègre, Habitation Gagneron, Le Lamentin, Martinique, French West Indies. Rows of slave cabins at the Gagneron Plantation. Photo by Nathalie Dessens.

social mobility was even possible, within their own sphere, for colored people in the French and Spanish societies, although not in the English societies.

The organization of these plantation societies was thus very similar in all the colonies, whether insular or continental. A principal difference remained, though: the continental colonies were definitely settlement colonies. In the North American colonies, the people, although they were at times mobile within the colonies themselves, settled for life. This was also generally true for the Spanish colonists, although they were likely to move from one colony to another (and often from an island to the continent). On the contrary, the Caribbean colonies of France and England were more often considered as places to make a fortune than places to live, and many big planters spent most of their time in Europe. Once their business was settled, they often entrusted it to a manager and lived off their revenues in their motherland. All the colonies were not equally affected by this trend; there was more absenteeism in the Greater Antilles than in the Lesser Antilles. In some islands, the practice reached incredible proportions. In Barbados, for instance, one-fourth of the planters were absentees in 1700; one-third in the late eighteenth century; while in Jamaica, the figure was over one-third in 1740 and reached two-thirds in 1800.[33] Craton cites three

interesting elements that promoted this trend. First, the habit of absenteeism enabled planters to reconcile the ideal of nobility with the commercial
constraints of business. Their property was also likely to be much more
prosperous if they simultaneously maintained a "strong metropolitan
base" and "efficient managers on the spot" (Craton 101). This explanation
is confirmed by the political importance of edifying a West Indian interest
in London and of being able to pressure the government for favorable legislation. Finally, as time went by, the profits of the plantations decreased
and diversification became a good way of counterbalancing this decrease.
The wealthier the planters, the more likely they were to be absent, which
explains why absenteeism was more common in the Greater than in the
Lesser Antilles and in Jamaica than in Barbados. This trend played a major
part in the differences found in the slave systems, and most certainly, as
will be seen later, in the development of a Southern cultural distinctiveness.

Before moving on to other aspects of the organization of the plantation
societies, a last population group must be dealt with. Although it played a
minor role in the development of the plantation societies *per se,* it had the
advantage of anteriority: the Indians. Although their role in the rise of
Southern difference was slight, their presence and interaction with the
colonizers require a few comments. The Spaniards either massacred or enslaved them, and enslavement was equivalent to murder. After decimating
those they found on the islands they first settled, they imported more of
them, from the Bahamas, for instance. Spain had no interest in the Lesser
Antilles, however, and the Indians remained there until the French and
English settlers reached the islands. Although the Europeans left them the
islands of St. Vincent and Dominica by treaty, colonization ultimately
caught up with them, and when the Europeans started occupying their last
two islands, their vital space was drastically reduced and their number decreased. The Caribs were ultimately either slaughtered or expelled, and the
treaties finally had no other function than that of delaying their disappearance. Thus, in the Caribbean, the Indians did not much influence colonial
history except during the first few decades, when their enslavement con-
tributed to the profit of the initial enterprises.

In the North American colonies, their presence was felt for a much
longer period, although some tribes became entirely extinct within a century of colonization. (The Florida Timucuans, for instance, had totally disappeared by the early eighteenth century.) Probably because there was
enough room, they were neither systematically massacred nor expelled at

once. Instead, the development of colonization resulted in their rapid demographic decrease. Although sometimes due to slaughters (the French of
the Chickasaw and the Natchez, for example) or rare removal projects,
most of the Indian mortality was due to two non-deliberate factors linked
with the presence of Europeans: diseases for which the natives had no
natural defense and the deleterious effects of alcohol which had not existed
in their societies. Their disappearance was thus much slower. It was not
until the land hunger of the colonists became unquenchable that they
started removing Indians on a large scale in the nineteenth century. There
were few attempts at enslaving them, except in the very early days. In the
Carolinas, for instance, in 1700, out of 5,500 slaves, there were 1,400 natives. This, however, was a marginal phenomenon, and natives remained
altogether present in these colonial societies for a much longer period,
whatever the European power in command. The "civilized" tribes sometimes assimilated into American society to such a degree that some of
them even became slave owners in the nineteenth century. In fact, there
was no systematic Indian policy until well into the nineteenth century,
during Andrew Jackson's presidency. The reaction of the settlers and of the
governments depended on the tribes, on the size of the territory available,
and on the number of settlers: in short, on the balance of powers. The European nations sometimes even used the Indians, taking advantage of their
taste for warfare to compete for territories through allied tribes. In Louisiana, the French used the Creek and the Choctaw to counter English expansion. The Anglo-Saxon tendency, which spread over North America in the
nineteenth century, was to neutralize them, remove them if necessary,
take their land when possible, and try to destroy their culture and way of
life through attempts at assimilation. This policy, peculiar to North
America, apparently had little to do with the development of the Southern
slave society. However, it has to be stressed for two main reasons. It would
be difficult to describe the organization of society without mentioning this
large population group; moreover, the settlers' relationships with the natives confirm the already-noted fact that, at first, the space left vacant for
colonists to settle was sufficient to avoid any major conflicts, either between foreign nations or between the settlers and the natives. Conversely,
Caribbean space was so reduced that proper colonization of the islands necessarily implied the destruction or removal of the native populations who
occupied the land.

To conclude, social organization, although very similar in colonial societies, in itself highlights a trend toward Southern difference. Very early in

the history of colonization, the continental colonies became settlement colonies, as opposed to the Caribbean ones, which remained, for a much larger part, places to exploit but not to settle. Planter absenteeism was a distinguishing feature, too; though common to the West Indian colonies and peculiar to the Caribbean basin, it was rarely met in the American South. To move forward on the track of Southern distinctiveness, it is indispensable to examine the economic development of the plantation societies of the Americas.

Plantation Economies

In economic matters, there were, again, many more similarities than differences. The first obvious common feature was the predominance of agriculture in the economy. In the Caribbean colonies, as well as in the American South, agriculture was first the main condition for survival and next, the main source of wealth. Throughout the colonies, the settlers first cultivated food crops to survive: corn and wheat in the continental colonies; potatoes, bananas, manioc, and rice in the island colonies, where animal raising also provided a large part of the food. Then, agriculture became more diversified. In Virginia, for instance, the natives showed the settlers how to cultivate tobacco. Other crops were later introduced in the southern colonies, including rice, indigo, and finally cotton, which became "King Cotton" in the nineteenth century.

Louisiana started in the same way, although it relied heavily on the fur and skin trade in the early years of colonization. The Louisiana settlers started cultivating tobacco, but their production proved to be of relatively poor quality, and the Natchez rebellion of 1729 almost entirely destroyed the industry. They subsequently turned to indigo and rice, as well as corn and peas, thus diversifying their production. If, like Virginia, Louisiana did grow cotton, it differed from the former in turning to the cultivation of sugar cane in the early nineteenth century." All the continental colonies ultimately grew sufficient food crops to feed their own settlers, as well as the inhabitants of the Caribbean colonies. Corn and wheat from the southern English colonies were sent to the West Indies, while Louisiana traded corn, rice, and peas for West Indian coffee, sugar, and rum.

Similarly, the Caribbean colonies first produced food crops. Then they started growing tobacco, indigo, cotton (especially the English islands), annatto, cacao, and coffee (introduced in the French islands in the eighteenth century), and, from the nineteenth century onwards, the breadfruit

Fig. 4. Slave Cabin, Rural Life Museum, Baton Rouge, Louisiana. Photo by Nathalie Dessens.

tree, and spices, especially pepper, cinnamon, and cloves. Spain turned early to large-scale sugar cane growing, although the Spaniards maintained some cattle breeding (as shown by the tradition of *latifundios ganaderos* [cattle ranches] in Cuba).[34] The Spanish colonists also cultivated tobacco in Cuba and coffee in Santo Domingo and Puerto Rico. As for the English and French islands, they turned to sugar around 1640 and relied on it progressively to reach a stage that was close to monoculture, especially in the late seventeenth century.

Even though the crops varied because the climates were different, the basic principles of agricultural economy were the same across the colonies. Instead, the main economic differential lay elsewhere. After the end of the colonial period, the South progressively tended to develop many fewer direct commercial exchanges with foreign countries. Despite their significant role in the national economy, the southern states increasingly depended on their northern counterparts for the organization of international trade. By contrast, the islands relied heavily on external commerce, favored by the small size of the territories and by the fact that most of the exploited land was located along the coast, which made sea transportation easy. This led the Caribbean colonies to a position of extreme economic wealth in the late eighteenth century, largely to the advantage of the French. At that time, France became the world's largest producer of sugar and coffee.

Concomitantly with commercial development, the colonies underwent a limited industrial evolution, unheard-of in the American South. Despite the invention of the cotton gin, because the main crops did not require instant treatment and could be sold as raw material, Southerners never developed transformation industries. They first relied on England and then on the North for the production of manufactured goods (the transformation of cotton, for instance). For obvious reasons, in the Caribbean colonies (and later, in Louisiana), where the main crop was sugar cane, the necessity of the immediate transformation of the cane promoted the development of an industrial model. The sugar plantations became industrial units with a definite organizational model and architectural specificity. The planters were both industrialists and businessmen, which promoted the economic surge of the West Indian colonies. They largely favored this diversity in their activity, sticking to their industrial role whenever it was threatened. In the French Lesser Antilles, for instance, the government attempted to concentrate the sugar cane transformation industry, believing that the building of a few cooperative sugar plants would be much more economical and profitable than the existing system, where each planter refined his own production. When the idea became public, the planters systematically opposed it, wishing to go on processing their sugar individually.

In short, all the societies studied evinced strikingly similar economic patterns based on agricultural production and plantation units. The West Indian colonies, however, tended to be more diversified economically and relied heavily on international commerce and industrial transformation of their products. This most certainly weighed on the later ideological developments of the antebellum South, where the agrarian ideal became a true profession of faith. Indeed, all these similarities and differences in the social and economic organization of the various colonies also implied equivalent common features and contrasts in the way of life of the colonists and in the cultural evolution of the societies.

Life and Culture

Like the other fields examined, way of life and cultural evolution reveal interesting developmental patterns. For instance, the industrial tradition of the sugar planters of the Caribbean colonies (and, from the late eighteenth century on, of Louisiana) had undeniable consequences for their way of life and culture. The plantation landscapes of the sugar societies were very

different from what could be found in the American South. The plantations of the American South consisted of the master's house, the houses of
the privileged workers (such as the overseer), some outbuildings, and the
slave cabins. This collection sometimes comprised the whole of the plantation, although if livestock were owned, barns and stables would be found as
well. The rest of the plantation consisted of fields for agriculture. In the
sugar societies of the Caribbean and of nineteenth-century Louisiana, the
picture painted by all the available evidence is altogether very different.
Describing a sugar plantation, Jean-Baptiste Labat cites the typical dwellings—the master's main house and slaves' cabins—but also enumerates,
among other buildings, the sugar mill; the boiling house and curing-house;
the still house for the distillation of rum (with its very characteristic chim-
ney); several sheds; workshops for the skilled workers; and the sheds for
the cane trash (which was stored to be used as fuel).[35] Plantation descriptions for the English islands, as precise as Labat's, are quite similar.[36]

The sugar plantation also generally had an area dedicated to food crops
and another to livestock, including the yokes necessary for picking up cane
and for turning the mill when animals operated it. Most of the planters
also used manure to fertilize the soil, which required intensive treatment.
In the Caribbean, thanks to the sub-tropical climate, it was possible to
grow two crops a year; this practice exhausted the land, and the surface of
the islands was too restricted to afford any uncultivated land. In the South,
because food could be easily imported from the North, food crops were less
essential than in the West Indies; there was also much less livestock. The
climate was less well adapted to this activity and, according to some historians, the bad treatment the slaves inflicted on the animals made breeding
an unprofitable activity.[37] Moreover, Southerners resorted much less to
fertilization techniques; having more space, they had opportunity to exploit uncultivated land. It is also to be noted that the large size of some
plantations made the use of these techniques unfeasible.

Despite these significant differences in plantation landscape, many
common features existed, among them the distribution of the habitat.[38] In
the South, as in the West Indian societies, the size and location of the
dwellings corresponded to the status of its occupants within the hierarchy
of the plantation organization. The master, his family, and house slaves
lived in the "big house," sometimes a mansion on the larger plantations,
and generally situated on the property's highest spot (for symbolic reasons, but also for defense and, especially in the Caribbean, because the
highest locations received the cooling eastern Trade Winds). The overseers

had a smaller dwelling, generally between the master's house and the slave quarters. As for the slaves, they lived in rudimentary cabins at some distance from the master's mansion. The distance between slave quarters and mansion was generally greater in the Caribbean than in the South, partly because of more distant relationships between masters and slaves in those colonies and partly because industrial buildings took space and relegated the slave quarters to more distant ground. The cabins could be arranged in a cluster in the form of a village, which was common in the South, or in a line, which was in general the tradition of the West Indies. In the latter case, they were regularly distributed on both sides of the very famous "rue case nègre" [literally, "Nigger Cabins' Street"], as it was called in the French West Indies.[39]

Masters' houses shared two common features in the South and in the Caribbean: their higher location and relatively larger size compared to other plantation buildings. Differences between the two were based principally on geography and social organization. Climate and ecology influenced the architecture and furnishing of the houses, for example. The uniformly hot tropical climate of the Caribbean obliged builders to figure out ways of preserving as best they could a certain coolness in the houses. Thus the implacable architectural tradition of kitchens located outside the main building. (Of course, detached kitchens were also found in many regions of the South, to avoid fire hazards.) The circular gallery around the Caribbean big house brought much appreciated shade around and into the dwelling, while wooden-louvered windows allowed air circulation and admitted refreshing Trade Winds. The climate of the South was different and, although hot in summer, much cooler in other seasons. The houses thus had windows and porches rather than galleries. They were more often constructed of harder materials than in the West Indies, which were more backward in the fabrication and importation of materials than the colonies of the northern continent. For their houses and furnishings, the West Indians used tropical woods not always found in the South, which also had a larger diversity of wood than the Caribbean colonies. The West Indian planters filled their houses with typical mahogany furniture adapted to their needs and handcrafted in Jamaica and Barbados.

The second source of difference lay in lifestyles. Caribbean plantation houses and their contents were generally more rudimentary than those in the South, partly because of the West Indian mercantile tradition; the planters often did not bring their families along when they spent time on their properties, and, as already noted, they were more often absentees. In some societies, even when they did not go back to Europe, planters tended to leave their plantations to the supervision of managers and live in the urban centers: this was the case, for instance, in the Spanish societies, and more particularly in Havana and Santo Domingo. In his famous study of Caribbean style, Jan Morris also mentions a certain pragmatism, which made the West Indian planters prefer solid massive buildings to elegant ones, probably because they were moneymakers rather than mythmakers and because they needed to protect themselves from frequent destructive hurricanes.[40] Altogether, it was more important for the Southern planters to tame the space where they and their descendants had every intention of spending their entire lives.

Common traits and differences also existed in social life. Occupations on plantations in the Caribbean were similar when planters were residents; horse riding and hunting were the leisure activities of the planters, being traditional activities of gentleman farmers. In travel narratives of the nascent plantation period, authors insist on the traditional hospitality offered by the colonists, a social habit which was probably the result of a craving for unusual company, especially when it came directly from Europe.[41] They all underline a relatively impoverished social life in the more rudimentary West Indian societies, where the main planters were not always residents.[42]

In the South, on the contrary, because it was an area of permanent settlement and residence, social life was highly developed. All the descriptions indicate an intense social life. Youngsters traveled both for pleasure and education. Weddings, balls, and receptions—to honor traveling celebrities and welcome neighbors—were abundant. The Southerners purchased fine furniture from Europe. They went to the theater, to watering spots, to race tracks.[43] In short, a true upper class social life was established and came to flourish in the eighteenth and nineteenth centuries. Consequently, cultural development was another main difference between the Caribbean and the American South.

The Caribbean colonies were not uniform as far as culture in the broad sense of the term is concerned. The Spanish colonies were relatively dynamic, with local newspapers and universities (both in Santo Domingo, where the first university on the American continent was established, and in Cuba, where the University of Havana was founded in 1728). In the French and English islands, culture was much less developed, and there were no real attempts at a specific local culture. The school system was unorganized, and there were no attempts at instituting one. When the planters were residents and had their families with them, they hired tutors for their young children and sent them to Europe for higher education. The level of organization and development depended on the island. Despite this relatively constant backwardness, the less absenteeism there was, the more organized the societies were: for instance, Barbados was much better organized culturally than Jamaica. With the notable exception of St. Domingue, where some dynamic intellectuals had launched several somewhat modest publications, the colonial newspapers were "shipping gazettes" rather than newspapers in the real sense of the word.[44] Even when there were some cultural events (as in French St. Domingue), there was no attempt at a local form of creation. In the theater, for instance, the plays performed were those in fashion in metropolitan France.

In the American South, the situation was quite different, even in the late colonial period. In the early days of colonization, the colonists' tasks were focused on other fields more urgent than culture. In the eighteenth century, however, a relative intellectual and cultural independence from the motherland began to take shape. Colleges were founded, and even if most of them were in the northern colonies, the South was not totally excluded. Williamsburg welcomed the famous William and Mary College, as well as the first theater in the British North American colonies in 1716. In the South, newspapers existed, although still in small numbers. This movement increased as the colonies started diverging from their mother country, a trend that accelerated after independence. Quite naturally, the birth of the new nation brought about the development of autonomous systems in all fields. Education was a priority for Americans, but the same development also concerned every form of cultural manifestation; newspapers and theaters were founded and, still more importantly, a completely new area of cultural development appeared. Americans now united their efforts to develop a specifically American culture, more distant from that of England. Literature, music, and all the artistic forms of expression took on a definite American flavor. This was also true in the early decades of the Southern states, which became involved in the creation of a specifically American culture. When oppositions became patent between North and South in the nineteenth century, this Southern cultural movement became autonomous, increasingly so as the two sections drifted apart. A Southern culture developed, first as a branch of American culture, then, after 1850, in a deliberate attempt at independence and difference.

In matters of culture, a few remarks should be made with regard to religion and churches, where various patterns of evolution can be found.

The colonial status of the Caribbean islands never encouraged, in their first centuries of existence, any religious independence. Be they Anglican or Catholic, the clergymen came from the metropolitan churches, most of the time as missionaries. Many accounts describe them as poor representatives of holy interests. The account of Jean-Baptiste Labat more often deals with good food and business than purely religious topics. Describing the Anglican clergy of the British islands, F. R. Augier contends that some of its members "were gamblers and drinkers," that there were "some unfrocked priests," and that "many were absentees." As was the case of the Catholic clergymen, "others engaged in the same pursuits as the more prosperous Europeans and became planters, merchants or even, in one case, the commander of a privateer" (Augier et al., 136). In the colonies of the northern continent, on the contrary, the churches grew in strength, organizational efficiency, and influence because of the religious mission of some of the colonies. The national existence of the United States increased the trend, the churches wishing, like the rest of the nation, to enhance their independence and characteristic features. As with other cultural manifestations (in the broad sense of the term), the growing divisions between North and South in the nineteenth century increased the development and strength of Southern churches, which became independent from their Northern counterparts.

This rapid examination of the political, economic, social, and cultural development of the slave societies of the Americas already shows, in a broad context of similarity, the existence of divergences between the Caribbean colonies and those of the American South. The examination of these differences already clearly hints at a nascent Southern difference. Whereas the colonists of the Caribbean persistently considered the islands as places to exploit, the North American colonies very early became places of settlement.[45] This pattern was encouraged by the availability of wide spaces, a more congenial and healthy climate, and the attraction for immigrants of much better living conditions. The political independence of the thirteen colonies and the acquisition of new territories on the American continent probably also spurred the trend toward settlement. As a result, the population of the South grew steadily, building a real society of elites, weaving a much tighter social fabric among a population that remained predominantly white. Concentrating on agricultural economy, the Southern whites organized a civilization that acquired real social and cultural autonomy, a society where their descendents would live and prosper as well.

The American South thus began quite early to display a number of distinctive features. This Southern difference was further enhanced by the divergences that appeared in the organization of the slave systems of the Americas. The latter, being at the core of the organization of plantation societies at large, require an in-depth scrutiny in order to reach viable conclusions concerning Southern distinctiveness.

Comparative Systems of Slavery

The organization of slavery is probably the aspect most often studied in a comparative perspective. Several authors have dealt with it either extensively or anecdotally in their works.[1] One of the reasons for this increased attention may be that comparison seems definitely appropriate and manageable for a topic that is much more factual and less fluctuating than other aspects of plantation societies. The present study is a comprehensive presentation, definitely comparative, bearing on all the societies of the Caribbean and the American South.

Many of the works that have attempted this type of comparison tend to concentrate on one type of society (either the South or the Caribbean,[2] or on a specific colony), mentioning the others comparatively only to delineate the specific features of the society studied.[3] Most of them deal with one precise aspect of the slave societies, and extensive comparative studies (on slave legislation, for instance) are still lacking. The purpose here is to attempt an impartial comparison and to examine as many aspects as possible of the question, including the legal principles of the codification of slavery in all the societies.

This chapter is at the core of the study of Southern distinctiveness, insofar as slavery is the first obvious similarity between all the societies studied. The African origin of the slaves; the organization of the slave system (plantation societies); the economic orientation of the societies (commercial agriculture); the slave's status (a legal, life-long, and transmittable status as chattel); and the organization of hierarchical social structures all tend to unify the slave societies. However, the thesis sustaining the present study is that, even if slavery was the main common feature, it was also what eventually divided the societies, although sometimes indirectly.

The central role slavery played in both unifying and diversifying the societies is easily understandable. Slavery was the constitutive principle:

when the "societies with slaves" became "slave societies," slavery in them became the modeling force.[4] As Ira Berlin puts it, the master-slave relationship, while ruling economic production, became "the social exemplar" (*Many Thousands*, 8). Slavery was thus the pivot of these societies, which is the reason why it is also the pivot of the present study, occupying the central position here. Up to this point, our comparative study of colonial settlement patterns and of plantation societies among the colonies of the Caribbean and the American South has indicated a slight Southern difference. However, everything that revolved around the Peculiar Institution— from the organization of slavery to its consequences for the further evolution of the societies; from the aftermath of the abolition battles to slavery's ultimate suppression—eventually pinpoint a potent Southern distinctiveness.

Transatlantic Trade

The founding element of American slave societies was, of course, the transatlantic trade that brought to the colonies their very special labor force. The first African slaves were imported to the Canary Islands by the Portuguese in the late fourteenth century and to the Americas from the Iberian Peninsula by the Spaniards in the early sixteenth century. The importation of African slaves was a common feature of Spain and Portugal long before they started colonizing the American continent. Almost three centuries before the first African slaves of the Caribbean reached Santo Domingo in 1508, slavery had been codified in Spain through the *Siete Partidas* or Seven Divisions, the major law code of Spain in the thirteenth century. In the West Indies, the needs rapidly became greater than the number of slaves the Iberian Peninsula could provide, and the Spaniards started importing slaves directly from Africa from the 1520s onwards.

As early as the first half of the sixteenth century, the Spanish crown delivered *asientos*, permits allowing the trading of slaves from Africa. The first such document known, referring to a direct importation, dates back to 1518. In 1540, the number of slaves imported to the Caribbean was about 10,000. In the last two decades of the sixteenth century, 11,300 and 40,700 African slaves, respectively, were brought to the Spanish colonies of the Caribbean.[5] The movement accelerated when the other European nations obtained the right to challenge the Iberian monopoly. The Dutch entered the competition first, then France and England, although these two nations obtained an official authorization through the Treaty of Utrecht only in

Fig. 5. Cabins where slaves were raised for market—The famous Hermitage, Savannah, Georgia. Library of Congress Prints and Photographs Division (Video Frame ID: LCPP003A-18408). Circa 1903.

1702 and 1713 respectively. In the eighteenth century, some two million slaves were imported into the Caribbean colonies, according to estimates.[6] The colony of Martinique can be taken as an example: from a population of 2,344 slaves in 1664, the figure increased to 23,260 by 1701,[7] and to 80,000 by 1754.[8] The other French and English colonies (for instance Guadeloupe, Barbados, and Jamaica) followed the same pattern.

In the English colonies of the northern continent, slavery came much later, which is consistent with the later settlement of these colonies. In 1619, twenty Africans were shipped to Jamestown. After the mid-seventeenth century, their status shifted from that of mere indentured servants to that of slaves for life. Slave importation remained, however, relatively limited compared with the West Indies, due to the natural reproduction of the slave population, a phenomenon that will be detailed below. The total importation figures are around 500,000 for the duration of the legal trading period, that is, until 1808.[9]

The Spanish colonies had been the first to rely on large-scale importation of Africans as slaves. They remained the main importers in the sixteenth and seventeenth centuries, but up to the time of abolition imported
fewer and fewer slaves. The eighteenth century was the era of French and
English importation. To illustrate this new trend, one example will suffice.
All observers describing the Spanish and French parts of Hispaniola in the
late eighteenth century (Sanchez Valverde and Moreau de Saint-Méry, for
instance) indicate the presence of about 15,000 slaves in Spanish Santo
Domingo compared to about 450,000 in French St. Domingue.[10] In short, if
African slavery was, in the beginning, a Spanish institution in the Caribbean, it rapidly expanded to all the American colonies of the European
nations.

The slave trade lasted until the nineteenth century when, one after the
other, the various nations abolished the practice. The Danish colonies led
the way, voting in 1792 for the abolition that took effect ten years later.
England did so in 1808, the same year as the United States. At the end of
the twenty-year moratorium set by the Constitution, Congress passed the
ban. Anti-slavery sentiment was just beginning at the time, but the natural
reproduction of the slave population made the trade less useful to the
Americans. France permanently ended the trade in 1815, and Spain followed, signing two suppression treaties with England in 1817 and (because
the first treaty was not respected) in 1835. England and Spain even organized mixed commissions, with members appointed by the two nations to
render sentences in case of illegal trade. The law prescribed immediate seizure of the cargo and emancipation of the seized Africans. To ensure its
enforcement, Spain voted in the 1845 penal law that instituted strong penalties for those who ignored the ban.

The trade, however, went on under other flags—all the more so since
evading the law was easy. In the Spanish islands, for instance, *cedulas*,
identity papers for slaves, were delivered to masters, but the latter found
ways to have additional, falsified papers created, and thus newly imported
bozals could pass for long-detained slaves.[11] The trade went on illegally for
several decades, although the numbers of slaves imported was much
smaller.

Throughout the three centuries of trade, although the slaves did not
have the same African origins in all the colonies, the system of importation
did not vary much and followed a similar pattern across the various nations. The acquisition of the slaves in Africa, as well as their transportation
to and subsequent sale in the colonies were organized in the same way

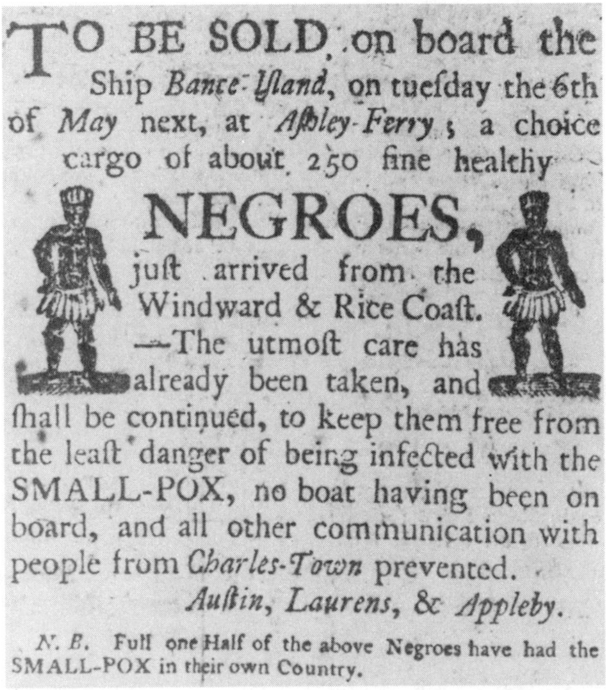

TO BE SOLD, on board the Ship *Bance-Island*, on tuesday the 6th of *May* next, at *Aſhley-Ferry*; a choice cargo of about 250 fine healthy

NEGROES,

juſt arrived from the Windward & Rice Coaſt. —The utmoſt care has already been taken, and ſhall be continued, to keep them free from the leaſt danger of being infected with the SMALL-POX, no boat having been on board, and all other communication with people from *Charles-Town* prevented.

Auſtin, Laurens, & Appleby.

N. B. Full one Half of the above Negroes have had the SMALL-POX in their own Country.

Fig. 6. To be sold, on board the ship Bance Island, . . . negroes, just arrived from the Windward & Rice Coast. Photograph of newspaper advertisement from the 1780s(?) for the sale of slaves at Ashley Ferry outside of Charleston, South Carolina. Library of Congress Prints and Photographs Division (Video Frame ID: LCPP003A-52072). Circa 1780.

throughout the trading period, no matter which nation organized the trading.[12] Very few dissimilarities existed, and they could be attributed to local exception rather than national rule.

The gender pattern of this mass transportation may be the only topic of interest here, since it had a direct influence on the demographic evolution of the slave societies in the various colonies. The first model is, as usual, the Spanish model. In the first half of the sixteenth century, the majority of slaves transported were young men. Very few women were imported at that time, although some had reached the colonies in 1518, coming, like the men, from Spain. Interestingly, at that time, there was no sex discrimination as far as prices were concerned.[13] Instead, the importation of women was more limited partly because Spain needed strong workers and partly because female and child slaves were in greater demand in Africa, which made the Africans more reluctant to sell them.[14] The Spanish crown, however, ultimately understood the necessity of importing women in order to put moral and social pressure on male slaves and consequently demanded that one-third of the importations be women.[15] The proportion sometimes went up to half a shipload, but was generally about one-third.[16] This evolution may be explained first by the belief that women would constitute a good social cement, a check to rebellions and marooning (that is, slaves' running away from the plantations), and second by their obvious utility in the natural reproduction of the slave population.[17] The other nations inflected the sex ratios of purchased slaves in the same way and for the same purposes. In all the colonies, at the very beginning, there was the same numerical imbalance between the sexes. The figures for Louisiana, for instance, give a ratio of three or four males to one female.[18] All the colonies later tried to redress the imbalance, to the point that the Spanish colonies were the most disadvantaged in this respect. All the colonies had in mind a way to ensure the natural reproduction of their slave populations, and although these reproduction schemes systematically governed the organization of trade, they were not equally successful in all the colonies.

Demographic Evolution

A deeply interesting focus in matters of demography is indeed the capacity of the slave populations to ensure their own reproduction. In this respect, the colonies were not equal and the differences created wide divergences among them, which may explain extremely different modes of further evolution. The English Southern colonies first experienced a slow process of reproduction among their slaves. In the 1680s, 2,000 Africans reached the colony of Virginia. In the next decade, this number reached 4,000 and in the first decade of the eighteenth century, 8,000. During that period, 90 percent of the slaves of the colony were born in Africa. At the time, the sex ratio still largely inclined to men (about 2 to 1), and natural reproduction was slow. The birth rate was very low among the newly arrived, and the death rate was extremely high. According to Berlin, within one year of their arrival, one quarter of the Africans would be dead.[19] The same can be said about Louisiana. Berlin takes the example of the *Venus*, a slave ship that reached the colony in 1729. Among the 450 Africans on board, 43 died before disembarking, and two-thirds of those sold died soon afterwards.[20]

A change occurred in the 1740s, although the new trend remained a relatively slow process as long as the proportion of newly imported slaves was much higher than that of native slaves. As soon as the proportion was reversed, natural reproduction sped up, in keeping with the general trend encountered in the North American colonies. The white settlers' reproduction rate was very high; that of the slaves was still higher. The native-born slaves were far healthier and lived much longer than those imported. The sex imbalance had been corrected by then, which favored reproduction. In Virginia, by 1730, 40 percent of the slaves were natives; by 1750, this figure had reached 80 percent; and by the 1770s, almost all of them were. If the process was slow at first, once triggered, it became steady. In the Carolina Low Country, the situation was very similar. At first, two-thirds of the slaves imported were men, and there was almost no natural increase; until 1760, deaths outnumbered births in the region. However, from then on, the slaves began to reproduce naturally. This was true of the entire South, the increase being especially strong in the nineteenth century. From a slave population of about 675,500 in 1790, the South reached a total of almost four million slaves in 1860, although the overseas trade had been legally suppressed.[21]

By contrast, in the Caribbean colonies, the natural reproduction of the slave population never compensated for mortality, and the islands had to keep importing large numbers of slaves throughout the slavery era. The death rate among the slaves ranged most of the time between 10 percent and 12 percent a year, while their birth rate, in the West Indies as a whole, did not exceed 8 to 9 percent.[22] The figures cited by historians are sometimes baffling. For Eric Williams, half the population of Barbados had to be renewed every eight years; for Jean-Paul Barbiche, an adult slave reaching the Antillean colonies had a life expectancy of five to ten years on the average.[23] For Craton, more than 2.5 million slaves were imported to the Caribbean over 180 years with only 670,000 remaining in 1834, while the 400,000 slaves imported to the South begot a population of almost four million by 1865.[24]

This fact, which is acknowledged by all historians, has been the object of many tentative—and sometimes contradictory—interpretations. It seems, however, that the chief difference between Caribbean and Southern slave populations may be accounted for by a sum of reasons difficult to organize in order of priority. Among the explanations is first the reality that constant importation constituted a kind of vicious circle. As previously noted, the *bozals* had a higher mortality rate and lower fertility rate than the "Creole" slaves.[25] As long as most of the slave population was imported, the natural reproduction of the population was checked. This is clearly visible in the colonies of the American South, where the phenomenon was only slowly reversed at first, but finally eliminated once birth, instead of trade, became the main factor in the increase of the slave population. The Caribbean planters never really tried to reverse the trend. Moreover, many fatal diseases developed in the Caribbean (yellow fever and malaria, probably worsened by the constant importation of slaves), and the climate was less healthy than in the South. Some historians also argue that malnutrition and bad treatment, partly due to absenteeism and to the huge size of the plantations, had an effect on the Caribbean death rates. Others try to refute this thesis, arguing that such conditions had no effect, because women remained fertile for about the same number of years in both regions. All historians agree that there was a clearly longer life expectancy for slaves of the northern continent. Thirty-five years was the average in the eighteenth century American South, while it was only twenty-five years in Brazil, for example. Similarly, taking into account the very high infant mortality rate, a five-year-old slave in Brazil had a life expectancy of thirty-five years, while in the United States, it was over forty. Historians cannot deny this evidence, but they contend that the same phenomenon existed among white colonists and free colored people.[26] Bad treatment alone cannot suffice to explain the trend. Other reasons should be considered, such as the persistent imbalance between men and women in the Caribbean.[27] Moreover, the difference in lactation periods, which were shorter in the South (following a European pattern) than in the Caribbean (up to three years), also permitted more frequent pregnancies.[28] For Santo Domingo historian Celsa Batista, a more precocious metabolism among Caribbean female slaves could also account for the lower birth rate found in the West Indian colonies. According to Batista, the adult female slaves of Santo Domingo, often newly arrived, may have reached earlier sexual maturity. They could thus give birth very early but did not, and their fertility ended earlier, at a time when they would normally have had children.[29]

Other more precise demographic studies can be considered here. Craton devotes a whole chapter to a detailed study of the slave population of several properties belonging to a single family in the Bahamas.[30] He shows that the age of the first childbirth was around 21.6 years, which may seem to confirm Batista's thesis. He also shows that there were numerous miscarriages and early deaths among babies. The lactation periods lasted about three years, which prevented pregnancies for the same duration. He eventually studies demographic differences according to the type of crop grown on the plantation, showing that cotton made fewer physical demands on the slaves than sugar, which could partially account for the discrepancies between the South and the Caribbean. His study is extremely interesting in the context of the present discussion, although it is important to add that the Bahamas had an intermediate position as its climate was far healthier than that in the rest of the Caribbean basin.

The consequences of birthrate difference are numerous. The constant renewal of slave populations in the Caribbean, for instance, affected relationships within the slave societies. The permanence of slaves on the plantation favored the type of paternalistic relationships between masters and slaves that tended to develop in the South. It also favored the existence of strong family cells in the slave population, as well as a definite social fabric among slaves in the South. The constant changes in the population of the Caribbean also slowed down (if they did not altogether prevent) the process of Creolization among West Indian slaves, "reafricanization frustrate-[ing] any notion of a linear progression from African to Creole"(Berlin 107). The demographic specificity of the American South and its social and cultural consequences would thus further account for the above-mentioned Southern distinctiveness.

Diverging demographic evolution was not the only feature separating the slave societies of the Caribbean and the American South. There was also a great imbalance in the white to African ratio in the Caribbean. In the South, the total slave population was never more numerous than the white population, although there were geographical exceptions to the rule. In 1790, the whole South contained 1,271,500 white persons, 675,500 slaves, and 32,000 free colored persons. In 1860, at the end of the slave era, the ratio was still about two to one, with 8,097,500 whites, 3,953,700 slaves, and 262,000 free colored people.[31] The figures vary slightly from one historian to the next (free colored people sometimes being counted with slaves), but the ratio fundamentally remains the same, although in the continental colonies there were differences between the rural and urban areas, with larger populations of African Americans in the latter. (In Charleston, for instance, the numbers were equal in 1720, but from the 1770s on, there were more blacks than whites.) There were also differences from one region to the next, with a balance in the Lower South, while the Upper South was more white.[32] The Carolina Low Country, with its huge rice plantations, evinced a Caribbean pattern, with the slave population outnumbering the white population by a ratio of two to one. The only region with a relative superiority of people of African origin (whether slaves or free) was Louisiana; as early as 1731, the black population represented about sixty percent of the total population.[33]

The West Indian model was very different from the Southern one, with the notable exception of the Spanish colonies, where slavery started earlier but did not develop in the same proportions. Puerto Rico had a proportion of blacks that barely exceeded ten percent, while in Santo Domingo, it verged on twenty percent.[34] In Cuba, whites represented over forty-five percent of the population. This does not mean, however, that slaves represented fifty-five percent, because there existed a significant free colored class.[35] The only exception was Trinidad, where slaves represented 53.3 percent of the population as early as 1790. This is because the island had always retained a large Amerindian population, which slowed the implantation of colonists and thus inflected the proportions. A comparison between the French and Spanish parts of Hispaniola in the late eighteenth century gives a good image of the peculiarity of the Spanish possessions. During this period, the total populations of St. Domingue and Santo Domingo were 570,000 and 103,000 respectively, with a corresponding 30,000 whites in the former and 35,000 whites in the latter. (Notice the slight advantage to the Spanish part despite the huge global disproportion.) To continue, St. Domingue had 40,000 free people of color and 500,000 slaves in contrast to Santo Domingo's 38,000 free people of color and 30,000 slaves.[36] In fact, the huge difference in number of slaves accounted for French Hispaniola's being over four times more populous than Spanish Hispaniola. Indeed, whereas the Spanish colony was divided into more or less three equal castes, there was a huge disproportion in the French colony (although the white and free populations were equal to those found in Santo Domingo).

The French and English models were very different from the Spanish one, although not always in such proportions as those recorded for the two parts of Hispaniola. In the whole British Caribbean, the slave population substantially outnumbered the free population. In Jamaica, for instance, the 1768 slave population consisted of 176,900 individuals, representing 89.2 percent of the total population. The 1775 ratio was the same.[37] In Barbados, the figures are 75.4 percent for 1746 (with 47,025 slaves) and 80 percent for 1768 (with 66,379 slaves).[38] The French colonies present a strikingly similar pattern with a proportion of 76.7 percent in 1726 (40,403 slaves), 77.7 percent in 1736 (46,062 slaves), and 83 percent in 1751 (65,905 slaves).[39] In Guadeloupe, the proportions recorded are 66 percent in 1710, 75 percent in 1730, and 82 percent in 1750.[40] These figures may explain some of the features and further patterns of evolution of the colonies.

The numerical superiority of the whites in the South, as well as the very early predominance of native slaves, certainly had an effect upon the paternalistic relationships that developed between the masters and their slaves. The larger disproportions noted in the Caribbean probably explain a number of differences that developed in the Caribbean colonies: many fewer personal master–slave relationships; a more culturally independent and Africanized slave society; and more numerous violent (or at least radical) reactions against the institution in the form of marooning, rebellion, or even total revolution as in French St. Domingue.

A last demography-related difference, with obvious consequences for the society at large should be emphasized: the presence of a much larger free colored class in the non-English colonies, especially of the northern continent. Although the phenomenon was not totally unheard of in the English colonies, it took on much larger proportions in the French and Spanish Americas.

Three-tiered versus Two-tiered Societies

In the British Southern colonies, the first decades of enslavement offered Africans the possibility to obtain their freedom. Indeed, their status was that of indentured servants, and there was no notion of life servitude in the legal sense. This model, however, endured only for forty years. In 1661, a Virginia law distinguished between white and black workers, indicating that the latter could not purchase their own contracts. In 1662, another law established that children's status would follow their mother's, meaning that all children born to slave women would immediately become slaves. The other colonies soon followed this example, Maryland as early as 1663.

The laws, even if they differed from one colony to the next, offered little space for emancipation once slavery had been legally instituted. As early as 1692, the colony of Virginia legislated against the possibility for black slaves to purchase their freedom. By 1723, Virginia law indicated that "a perpetual brand upon Free Negroes and Mulattoes by excluding them from the great privilege of a Freeman" should be fixed by the planters "to make the free Negroes sensible that a distinction ought to be made between their offspring and the Descendants of an Englishman, with whom they never were to be Accounted Equal."[41] Altogether the Southern colonies legislated to deny slaves access to freedom and reduce the rights of free colored people; the latter were no longer allowed the possession of white indentured servants; they could not hold office, bear arms, be militia members, or vote. Special taxes were sometimes imposed on them, and they incurred more severe penalties under the law. By 1691 in Virginia, manumission was no longer a master's power alone; it had become a legislative prerogative, and the emancipated slave had to leave the colony. The law also specified that the children born to white women and black slaves would be enslaved for thirty-one years, as would children born to these "part-time" slaves during their thirty-one years of enslavement. This, of course, reduced the possibility of increase in the free black population.

It would be time-consuming and pointless to detail all the different laws that were passed in the various colonies and states. Manumission remained possible, although difficult and rare, until the end of the eighteenth century, since at the time of the Revolution, the states one after the other lifted the bans of the colonial period. (Virginia, for instance, did so through the Virginia Manumission Law of 1782.) By 1790, all the Southern states except North Carolina had done so. In the late eighteenth and early nineteenth centuries, new measures were passed, though, preventing or even altogether banning any slave manumission by masters. The Haitian revolution and such events as the 1800 Gabriel Prosser rebellion in Virginia had made Southerners fearful that an excessively large free black population might endanger the whole system of slavery. This fear was reinforced in the nineteenth century by the development of the pro-slavery argument, which attempted to demonstrate that Africans had to be enslaved because they were incapable of independent thought and action. A 1793 Virginia law prohibited the access of free blacks to the state, and in 1808, the state legislature ruled that slaves manumitted in the future would have to leave the state within one year or upon their majority. As a result, such neighboring states as Maryland, Delaware, and Kentucky forbade the settlement of free blacks. In the early nineteenth century, all the states took constitutional measures preventing legislatures from freeing slaves without the consent of their masters.

This trend seems typical of the Anglo-Saxon societies. Indeed, the legislation of the English Caribbean constantly tried to prevent manumission. Slave status was matrilineal and so systematically passed from one to the next generation. Evidence of this Anglo-Saxon tendency is the case of Louisiana after its purchase in 1803 by the Americans. In colonial Louisiana, there was room for free colored people and for manumission, especially under Spanish rule. When the United States took control of the territory, the situation changed radically. Several restrictions were passed, including a ban on the manumission of slaves under the age of thirty, and in 1807, slaves' ability to purchase their own freedom was eliminated altogether. The Louisiana legislature ruled in 1830 that any emancipated slave would have to leave the state within the following month and ruled again in 1852 that he or she would have to leave the territory of the United States within one year. In 1857, Louisiana law banned manumission entirely. Facing risks mentioned in several primary sources—risks of being kidnapped and reenslaved—the free blacks' situation significantly worsened. The legislation shows Anglo-Saxon reluctance to let the free black population increase, a reluctance also evident in Martinique where manumission was strongly limited whenever England temporarily wrested control of the island from the French.

There was a free black population in all the English colonies, but it remained relatively limited in numbers. In Barbados, for instance, free blacks represented only one percent of the population in 1786, while in 1775, Jamaica counted 4,500 free colored people for 18,700 whites.[42] This is far from the quasi-parity of St. Domingue and Santo Domingo mentioned earlier. In 1860 in the United States, there were altogether 260,000 free blacks (to about four million slaves and eight million whites), and they were found in geographically restricted areas: in Louisiana (because of the state's French and Spanish colonial past) and in Maryland (about 84,000 of them). The rest were located mostly in towns, where sometimes one-third of the population was composed of free blacks. In New Orleans, in the early nineteenth century, the numbers were higher still, with free blacks accounting for 10,700 of the 18,600 people living there. In the whole South, they represented scarcely six percent of the population of African origin, and more than half of them lived in towns of over 2,500 inhabitants.[43]

At any rate, the status of the free blacks was never high in the Anglo-Saxon societies. Mostly craftsmen and skilled service workers, they remained a second-class, disfranchised populace. Mulattoes could not inherit their white fathers' property, for instance. In St. Vincent (which had become English at the end of the Seven Years' War in 1763), a 1767 law indicated that they could not own more than eight acres of land. Unlike their Spanish and French counterparts, mulattoes did not form an intermediate class in the English societies. These populations were not divided into three classes, and there was a single inferior caste composed of all those of African origin. There was miscegenation, but color prejudice was such that it remained a marginal phenomenon compared with its occurrence in the other societies. Moreover, the offspring of mixed unions retained the inferior status of the African parent. To show how little room there was for free blacks in the South, a single anecdotal example suffices. So unwelcome were free blacks in the English South that they built a small community in Gracia Real de Santa Teresa de Mose in Florida, but followed the Spaniards to Cuba in 1764 when England took control of that part of Florida.[44] Those who remained behind lost their freedom within an English colonial society.

The French and Spanish societies were quite different. Both were more favorable to free blacks, although the Spanish colonies afforded them a slight advantage. Louisiana provides an excellent example; there was room for emancipation during the French colonial era, but still more under Spanish control. Spain officially encouraged manumission. In 1779, for instance, 320 manumissions were recorded in Louisiana.[45] These manumissions extended primarily to women and children, who represented sixty-three percent of the total emancipated slaves.[46] The freed children were sometimes, though not necessarily, born of mixed unions. The practice of self-purchase (*coartación*)—not based on law, but having the force of a law—was expanded, and if the master refused, the slave could petition the governor, since Louisiana slaves could take their masters to court.[47] In New Orleans alone, in the first decade of Spanish control, two hundred slaves initiated the self-purchase processes, and 166 obtained satisfaction. Throughout the Spanish period, 1,330 slaves were freed, including planters' children.[48] The free colored population became much more visible under Spanish rule and played an important economic role. Free blacks were often craftsmen, which enabled them to become relatively wealthy. They could even be planters, and the Spanish government created a free colored militia to defend the colony. Although emancipated slaves could not hold any public office or enlist in the army, their descendants could. They could even accede to the priesthood.

The same trend was witnessed in the Spanish Caribbean colonies. Free colored people were roughly the same in number as whites and had a definitely higher status than in the Anglo-Saxon societies. Free colored militias, such as the Batallon de Pardos y Morenos in Santo Domingo, were formed. They were thus granted a special status, which gave them a real social, economic, and political function in the colony. Nonetheless, their legal status remained inferior to that of the whites. A number of interdictions denied them access to total civil equality, although the black bourgeoisie could vote in the Spanish (and Portuguese) continental colonies. There were also clothing restrictions imposed on them. In Santo Domingo, for instance, chapter 9 of the *Leyes Suntuarias* prevented them from wearing pearls, emeralds, precious stones, or even gold and silver.[49] They could neither wear *mantillas* or *sombreros*, nor carry spears.

In the French colonial societies, there was a large class of free colored people as well. In Martinique, for instance, they represented one-third of the free population. In St. Domingue, they were roughly equal in number to the whites. There were many acts of manumission, and unions official or not, between white men and black women, also produced a large mulatto class. White women being scarce, men had to choose their companions among the female slave population if they wanted a family life. A study of the registers of three parishes in the south of St. Domingue shows that in 1730, mixed unions represented seventeen percent of all unions. That figure increased to thirty percent by 1770.[50] Children, in most cases, were legally recognized, and their fathers very often ensured their futures. They were educated, sometimes in metropolitan France; daughters received dowries; and fathers sometimes gave their sons plantations, either as gifts or as bequests. As a result, the free colored population formed a diversified group representing a cross-section of society. This was more often true in St. Domingue than in the Lesser Antilles, but the latter followed a similar pattern. Colored people were often mulatto children with one white parent. There were also numerous cases of emancipation as the result of testamentary provisions or because a given slave was physically unable to work or was a non-French runaway. There were, for example, 507 manumissions in Martinique in 1701 and 772 in 1709, even if some restrictions were voted into practice soon afterward. A 1713 decision of the state council made the permission of the administrators a prerequisite to manumission; a manumission tax was instituted in 1742; and a 1768 law forbade fictitious sales to other islands, a ruse organized by some masters to free their slaves. Despite such legal restrictions that often went unheeded, the number of free colored people increased considerably in the eighteenth century, with the notable exception of the periods of English rule, when the shift in control brought about restrictions on manumissions. There were 13,181 free blacks in Martinique alone in 1762.

Their place in society was similar to that of their Spanish counterparts. They had a definite social and economic role, although they were subject to numerous legal restrictions as far as their status was concerned. They were not entitled to donations from white people and could not bear arms or buy gunpowder without a permit. They were not allowed to gather without authorization (ordinance of 25 December 1783); could not become apothecaries, lawyers, bailiffs, or clerks of the court (by decision of the Superior Council of Martinique, 9 May 1765); and were subject to clothing restrictions as in the Spanish colonies (ordinance of 4 June 1720). They could not bear white people's names, sit with them at church, or walk with them in processions. They were not allowed to work as mechanics or in the wholesale trade and were denied access to the professions. Most of them were artisans and, as in the Spanish colonies, they could be members of the militia. There were also many planters among them: in St. Domingue, for instance, they possessed up to one-third of the land in the late pre-revolutionary era. In the French colonies, they even enjoyed political rights at times, although they lost them all on 2 July 1802, when the French government issued new legislation.

There was thus a marked difference between the Spanish and French societies on the one hand and the Anglo-Saxon ones on the other. In the former, there was a large free colored population, sometimes as large as the white population. Although their legal status marked their inferiority, they had a definite social and economic role in the life of the colonies. Theirs was a constantly growing class with a real intermediary position. Its members were not totally segregated, and race prejudice was much less significant than in the Anglo-Saxon societies. Mulatto children of white colonists were rarely enslaved and often occupied a quite decent position in society. In the British colonies and in the Anglo-Saxon South, on the contrary, except in the very early colonial period, free blacks were never numerous, their number did not significantly increase, and they were relegated, together with the slaves, to a true sub-class as a result of color prejudice. Their social role was almost nil as was the economic part they played, facts that influenced the type of slavery that developed in the South. The three-tiered societies permitted relatively easier access to freedom, and there was much more social fluidity: Freedom was not an unattainable ideal. By contrast, in the South, there was little hope of freedom for anyone born in bondage. Race prejudice condemned those with African origins to forming the substratum of society. Even though the legal status of free colored people was limited in the French and Spanish societies, it was almost entirely restricted in the Anglo-Saxon ones as the status of free blacks in the American North proves.[51] The consequences for the evolution of the slave societies of the Americas were still more considerable, since the existence of this intermediary class later influenced the process of abolition, as well as the post-abolition era in many ways.

This difference was further heightened by the codification of slavery in the various colonies. Here again, the Anglo-Saxon model diverged sharply from the French and Spanish models, a contrast which justifies a closer study of the legal aspects of slavery in the Americas.

Slave Codes

Close examination of codification is of interest, although it does not permit an exact description of the organization of slavery. Few of the legal provisions were strictly implemented, whether they restricted masters or slaves. The *modus vivendi* established was very often far from what the law stipulated. However, although codification does not lead to a clear perception of what slavery really was, it does allow insight into the way the institution was perceived by the various countries that practiced it.

Moreover, codification in the colonial societies of the Americas is the step that turned "societies with slaves" into "slave societies." At first, all of the non-Spanish colonies established similar patterns of organized labor, which placed indentured servants from Europe and Africa side-by-side under similar working conditions. It was not until codification began that the fate of the two groups really diverged, thus marking a turning point in the history of the institution and of the colonies more generally.

The necessity of examining that codification closely is thus unquestionable. The difficulty here lies in the fact that not all the colonizing powers codified the institution in the same way. The French 1685 *Code Noir* was state legislation that applied to all the Caribbean colonies before being expanded to Louisiana, in a slightly revised version, in 1724. The Spanish code was somewhat less centralized; in the early era of colonization, it largely relied on the thirteenth century *Siete Partidas*. It was refined, however, in the sixteenth and seventeenth centuries by successive royal ordinances and partial codification, but was not officially centralized and adapted until the 1789 *Codigo Negro*, which was specific to the American colonies. In the British Caribbean, slavery was even less codified. Self-government implied independent laws that were not gathered within a single code. These laws could vary from one colony to the next, were not immutable, changed over time, and were pragmatic (being determined by the planters rather than the motherland). In the English Southern colonies, the laws similarly varied from one colony to the next and over time, although they were sometimes presented in the form of a code, as in Virginia in 1712. After the American Revolution, each state had its own constitution and its own legal measures. This diversity needs to be borne in mind throughout the following discussion.

While a general study will be relatively straightforward concerning the French and, to a certain extent, Spanish colonies, several models will require examination for the Anglo-Saxon possessions, both during colonial rule and after Independence. Examples will be drawn from Virginia legislation and from the South Carolina slave code of 1712 for the colonial period; and from the Alabama slave code of 1852 for the post-revolutionary era, with an extension to the rest of the South in a more general presentation. Finally, an extrapolation will be made from various individual laws for the English Caribbean colonies, since the conception of the institution as well as the general provisions were the same in all of them. To some extent, although this assertion will be qualified later, the spirit was the same throughout the Anglo-Saxon territories, and the provisions of the Southern codes corresponded, in many ways, to what could be termed "the English spirit."

At this point, a few words should be added about the principles that determined codification in each individual nation present on the American continent. The French started defining and refining the practice of slavery through decrees of the sovereign council (*Conseil Souverain*) and lieutenants general. This means that provisions could vary slightly from one colony to the next. Uniformity came through the *Code Noir*, drawn up by Colbert for Martinique in 1685, signed by Louis XIV, and then expanded to all the French colonies of the Caribbean and to Louisiana, with some alterations, in 1724. The code was largely borrowed from Roman law (negating the slave's personality and branding him or her with utter incapacity) and from canon law, although, of course, in a Creolized form. Superficially, the *Code Noir*—most centralized of all the codes and maintained under the strictest state control—apparently endeavored to reduce abuses, guarantee slaves certain rights and forms of justice, and to protect them by ensuring more humane treatment. On a closer reading, it appears both dehumanizing and reifying for the slave and does codify the institution.

The Spanish principle was both similar and slightly different. It also borrowed from Roman law, but defined the slave as a member of a large family, an integral part of the *Casa Grande* [literally, "the Big House," meaning extended household]. The legislation adopted throughout the colonial period and collected in the *Código Negro* attempted to humanize the master/slave relationship by endowing the slave with a moral personality, along with all the legal, familial, and patrimonial consequences implied therein. It originated from the principle that the slave was a human being created by God, which conferred upon him a number of rights. Spanish law defined the institution of slavery as a frame that was not necessarily immutable, providing for a possible way out. It instituted a very peculiar social and racial order that was unmatched in any other codification.

In the British Caribbean, codification was less general and much more pragmatic: slavery was regulated by a set of laws voted only when absolutely necessary. Very strict laws were not passed until the late seventeenth century. Although there was no unity in the legislation itself, it evinced across the colonies of the British Caribbean a remarkable homogeneity of spirit, based on a common culture, on comparable economic orientations (requisite to sugar cane cultivation), and on standardized organization of labor. There were also permanent population movements between the colonies, which accounts for the relative uniformity palliating the absence of centralization. As David Lowenthal explains, the differences among English Caribbean societies were fairly "trivial or inconsistent" and were more the result of differences in individual practice than in legislation, reflecting "the character or circumstance of the slave-owners more than any territorial distinction" (40).[52] The institutionalization of slavery came progressively and relatively early. In 1664, for instance, the Antigua Assembly voted the first law against miscegenation, establishing different penal remedies for different classes of law-breakers: fines for free persons; extensions of indenture time for servants; and branding and whipping for "heathens." In 1650, servitude became a lifetime condition for Africans and was extended to their children and posterity.

English slavery legislation, like the French and Spanish codes, borrowed from Roman law, but was mainly legislation of restriction, obligation, and punishment. In 1661, Barbados voted a set of laws—expanded to Jamaica in 1664 and to Antigua in 1702—ostensibly justified by a need to protect the whites from "an heathenish, brutish, and an uncertaine, dangerous kinde of people" (1661 Barbados slave code). It was almost solely devised to ensure order and obedience, as very few laws were aimed at protecting the slaves or at introducing more humanity into the master–slave relationship. Such provisions were not added until the very late eighteenth century, when the *Consolidated Slave Act* was issued. This act ensured that the most basic needs of the slaves (food and clothing) fulfilled, offered them some kind of relief in the Christian religion, and protected them from the most barbaric repression. These protecting clauses never went very far and were usually voted "incidentally," to use Michael Craton's words, under pressure from philanthropists outside the colonial societies.[53]

The restrictive tendency of the Anglo-Saxon codes is confirmed by a close examination of English colonial rule in North America. As in Virginia, where the progressive institutionalization of slavery occurred from 1661 to 1705, the laws were voted individually. First the difference between blacks and whites was established in 1661: whereas white indentured servants could repurchase their contracts, blacks could not. Next, slave status was made hereditary in 1662. In 1669, another law went so far as to state that the death of a slave under castigation was not a felony. A more coherent codification did not occur until 1705 in the form of a slave code that recapitulated, systematized, and expanded the existing legislation.

The other Southern colonies followed Virginia's example with only minor differences, although legislation was voted individually by each colony. As in the Caribbean, codification was aimed solely at repression and contained almost nothing to protect the slaves. This condition is exemplified by the *incipit* of the 1712 code of South Carolina. When enumerating what necessitated the code, the Carolina legislators explained that the "Negroes (...) are of barbarous, wild, savage natures," and that the legislation was meant "to restrain the disorders, rapines, inhumanity, to which they are naturally prone and inclined," and to "tend to the safety and security of the people of this Province and their estates."[54] The 1712 code ostensibly addressed these needs by restricting the movements of slaves outside the plantation; by prohibiting slave gatherings, as well as their bearing of arms; and by punishing their crimes. In truth, the code resulted in the total dehumanization of the slave.

After Independence, although each Southern state had its own legislation, codification was remarkably uniform. There were minor local and regional differences (the rules were generally stricter in the Deep South than in the Upper South), but these differences are largely insignificant when the codes are considered in their totality. American as opposed to colonial legislation made more allowance for the protection of the slaves, though never going as far as the French and Spanish codes. This was, of course, largely due to time and to development differentials, the American legislation of the nineteenth century being strongly influenced by the debate raging over slavery.

Detailed comparison among legislation of the various nations shows a number of interesting common features. The codes were all aimed at regulating slavery, at setting rules, at making slavery a real institution whereby "societies with slaves" were transformed into "slave societies." First, the codes proclaimed the existence of slavery and made it a hereditary servitude for life. The introduction to the 1712 South Carolina slave code states: "they, and their children, are hereby made and declared slaves, to all intents and purposes." All of the codes also defined slave status. Slaves were property, and more specifically, chattel: the French code (as well as the colonial code for South Carolina) uses the term *"biens meubles"* (or "movables"), while Article 2042 of the 1852 Alabama code (like most of the other state codes) calls them "property." Slaves were thus subject to the general rules concerning chattel. They could be sold; they were "part of the community of acquests between husband and wife" (Louisiana, art. 40); and they were considered movables in matters of inheritance.[55] The Barbados law of 1661 explains in its preamble that it has been devised to "protect [the slaves] as wee doe men's other goods and chattels."

From the seventeenth to the nineteenth century, all the codes prohibited the movement of slaves within the territory without the special authorization of the master. All of them banned gatherings, whatever the form, although slight differences appear among the various codes. The French code for Louisiana prohibits gatherings with slaves from other plantations and implies that any violation of this law will be met with punishment, for the master as well as for the slave (art. 13). The South Carolina colonial code states that slaves who go to "Charlestown" will be whipped. Even in the Spanish possessions, gathering was forbidden (Ordinance of 30 October 1695), as was the existence of secret slave societies. The nineteenth century Alabama code also prohibits the gathering of more than five slaves from different plantations (art. 1007), as well as any other gathering of more than five male slaves unless for worship and in the presence of the master (art. 1020).

In all the codes, the bearing of arms is narrowly restricted, most of the time to the purpose of hunting, and requires a special permit from the master and (Louisiana, art. 15; South Carolina, art. V; Alabama, arts. 1012 and 1017). All the codes, including the most protective ones, indicate that some functions or offices are forbidden to slaves. For example, they could not hold public functions or serve as arbitrators or experts in French Louisiana and could not serve as mechanics according to Spanish legislation.[56] Similarly, from 1676 on, the English Caribbean colonies prevented slaves from practicing such skilled trades as those of cooper, smith, carpenter, tailor, and boatman. On the other hand, slaves were allowed to sell goods almost anywhere, although certain restrictions were made. The South Carolina colonial code does not mention vending, but the practice was authorized in the Caribbean. Take English Martinique, for example, which—with the single exception of meat—permitted broad scope to slaves as vendors. In the French colonies, slaves were also allowed to sell goods, but only after receiving special permission (Louisiana, art. 15). Likewise in the Spanish colonies, vending was perfectly legal, and slaves could even have a share in the profits on condition that they kept a register of what they sold and had a permit from the council. Thus, slaves could save enough money to purchase their own freedom with their earnings. Vending was also permitted in the nineteenth century American South, as was the practice of hiring out, although both had to receive the permission of town authorities (Alabama, art. 1005).

A large part of each of the codes, whatever the nation or time period, was devoted to offenses and punishments. Every code punished acts of violence against white people, especially masters, as well as theft in any form. Most of the time, capital punishment was clearly indicated for the murder or assault of a white person (Louisiana, arts. 27 and 28; 1661 Barbados slave code; South Carolina, art. IX, for instance), and various forms of whipping were prescribed when the offence was less serious (Louisiana, arts. 29 and 30; South Carolina, arts. IX and X; *Código Negro*, Capítulo 3, ley 8).

Provisions were also made in all the codes for severe punishment for running away or trespassing. The French code threatened the runaway slave with having his ears cut off and a "flower de luce" branded on one shoulder. For a second offense, the slave could be hamstrung and branded on the other shoulder, and capital punishment was incurred the third time (Louisiana, art. 32). The South Carolina English code threatened "death or any other punishment" (art. XII); the Barbados law, whipping, branding, or nose slitting; and the Alabama code devoted nine articles to the issue (1023–1032), threatening reenslavement and a whipping of up to one hundred lashes. The Spanish code permitted slave hunting; granted rewards for anyone returning a runaway slave; promised two hundred lashes for the first escape and one hundred more if the slave took another slave with him; and warned that, for a second offense, the slave would be "desterrado de la Isla" [exiled from the island]. The code even stated that anyone helping a slave to run away incurred penalties: the same number of lashes for slaves; the loss of half their fortune for free colored people; and, for Spanish people, the loss of all their fortune together with being "desterrado de todas las Indias perpetuamente" [perpetually exiled from the colonies].

Other points were systematically mentioned in all the codes, although provisions differed widely from one nation to the next. Among these common points was religion, discussion of which was generally very detailed in the Catholic territories, while in the Protestant societies it was treated more allusively. The English colonies authorized some forms of worship, but with strict limitations. The South Carolina code made no provision for religious practice, but later in the development of the colonies, in the Caribbean for instance, some laws stipulated that the slaves would share the benefits of their masters' religion. Worship was sometimes allowed, although always in the presence of masters. Post-Independence Southern states took similar measures: the Alabama code, for instance, forbade any meeting of five slaves coming from outside the plantation, unless it was "for the worship of almighty God, or for burial service," in which case it had to be with the consent of the owner (art. 1007). In the same way, the gathering of more than five male slaves was forbidden, except "for a public worship of God, held by white people" (Alabama, art. 1020). Catholic societies were more liberal and more precise in their codification. Article 2 of the French Louisiana and Caribbean codes made it compulsory to instruct slaves in the Catholic religion. Article 4 obliged the masters to respect Sundays and religious holidays. Article 11 added that the slaves had to be buried in consecrated ground. For the Spaniards, slaves were human beings created by God, endowed with a moral personality, and thus entitled to the moral and religious support of the church. Slaves were Christianized as early as the mid-sixteenth century and were maintained in the Catholic faith throughout the colonial period.

Another among the points common to all the codes was the issue of emancipation. It was not viewed favorably by the Anglo-Saxon codes, although it was systematically mentioned. Interestingly, manumission was mentioned in the South Carolina colonial code of 1712 as the only measure favorable to slaves. According to Article 1, a slave could be "for some particular merit, made and declared free" by the governor and council of the province or by his or her master. It was even possible for a slave to request manumission, in which case the governor and council of the colony made the final decision. The Alabama state code left the possibility open, although manumission was submitted to the permission of the county probate judge and had to be fully justified (arts. 2044–2046). Like the other state codes of the period, it required the slave to leave the state within six months of manumission (art. 2047). The Alabama code also made it possible for a slave to "claim his freedom . . . by petition in the circuit court of the county" (art. 2049). Manumission was drastically restricted in the nineteenth century South and became utterly impossible on the eve of the Civil War.

In contrast, the French code gave masters over the age of twenty-five the possibility of manumitting a slave "by testamentary disposition or by acts inter vivos" (Louisiana, art. 50), although it was conditional on the agreement of the superior council. A slave also became automatically free if he or she was appointed tutor of the master's children (Louisiana, art. 51). An act of enfranchisement being an act of naturalization, the freed slaves were to "enjoy all the rights and privileges inherent" to that naturalization and "the same rights, privileges and amenities" as free persons, save the possibility of obtaining a donation from a white person (Louisiana, arts. 52 and 54).

Finally, manumission was possible, and even easier than elsewhere, in the Spanish colonies. As in French legislation, masters could free their slaves as a reward for services or good conduct,[57] and this immediately conferred on the slave the same rights as any other free citizen.[58] The great benefit of the Spanish code compared with the others was that it gave slaves the right to save money and purchase their own freedom (*coartación*). Slaves were also sometimes manumitted when their master died and they could receive donations.

Another principle that was generally common to all the codes was the slaves' obligation of obedience, respect, and deference to their masters and to any free person, especially white. Some codes even expanded the provision to free blacks with respect to whites. In English and American legislation, this principle was clearly stated. The French code specified that even manumitted slaves had to "show the profoundest respect to their former masters, to their widows and children" (Louisiana, art. 53). Failure to observe this provision warranted severe punishment, as did disrespect shown to any other white person. The Spanish code carried exactly the same provision (Capítulo 20, ley 2) and even stipulated that this respect had to be shown by any colored person to any white. Eleven laws detailed this obligation: "amor y veneración a los blancos" [love and veneration of whites] (Capítulo 3, ley 3); "subordinación y disciplina" [subordination and discipline] (ley 4); "tan sumiso y respectuoso a toda persona blanco, como si cada una de ellas fuera su mismo amo o señor del siervo" [show submission and respect to any white person as if each of them were his/her master] (ley 6).

All the features common to the codes reveal a manifest intention to institutionalize the labor system by reifying slaves and subjecting them entirely to the ruling class of whites. Interestingly, the codes' rigid frames denote an intention to closely regulate relationships between masters and slaves. The desire to make the colonies safe is obvious through the codification of offenses and punishments, and a definite, racially determined structure is set up by making any colored person (including free persons or manumitted slaves) subservient to the white ruling class. In all these respects, there is notable uniformity throughout the slave societies of the American South and the Caribbean. Despite this very homogeneous basis, which clearly delineates the conceptions these societies had of slavery, there are marked differences that reveal much about the different nations. Some small differences in specific provisions concerning religious worship and manumission have already been mentioned. There are more serious divergences, however, that testify to a disparity in the general conception of who and what the slaves were.

To generalize, the French and Spanish societies seemed to offer much more protection to their slaves, be it because of Catholicism or because of different traditions. Both in the British Caribbean and in the American South, the Anglo-Saxon laws, which early on had very few, if any, protective measures for slaves, also changed over time, but only late in the period and only under pressure from the developing abolitionist movement. Whereas the South Carolina code of the colonial period did not contain any protective clauses, two-fifths of the articles in the American Alabama code regulated the behavior of slaves, two-fifths were devoted to master–slave relationships, and one-fifth was dedicated to the treatment of offenses against slaves. It is necessary to examine these changes, but also, as a kind of confirmation, to study the modifications that occurred in codification when some colonies shifted nationalities.

In general, the Spanish and French codes contained, from the start, provisions concerning the basic survival of the slaves, thus including a touch of humanity in their conception of the institution. The French code detailed the way the slave should be cared for, giving lists of foods to be provided, as well the exact quantity of each product.[59] Slaves had to be taken care of when they grew too old or sick to go on working (Louisiana, art. 21). The Spanish code even contained provisions protecting pregnant women. (One may reasonably contend that such a provision was made less for humanitarian than for business reasons, to ensure the reproduction of the slave population.) In any case, pregnant women were allowed to start working later in the day (to leave time for the dissipation of the noxious vapors of the earth), were given shorter working hours, were better fed, were granted separate lodgings, and were not to work at all during the last month of pregnancy (*Codigo Negro*, Capítulo 26, ley 2).

The early English laws did not include any provision to ensure attention to slaves' vital needs. The Barbados and South Carolina codes, for example, are absolutely silent on such matters. This theme was dealt with in later codes, both in the English colonies and in the American South, although in a very discreet way. The Alabama code, for instance, simply mentions the necessity of providing slaves with "a sufficiency of healthy food and necessary clothing" (art. 2043). The language here is vague enough to allow for interpretations as varied as owners' temperaments and qualities of conscience. The same article adds, in a similarly imprecise formulation, that the slave "must be properly attended during sickness and provided for his necessary wants in old age."

The slave's legal protection against excessive severity is also manifest in the French and Spanish codes. Only one advantage over these is to be found in the American codes, where runaway slaves do not necessarily incur the capital penalty, although this leniency could be interpreted as a will to protect the master's property rather than the slave's life. Two provisions of the colonial South Carolina code suggest this kind of mercenary motive. When a slave was punished by law for a rather serious offense, but one not deserving capital punishment, the court was left to decide what penalty would be inflicted, provided it did not extend "to limb or [to] disabling him" (South Carolina, art. IX). Very severe punishments devised for petty larceny further prove that protections did not concern slaves themselves, but what they represented as property for the master. For a first offense, the slave could be whipped; for a second, he could have "one of his ears cut off or be branded in the forehead with a hot iron"; for a third, he could have his "nose slit"; and for a fourth, the offense was treated like murder, burglary, or any other very serious crime, and the slave could incur "death or other punishment" (South Carolina, art. X). Similarly, if a slave was accused of theft and whipped, the whipping must not "exceed forty lashes" (South Carolina, art. X). According to Barbados law, the master was allowed to punish his slave, and no penalty was incurred if the slave died during punishment.

Following the evolution of ideological and political objections to slavery in the nineteenth-century United States, the Alabama code of 1852 was somewhat less inhumane, although it still clearly reified the slave. Article 2043 states, in relatively vague terms, that the master "must treat his slave with humanity and must not inflict upon him any cruel punishment." The code also stipulates that it is forbidden to kill a slave, and the person who does so "by cruel whipping, or beating, or any inhuman treatment" will be considered "guilty of murder in the first degree" (Alabama, art. 3295). However, this order is mitigated first by the stipulation that death must be inflicted "with malice aforethought"—hardly provable in the context— and second by the provision that if the person had "the right to correct" the slave, his or her death becomes murder in the second degree (Alabama, art. 3296). Moreover, if someone other than the master committed "assault or battery" on the slave, it was considered a mere "misdemeanor" (Alabama, art. 3300). Finally—and this is probably the most dehumanizing provision because the punishment incurred is only a fine—in cases of cruel punishment or gross neglect, where a master fails to provide his slave with "sufficiency of healthy food or necessary clothing, or to provide for him properly in sickness or old age, or treats him in any other way with inhumanity," he will be fined (Alabama, art. 3297). Archival documentation of such abuse is largely non-existent. In the first place, slaves could not lodge official complaints against their masters. In the second, slaveholders themselves made up two-thirds of the juries designated to judge such matters (Alabama, art. 3299), and the remaining third, given the stratification of Southern society, probably primarily acted on pro-slavery, pro-master bias.

The French code, on the contrary, although it was written very early in the history of the colonial societies of the Americas, was very precise on such matters and seemed to protect the slave by restricting the master's prerogatives. Such legislation was apparently not inspired solely with respect to the master's property rights. Article 38 of the Louisiana code indicates that there should be "no mutilation on their own [the masters'] private authority," while article 39 makes civic authorities responsible for punishing anyone who transgresses this prohibition. The language of article 39 is severe, especially in its initial use of a verb of compulsion, the verb "to command": "We command our officers of justice in this colony to institute criminal process against master and overseers who shall have killed or mutilated their slaves . . . and to punish said murder according to the atrocity of the circumstances." Pardon for such crimes was still possible, however. Like the French code, the Spanish code legislated against overly severe punishments and limited to twenty-five the number of lashes that could be imposed. (In cases of assault on a white person, however, this limit went up to a hundred). A special protection—unheard of in Anglo-Saxon America, either colonial or post-revolutionary—existed in the French and Spanish societies: the possibility for a slave to appeal to justice in case of mistreatment. The Spanish code allowed a slave to show his injuries to a judge or to have the effects of malnutrition publicly revealed in order to obtain the authorities' protection. In the same way, article 20 of the French code theoretically allowed complaints from slaves to the attorney general and to the superior council (or any officer of justice) in case of barbarous treatment.

Another typical feature of the French and Spanish codes was their protection of slave families; both nations acknowledged the family unit and tried to protect it against fragmentation through sales. The English colonies did not legally recognize slave families and thus did not attempt to protect this officially indefinite institution. No mention of it is made in the early English codes, as the slave was not considered a human being. The nineteenth-century Alabama code mentions it briefly in article 2057, indicating that the slaves "must be offered, and if practicable, sold in families" (the significant "if practicable," of course, lessens any real degree of obligation), but the stress is laid on the mother–child unit. Article 2056, indeed, states that children under age five must not be separated from their mothers and that children under ten should not be sold separately unless the master can prove it will be prejudicial to him not to do so. The last clause, with its nod to ownership, shows that financial interests superseded humanitarian ideals. In the French and Spanish codes, the provisions were more clearly stated and more protective of slaves' families. Similar to the provisions of the Spanish code, Article 47 of the Martinique code (which became article 43 in Louisiana's) states that husbands and wives "shall not be seized and sold separately when belonging to the same master" and that children under fourteen must not be separated from their parents. Moreover, the measure is not mitigated by any exception based on financial considerations, and the parental unit is clearly respected. It is quite exceptional that a master who transgressed this provision was required to give the remaining members of the family to the person who purchased one of them.

Humanitarian provisions of this nature are perhaps unsurprising in the Spanish and French codes where the slaves were officially considered human beings endowed with a certain moral personality. While slaves had no legal existence in the Anglo-Saxon societies, they were slightly more fortunate in French and Spanish legislation. Marriage was not recognized in the former, since slaves had no right to sign any contract. Under French and Spanish legislation, on the contrary, slaves could marry. Article 7 of the Louisiana code (10 of the Caribbean one) acknowledges marriage between slaves, though adding in article 8 the necessity of obtaining the master's permission. Article 9 of the Louisiana code even makes wedlock possible between slaves belonging to different masters. Capítulo 26 of the Spanish code expressly states that marriage between slaves must be encouraged.

The legal non-existence of slaves in Anglo-Saxon societies also informed prohibitions against a slave's right to bear witness in court. The French code, by contrast, states that slaves cannot give their testimony in civil or criminal matters "except if matter of necessity" (Louisiana, art. 24). By forecasting a possible "matter of necessity," the French code positions slaves as human participants in a larger society. Article 25 of the French code prohibits slaves from being parties in civil suits, unless the master has lodged a complaint against someone who has harmed one of his slaves. Though it is limited in scope, this article nonetheless confers upon the slave a degree of legal recognition. Such recognition is also clearly visible in article 26, which states that a slave "may be prosecuted criminally, with the same rules, formalities, and proceedings observed for free persons." The Spanish laws went even further, since slaves could apply to courts and bear witness before any judge.

A similar analysis may be made concerning the question of property rights. The English codes seldom mention property for slaves. Maintaining that slaves were property themselves, the codes made obvious that slaves could not, in turn, own property. In fact, when the English codes mention property rights at all it is to strictly forbid them. The same is true of the American codes. The Alabama code, for instance, states, in article 1028, that "no slave can own property." A slave cannot even own a dog (article 1014). The French code, which is more liberal in certain respects, is equally strict with regard to property; a slave cannot own or inherit property, and any acquisition made by a slave becomes his master's property. In the Spanish possessions, on the contrary, slaves had patrimonial rights, could inherit property, and possess money. This is made quite clear from the very fact that they could have financial interests, sell goods for themselves, save money, and purchase their own freedom, which lessened the impression of permanence that was attached to slave status in the Anglo-Saxon societies.

It is impossible to detail all the provisions (which vary from one English or American code to the next), but it is interesting to quote other differences attributable to the same denial of any human condition to the slaves in the Anglo-Saxon societies. For instance (although there is no mention of it in the Alabama code), many later American codes forbade teaching of reading and writing to slaves, since experience had proved that all the slave rebellions had been led by educated and skilled slaves (Gabriel Prosser and Nat Turner, for instance). Neither French nor Spanish codes contained such measures. On the contrary, they favored the education of slaves, especially to give them access to the Catholic religion.

In general, Anglo-Saxon codes never acknowledged the hardship of the slaves' condition, whereas the other nations seemed to accept the existence of the institution reluctantly. The Spanish code is probably the most expressive in this respect, where several articles mention the sadness of the slaves' fate ("penas y fatigas," "triste suerte y condition" ["suffering and fatigue," "unhappy fate and condition"], Capítulo 26, ley 4), along with the necessity to mitigate the effects of that condition ("humanidad a favor de estos miserables" [to show "humanity in favor of the miserable"]), by trying to make their daily tasks easier through the use of appropriate tools ("simplificar los instrumentos más adaptables y proporcionados para sus trabajos diarios" [using the most adaptable and suitable tools to simplify their daily tasks]).

The last divergence in national codifications lies in the existence in the French and Spanish societies of the three-caste conception of racial organization. This social feature has already been examined, but codification interestingly reveals how the various societies regarded miscegenation. Not officially recognizing marriage between slaves, the Anglo-Saxon codes did not accept it between slaves and free persons either. In many codes, miscegenation was strictly forbidden (although neither the colonial South Carolina code nor the later American Alabama code refer to the topic). On the contrary, the French Louisiana code permitted unions between free colored people and slaves, such marriages bringing about the liberation of the enslaved spouse and of the couple's children. The Spanish code did not forbid marriage between free people and slaves, although it stated that it was harmful and that the masters should try to dissuade their slaves from contracting such unions by offering them a more suitable spouse among the other slaves (Capítulo 26, ley 4). Throughout the Spanish colonial period, marriages between white people and white slaves (a category specific to Spanish society) were tolerated. Marriages between white men and indigenous women were similarly accepted as early as 1514 (due to the high number of single males and the scarcity of white women in the colonies), but marriages of whites to black slaves had been officially forbidden since 1527. The law thus denied any possibility of mixed-blood descendants, despite explicit recognition of a mulatto population issued from apparently illegal unions between white masters and black slaves. Indeed, the code made possible the freeing of slaves and their children for motives that cannot be decently detailed, to paraphrase the wording of the code ("libertad a siervas y hijos por motivos que silencia el pudor," Capítulo 19, ley 5). The code also states that such children were born slaves, but that their freedom could be purchased (ley 9). The French Caribbean code went even further (and this is one of the main differences between the Caribbean and Louisiana codes and between the French and Spanish codes). Article 9 forbids any cohabitation between free men and slaves on penalty of fine, but accepts marriage between them if contracted by the rules of the Church, without—and this is essential—the least restriction on color. It even adds that such marriage results in the emancipation of the female slave and that children born of such unions are free and legitimate.

Finally, Spanish legislation displays an interesting feature by introducing distinctions between colored people according to their degree of "whiteness." In many articles, the mulattos (sometimes called "mulatos primerizos") are classified with the blacks, both male and female ("negros y negras"), while these are clearly distinguished from the quadroons and other more mixed colored people ("tercerons y quarterons"), that is all who are more than half white. This distinction appears in the article that prevented blacks and mulattos from being mechanics, as well as in the article that fixed penalties for those helping maroon slaves "mulato o mulata, libre o cautivo" [mulatto male or female, free or captive] (Capítulo 34, ley 9). This difference is further reinforced by complementary codifications (such as ordinances specifying the goods women were allowed to sell) and by sixteenth-century *Leyes Suntuarias* [sumptuary laws]. For instance, blacks and mulattos, be they slave or free, were denied the right to wear pearls, emeralds or other precious stones, as well as gold and silver (Capítulo 9, ley 1). Similarly, they could not carry spears or sticks and could not wear mantillas or "sombreros de galón de oro o plato" [hats adorned with gold or silver] (ley 2).

To summarize, regardless of nation or era, strong similarities inform the basic principles behind the various slave codes: institutionalization of slavery; regulation of the master-slave relationship; authorization of punishment for crimes committed by slaves. Nonetheless, different societies' conceptions of the institution obviously varied. The French and Spanish organization of slavery tended at all times to be looser, leaving individuals the possibility of escaping their slave status. The French and Spanish were apparently more likely to protect their slaves and to grant them a certain degree of moral and legal existence. Finally, the boundary imposed between the races was much more fluid, leaving room for interracial relationships and thus for the existence of a third class of colored people. It is interesting to note that, even if the Anglo-Saxon codes tended to become more protective in the later slave era (probably as a result of abolitionist pressure), they never matched the apparent leniency and benevolence of the very early French and Spanish legislations.

A final confirmation of nationally distinct conceptions of slavery can be made through brief study of the ways codifications changed when they came under the authority of another European nation. For instance, when Martinique turned from French to English control, several measures instantly restricted the potential emancipation of slaves. The Capitulation Act of March 1794 stated that slaves who had been in the National Guard would not be freed and would be returned to their masters. It also became impossible to free a slave by testament or purchase. In 1800, any manumission became subject to the approval of the governor general, thus confirming the wish of the English societies to check the progression of any intermediate category of free colored people.

Just as interestingly, when French Louisiana became Spanish, the Black Code remained valid and was even confirmed by General Alejandro O'Reilly in 1769. It was superseded, however, by the code enacted by the Cabildo in 1778. It is interesting to examine the spirit of this code, even though it was relatively short-lived, suspended in 1794 due to planter opposition. Some of the French articles remained intact (such as article 61 on religion), indicating the role Catholicism played in uniting French and Spanish conceptions of slavery. Some provisions, however, changed. Spanish rule opened up the possibility of voluntary work for slaves, while discouraging unions between whites and black slaves. (The white partner in such a union would be driven from the colony in shame.) Spanish colonial authorities also allowed slaves the possibility to purchase their own freedom; permitted blacks to inherit property from whites; and authorized marriages between slaves belonging to different masters. (The master who had authorized the marriage was legally obligated to sell his slave to the other master.) That some provisions were more protective, while others were somewhat less so created a balance between the French and Spanish codes, at least in spirit. (Details concerning slave nutrition were left out of the Spanish code, but the issue of obligatory pensions for old and sick slaves was included, for instance).

In the same way, when Americans took control of Louisiana, legislation was modified. In this case, change was both more rapid and more drastic. A new code was adopted in 1806 and an addendum voted in 1827. Although the code remained basically less strict than those of other Southern states of the Union, it was far less favorable to slaves than either the French or Spanish codes. Protective provisions concerning food, clothing, rest periods, and care in sickness and old age remained intact. The police measures of 1751, 1778, and 1795 ensuring law and order among the slaves were also retained, filling thirty sections. Among significant changes to the Louisiana code, Article 16 forbade slaves to bear witness against white people in court. Several sections were designed to institute a separate criminal code for slaves, leaving matters in the hands of the slaveholding class. In cases mandating the death penalty, a county judge and a jury of three to five slaveholders rendered judgments; for non-capital crimes, a committee of three slaveholders made the decision. Several laws were added to the code, including an ordinance of 1807 that abolished self-purchase and limited manumission by requiring a special act of the legislature (article 1); a minimum age of thirty (article 2); exemplary behavior for over four years (article 3); and opportunity for a master's creditors to prevent the emancipation (article 4). An 1807 law also banned the entry into the territory of free blacks, while a law of 1808 made it compulsory to indicate the color of a free person on any official document. The civil code prevented any union between a slave and a free person, whatever his or her color, and a law of 1830 made it compulsory for any emancipated slave to leave the state within a month after his manumission. In short, the legislation made the barrier between races much more difficult to cross and tried to restrict the rights and expansion of the intermediate class of free colored people, which perfectly confirms the Anglo-Saxon tradition of racial exclusion, as opposed to the way the French and Spanish considered racial difference.

National differences were thus undeniably reflected by varied codifications of the institution of slavery. However, as already stated, legislation was never strictly enforced, and many examples of code infringement can be found. If codification clearly indicates what a given nation considered society's ideal organization, it never provided an accurate representation of how a society actually functioned. It is thus necessary to devote the last part of this chapter to the enforcement (or rather non-enforcement) of the codes and to give a more exact picture of the societies studied. This discussion, although indispensable, will tend toward generalization. Indeed, solely for comparison's sake, we will assume that slavery in a given territory was a non-evolving institution, although I fully concur with new historiographic trends that critique and rigorously query such assumptions.[60]

Slavery in Practice

Records of daily life indicate that the reality of slavery differed significantly from the impressions conveyed by the codes. The codes of the Spanish and French societies were, apparently, much more humane than those of the Anglo-Saxon societies. Recognizing that slaves had souls, granting them certain rights (to self-purchase and to marriage, for example), these codes appeared to reject maintaining slaves in a state of permanent inferiority. In fact, in spite of this greater social fluidity (so ostensibly at odds with the impassable racial barriers set up in Anglo-Saxon societies), the living conditions of the slaves on the islands were usually much worse than those of the Southern slaves, rendering suspect and relative the actual validity of the codes. Whereas many of the protective measures of the French and Spanish colonies were not implemented, the more austere Anglo-Saxon codes of the South seem to have been largely mitigated in practice. Importantly, there were various models of slavery, not necessarily linked with the nation in control of the colony, but rather with geographical location and with certain external conditions that influenced social organization.

Some differences also depended on the work status of the slave. Everywhere, whatever the national authority, domestic slaves were better treated than field slaves. Domestic occupations along with residence in the main house entailed a closer proximity with the masters. These slaves were better fed, better clad, better lodged, much less overworked, and had privileged relationships with white people. In addition, conditions were everywhere different for urban and rural slaves. City slaves were generally servants or skilled laborers, women working as seamstresses or weavers, for instance, and men working as carpenters, coopers, or shoemakers. Urban slaves had more freedom and were more often rented out, which permitted them to work overtime and save money, even though such privileges were not necessarily included in the codes. City slaves also lived much closer to white people and could socialize more easily with one another. It is essential to remember, of course, that everywhere conditions varied according to who exerted authority: the slaves' fate largely depended on the master himself or on the overseer who directed the plantation.

Moreover, many provisions were not or could not be implemented. Marooning was everywhere prohibited, and the codes contained severe punishments for anyone who transgressed the law. This never prevented relatively large maroon societies from developing wherever geographical and social conditions permitted. Historical studies of Spanish Santo Domingo, for instance, record a population of six hundred maroon families—a total of about two thousand persons—in the sixteenth century.[61] Similarly, miscegenation was severely restricted or even forbidden, but this never prevented its occurrence, although with differences in proportion throughout the different slave societies of the Americas. Despite the ban on mixed unions, there was a tolerance for them everywhere, including in the South.

In many cases, codified protective measures were not respected either. Although the Spanish and French codes were very strict with regard to humane treatment of the slaves, reality was much bleaker. Despite detailed provisions concerning food, lodging, clothing, and decent treatment, everything attests to the poor living conditions of the Caribbean slaves. All the travel narratives by Europeans visiting the islands depict the astoundingly harsh living conditions of the island slaves. Travelers describe them as overworked, ill-fed, isolated, severely castigated. Despite the more lenient codifications described earlier, the lives of Caribbean slaves were, according to all testimony, the worst in the Western Hemisphere.[62] The large proportion of people of African origin living in the islands terrified the whites and made repression of slave rebellions horrifyingly harsh, all the more so since revolts were relatively numerous, due precisely to the poor living conditions and bad treatment the slaves were subjected to.[63]

Moreover, in the West Indies, there were neither hospitals nor doctors to tend sick slaves; in the French islands, for instance, the first hospitals were not built until the nineteenth century, and even then only in small numbers. The obligation in the French code to provide religious instruction to slaves was never implemented either, since most masters were opposed to such evangelization. Moreover, planters too often found deceitful reasons to get rid of slaves who, through disease or old age, were unable to work, sometimes inventing accusations against them in order to collect the compensation awarded to masters when the authorities executed a criminal slave.[64] The fate of a Caribbean slave was thus hardly enviable.

Several reasons may explain this administrative failure. Control by the authorities was almost impossible due to the enormous size of the plantations and to the large number of slaves working on them. Slave owners were sufficiently powerful to protect themselves and each other. The European governments, whatever their good intentions, were too far away to ensure the implementation of provisions unfavorable to the masters, all the more so since, if there was a complaint to the verifying agents, a jury of planters judged its validity and it was almost impossible to find witnesses for the defense. Most of the time, masters were acquitted because a trial entailed the master's against the slave's word.[65] Often, even if a code permitted a slave's complaint, the records prove that this provision was rarely invoked. The Louisiana judicial records, for example, do not offer a single case of a slave appealing to the superior council for protection or redressing of wrongs.

Another reason for the poor situation of Caribbean slaves may lie in the mercantilist attitude of West Indian planters. They rarely had a resident mind; even when they had established physical residence in the colonies, their main purpose was to increase their wealth, even if that meant sacrificing human lives. It was more economical to buy new slaves than to provide for the well-being of those already present. Moreover, the huge numbers of slaves and the size of the plantations made personal relationships between masters and slaves much more exceptional in the Caribbean. The tremendous need for manpower also made the overworking of slaves inevitable: sugar cane required a large work force and days were very often long on Caribbean plantations. Male or female, slaves worked all day and sometimes part of the night. Even pregnant women and those with very small children worked, along with children as young as twelve years old.

What was true for resident masters was even more frequently the case for non-resident ones. Absentee owners delegated their responsibilities to overseers who did not hesitate to mistreat the slaves. Statistically, there were more runaway slaves on the plantations of absentee owners, where overseers did not pay great attention to slaves' well-being.

This was the general condition of the French and Spanish Caribbean slaves, although better situations did exist depending on the colony or on the master himself. Spanish masters, for instance, were said to be much closer to their slaves than the French and West Indian English ones, but too often the subsistence of the slaves was not really ensured. The clothes provided were poor, and medical care rare. The conditions also largely depended on the good or ill graces of individual masters. They were much better when the masters were resident, concerned with the development of their property, and endowed with kindness. Some travel narratives mention the example of masters who tried to alleviate their slaves' labor by providing them with better tools.[66] Even so, instances of kindly paternalism and close master-slave relationships found in the travel narratives were apparently far from the norm.[67]

By contrast, the English and American codes, which appeared much stricter, were often mitigated in practice. The principal Anglo-Saxon distinction was the development of a peculiar form of paternalism. This attitude appears to have been based in an English relationship model, because it could be witnessed even in the Caribbean. This was the case of Barbados, for instance, until the plantations grew so large that it was no longer possible for a master to ensure this type of relationship with all his slaves. All the historians of the British West Indies acknowledge that practice strongly mitigated the austerity of the codes. Protective laws introduced under the pressure of metropolitan abolitionists were mere enactments of current practice, a formal codification of changes that had occurred independently.[68]

This was still more obvious in the American South. As previously stated, the living conditions of the slaves were even better there than in the English Caribbean colonies. Although less protected by the codes and more secluded in their status, slaves often lived much better than their West Indian counterparts. They were better fed, better clad, better cared for, and better treated as their greater longevity and natural propensity to reproduction prove. They also developed relationships with their masters that were much more favorable to their well-being.

For many reasons, Southern planters considered their agrarian world as some kind of Edenic model and regarded their slaves as powerless children who should be taken care of. Some historians contend that this concept was linked with certain Anglo-Saxon traditions and with a special turn of mind.[69] It may also be traced in part to facts of residency. Southern planters were not only more often physically present, but they also saw to the management of their plantations themselves. They had the most definite intention to remain on the American continent and never return to Europe. Moreover, paternalistic attitudes and behaviors were easier to maintain given the generally smaller size of the plantations and the smaller number of slaves per master. Conversely, the exercise of paternalistic attitudes was less common in regions where large plantations prevailed. In Georgia, coastal South Carolina, and the area around Charleston, rice plantations more closely resembled the Caribbean model in size and organization. Masters were also more often absentees, since they sometimes had several plantations and tended to reside in the cities of Charleston, Georgetown, or Savannah during the summer months to flee malaria. In their absence, overseers tended to rule the plantations, and there are many more examples of mistreatment in these situations than in the rest of the South.

Among the reasons given to explain the birth of Southern paternalism are also the different white to black ratios found in the South and the fact that almost all of the slaves were Creole and partly Americanized, because their African origins were further away from their immediate experience.[70] This paternalism has been largely documented in the literature on North American slavery, although it has not necessarily been interpreted in the same way throughout history. For decades, historians of the South, following the pro-slavery ideologists of the nineteenth century who used this argument to justify the institution, showed that paternalism, which appeared to be part of the Southern honor code, produced a better form of slavery and meant more humanity and affability. A recent interpretive trend, although it still acknowledges the existence of such a concept, tends to be less positive about its subtext. Ira Berlin, for instance, calls the first stage of this paternalism "domestication of domination" (*Many Thousands Gone*, 99), showing that it is part of a long process of depriving slaves of their individuality (through forced rejection of their given names, harsher living conditions in the early days of enslavement, codification, and so on). For Berlin, Southern masters then simply turned "patronage into paternalism."[71] Improvement of conditions, respect for family ties, development of some forms of privacy, the return of naming practices to the slaves, and other consequences of this paternalism tended to further reduce the autonomy of the slaves and to prevent them from resisting slavery (by running away, for example). Similarly, Drew Gilpin Faust indicates that paternalism represented a form of "intrusiveness," which "constrained the independence of both masters and slaves" (14).

Whatever the unconscious or unstated motives, such paternalism led to many benefits for slaves. A closer relationship with the master resulted in a certain humanization of the institution. It also enabled the filling of gaps left in the code and the easing of its severities. The slaves obtained much more from their masters than what the law granted or even authorized. Food and clothing were provided; the maintenance of the cabins was better ensured; slaves were granted more medical care; holidays were often respected; and the custom of giving slaves Christmas gifts was common. Because the cultivation of cotton or tobacco was less demanding than that of rice or sugar cane, young children were not put to work, and there could be special provisions to protect pregnant women, whether for humanitarian or economic reasons. Slaves were often allowed to have gardens and even poultry, although this again was not included in the codification. A relatively complex master-slave relationship moreover implied a slave's permanent negotiation with the master, a negotiation perhaps made more palatable because masters understood that advantages granted to slaves tied them to the plantation, prevented them from running away, and reduced the risk of rebellion. Nonetheless, Peter Kolchin, who has made a detailed and largely comparative study of Southern exceptionality in matters of slavery, confirms the conclusions of Berlin and Faust, arguing that paternalism reduced the slaves' autonomy, making them more dependent on the master, who interfered with every aspect of their daily life.[72]

A closer examination of daily life in the various plantation societies thus proves that, even though the codes have a real importance to a comparative perspective by indicating the sundry conceptions these societies had of the institution, practice very often changed the conditions of the slaves in one direction or the other. A study of exceptions to the rules reveals that the power of the codes was relative. Practice often deviated from the general model, because of specific conditions or influences. A few words here about singular areas of the American South will confirm the ascendancy of practice and external conditions over codification.

As already suggested, although the American codes were, despite slight divergences, basically the same, some regions followed a model that was somewhat different from that of the rest of the South. Parts of Georgia, South Carolina, and even East Florida (which became British in 1763), followed a model that was closer to the Caribbean model. Large rice plantations required more manpower, resembled factories rather than farms, and involved an important product transformation component similar to that involved in the processing of sugar cane. The work was more exhausting than that required by the cultivation of cotton and tobacco. The demographic features of the slave society were also closer to those of the West Indies, due to epidemics of tropical fevers, among other things. The organization of slave life was often left to an overseer, and relationships between masters and slaves were often diluted. This clearly shows that differences in codification cannot entirely account for variations in slave life or in the master-slave relationship and that external, material conditions can play an essential role. Thus, while these particular regions tended toward a Caribbean model, they also slightly diverged from it, thereby attesting to the importance of ethics in the regulation of the daily lives and conditions of the slaves. Even though the large-scale planters were more often absentees, it was not the same kind of absenteeism found in the West Indies. American planters were firmly and exclusively rooted in America, and their absenteeism was therefore "local." For several reasons, as Berlin suggests, local absenteeism "did not breed the callous indifference of West Indian absenteeism" (*Many Thousands Gone*, 152). The masters resided on their plantations for at least a few months every year and were never geographically very far from them in the first place. Whereas Caribbean absentee planters lived in Europe, Southern ones were rarely farther than a day away from their holdings. This implied both a physical proximity in case of necessity and a clearly different vision of the role and obligations of a master, which gave birth to what Berlin interestingly calls "paternalism-at-a-distance" (*Many Thousands Gone*, 152). This comparison of several regions of the Deep South thus indicates the two-fold conclusion that— more than legislation—peculiar external conditions as well as practice and a certain ethical vision had an influence on the lives of the slaves.

Another significant deviation from the principal Southern model is found in the case of Louisiana. It was ruled by the same French (then Spanish) code as the French and Spanish Caribbean colonies. Nevertheless, the territory often followed a model closer to the American one, which may account for the very easy integration of the territory within the American fabric in the early nineteenth century. It was an intermediary colony, partly following the French and Spanish models and partly following a continental model.

The French and Spanish models were perceptible. Slaves lived outside the plantations and hired themselves out more often than elsewhere in the South. Unlike the Anglo-Saxon areas, Louisiana had a separate slave economy parallel to that of the whites. The slaves labored for themselves on Sundays, sometimes on Saturdays, or even a few hours every day. They had relative freedom of movement and lived closer to one another with opportunities to socialize (in the marketplaces, for instance). There were even specific slave celebrations, as the New Orleans tradition of slave dances in Congo Square demonstrates.

At the same time, there were much more favorable demographic conditions for the Louisiana slaves than for their Caribbean counterparts. As parish registers show, planters encouraged family life, reproduction, sometimes even marriages and christenings, even serving as godparents to the baptized slave babies. For this reason, but also on account of better living conditions, there was a high natural increase of population. In 1740, while the Caribbean colonies had to replace their slave populations constantly, and while most of the Southern colonies had a large American-born slave population, two thirds of the slave population of New Orleans were of Creole origin.[73] When Louisiana became Spanish two decades later, the population of the colony was almost exclusively native to Louisiana.[74] The slave population of the Lower Mississippi Valley grew altogether by about 36 percent between 1731 and 1766, mostly by natural increase.[75] In his close study of the evolution of Louisiana, Ingersoll contends that this might be partly due to the reduction of diseases, following the lower rate of importation of slaves from Africa (119).

Other manifest differences made the Louisiana colony depart from the Caribbean model. There was very little marooning in Louisiana—although slightly more than in the rest of the South—much less planter absenteeism, and closer relationships between masters and slaves. Thus, as a consequence of demographic conditions, among other things, the Anglo-Saxon paternalist model exercised more influence here than in the other French and Spanish colonies. The creolization of the slaves implied their much better integration into the cultural milieu of the colonists and less distance between slaves and masters. Moreover, proximity was made possible by a white-to-black ratio that bore no resemblance to those of the West Indian colonies. Because blacks outnumbered whites only by a margin of two to one in the 1760s, the white population was less frightened of them. There was also a lower rate of slave importation and less slave trade, which probably necessitated masters maintaining slaves in good conditions. The Louisiana slaves were thus much better treated, better fed, and better accommodated.

This situation changed slightly at the end of Spanish rule with the development of sugar cane, an increase in the size of plantations, and a necessary influx of new slaves. With different cultures and different languages, new slaves were more isolated from their masters. The increase in slave importation and in the number of slaves per plantation worsened living conditions, indicating again that external factors influenced the particulars of slavery more than the slave codes, which did not drastically change when Spain took control over the colony. The Spanish regime simply tended to be more mercantilist and more profit-oriented to the detriment of the slaves and their relationships with the ruling class.

While the codes themselves lend insight into the conception each society had of slavery, it is essential to keep in mind that a theoretical vision of society does not necessarily reflect reality. Practice may differ significantly from legislation, as the result of varied ethical systems and in reaction to different external conditions. Ethics and living conditions might sometimes provoke larger divergences between the slave societies than the legislation itself. The absence of three-tiered organization in the Anglo-Saxon societies, for instance, was partly due to a differing vision of interracial relationships, but was enhanced by special conditions. Some historians contend that it was also the result of specific demographic conditions, and more particularly of the presence of a large population of whites not involved in slavery in the South.

It is thus important to remember that, even though the Anglo-Saxon codes were the strictest and the least favorable to the slaves, the conditions of continental North American slaves were, apparently, by far the best in the region. Moreover, the special type of slavery that developed in the South (although this does not involve any value judgment on the "quality" of that slavery) brought about the birth of a very special cultural specificity. The presence of resident masters with "resident" minds and clearly determined to build a society in which they and their descendants would live, along with the paternalism such attitudes fostered, led to the development of relatively better living conditions for the slaves. The slave population thus developed without any sizable influx from Africa, and this led to the appearance of a very distinct African American culture. The slave population was not "re-Africanized," which might also explain some specific traits of the South. Historians, for instance, explain the absence of large-scale marooning in the South by material conditions—the higher density of the population and the less favorable geographic distribution of that population—but also by the emergence of a culture distinctly different from the African ones.[76] They contend that maroon colonies recreated typically African social organizations, which could not have had an equivalent in the South, because there the African patterns had been partly lost for several generations.

The definite proximity between masters and slaves, the special paternalist model that developed, and all of the conditions mentioned above led to the development of a distinctive African American culture during the era of slavery: a culture modeled by slavery that gave birth to an original pattern. The study of this model would be irrelevant here. However, it is important to note that the family pattern was Europeanized and that the culture, although it kept its African roots, synthesized regional character- istics and quirks. Celebrations, for instance, were unique amalgamations of indigenous and European traditions. African American music combined European instruments with instruments based on African tradition (the violin, the tambourine, and the banjo, for instance). Slaves so successfully assimilated the language of the masters that their songs were generally sung in English.[77] Even though differences between them remained strong, a kind of cultural continuum was thus created between masters and slaves, a continuum that reinforced the links that tied them together. Moreover, a highly singular society emerged, or, more importantly for this study, an extraordinary vision of slave society. Out of this vision, the South fashioned a specific cultural image that informs the Southern dis- tinctiveness with which this study is concerned.

This singularity was further enhanced by the development, in the nine- teenth century, of a real internal debate on the validity of slavery, which directly pitted the contenders against one another. The birth of an increas- ingly virulent abolitionist movement obliged Southerners to elaborate a defense and illustration of the institution—and of all the social, political, economic, and cultural developments that went with it—thereby giving a new impulse to the exceptional cultural construction that was being elabo- rated. At this point, it is therefore crucial to review the ideological debates on slavery, both in the Caribbean colonial societies and in the American South, to come closer to the elusive nature of Southern distinctiveness.

4

Ideology, Ideologies

Abolitionist positions can be traced back to the creation of colonial empires and to the institutionalization of slavery on the American continent. The development of abolitionist theses was a consequence of the Enlightenment and of the French Revolution in eighteenth-century Europe. Opposition to the very institution that lay at the core of colonial expansion increased in the nineteenth century. Its particular evolution in the United States produced the new form of an elaborate anti-slavery ideology.

A real difference between the American South and the Caribbean colonial possessions emerged after the American Revolution; the West Indies remained colonial possessions of far away European powers, while the United States started elaborating a national fabric. Once it had integrated the French and Spanish continental colonies, the United States became a united and supposedly indivisible nation. Any discussion of an existing institution was thus a matter of national interest. In the Caribbean, on the contrary, the territories remained in the hands of European powers, which implies that they were dependent on their mother countries in all matters. Their persistent colonial status reinforced their relative uniformity, especially where institutions specific to them were concerned. From the start, this created a difference in the birth and development of ideologies related to the institution of slavery on the American continent.

Conflicting Ideologies

The development of ideological debates in all the slave societies followed the same general pattern. Very logically, the anti-slavery ideology started developing first in reaction to an existing institution: in the 1770s for the Anglo-Saxon societies; in the late 1780s for the French colonies (corresponding to revolutionary ferment), and for the Danish and Dutch colo-

nies; and in the first decade of the nineteenth century for Spain. Predict-
ably, the pro-slavery argument developed later in response to abolitionist
attacks.

There was also the same gradation in the scope and strength of the argument throughout the Americas. The opponents to slavery first tried to
obtain the abolition of the Atlantic trade. This was the object of all the first
abolitionist societies as their names sometimes indicate: the English Society for Effecting the Abolition of the Slave Trade (founded in 1787 under
the lead of Grenville Sharp) and the French *Société des Amis des Noirs*
(created in 1788 by Jacques-Pierre Brissot). Both primarily aimed at dealing with the question of the importation of new slaves into the colonies.
The first opponents to slavery succeeded in obtaining what they wanted:
trade was abolished first in Denmark in 1792, taking effect in 1796. The
clause in the United States Constitution of 1788 caused the postponement
of the ban for twenty years, at the end of which period the trade was abolished. England—after a first unsuccessful attempt in 1792 when the House
of Lords rejected the bill—voted for abolition of the trade in 1807, which
also took effect in 1808. In France, the slave trade was first abolished in
1794 by the revolutionaries, then restored by Napoleon in 1802, and at last
decisively abolished (also by Napoleon, in a decision confirmed by Louis
XVIII) in 1815. Finally, Spain, under English pressure and after a first unsuccessful attempt in 1812, signed a treaty with England in 1817, abolishing the slave trade in 1820.

The second step of abolitionist ferment turned to the institution itself.
Often the same societies, sometimes under slightly different names, but
led by the same persons, started fighting against slavery itself. Everywhere, this second crusade was organized into two successive steps: the
struggle for gradual emancipation first, then a hardening of the opposition
and a radicalization of the argument, leading to the demand for a total and
immediate abolition of slavery.

In the United States of the 1810s, there was also the intermediary step
indicated by the American Colonization Society, which, by purchasing
Liberia in 1818, tried to foster the return to Africa of the emancipated
slaves. The ultimate aim of most of its members was in fact a gradual disappearance of slavery, and when the society broke up in the late 1820s, its
most militant northern members (including William Lloyd Garrison) began to demand gradual abolition of the institution. In England, the English
Society for the Mitigation and Gradual Abolition of Slavery was founded
in 1823, a step taken by France in 1834 with the creation of the *Société*

Française pour l'Abolition de l'Esclavage (led by such people as the Duc de Broglie, Alphonse de Lamartine, and Victor Schoelcher). As for Spain, it was not until 1865 that the *Sociedad Abolicionista Española* was founded by Rafael María de Labra.

As in the United States, all these societies first fought for gradual abolition before demanding total and immediate abolition. The change occurred in the United States at the turn of the 1830s. Garrison founded *The Liberator* in January 1831 and, in his first editorial, apologized for militating for gradual abolition of the institution.[1] In England, this change occurred at the same time, since from May 1830 on, the antislavery society called for the end of gradual measures and for immediate abolition. That year, it even changed the "Gradual Abolition" in its name to "Immediate Abolition." This trend was emphasized by the strong repression exerted after a few rebellions (the Christmas rebellion of 1831 in Jamaica) and the expulsion of missionaries from the Caribbean islands. In France, the change occurred in the 1840s, essentially under the lead of Victor Schoelcher, who, after fighting for gradual abolition in the 1830s, toured the Caribbean twice, came back with an overall view of the situation, and started criticizing the English system of progressive abolition.[2] In two books published in 1842 and 1843, he advocated immediate abolition of the institution.[3]

The second common feature of abolitionist attacks everywhere was their invocation of religion, morality, and humanity to fuel debate; revolutionary ideals were often appealed to. This was the case in France, where slavery was abolished for the first time by the Convention (French Revolutionary Assembly) in the name of liberty and equality: the ideals of the Revolution. The second abolition law was passed and implemented in 1848, after a second revolution had inaugurated the Second Republic. In the United States, all the abolitionists called forth the democratic ideals of the American Revolution and Constitution, often quoting its preamble as well as parts of the Declaration of Independence.[4] In Spain, the final move towards abolition was similarly triggered by the Revolution of 1868, the ideals of which were regularly evoked in the process. Indeed, the liberal constitution of 1868 granted equal rights and liberty to all Spanish citizens, thus creating a disparity between the peninsula and its colonies. The abolitionists instantly requested implementation of the constitution in Cuba. In all these societies, economic arguments were also put forward, all the abolitionists using the non-profitability argument to oppose the institution.

Finally, and very importantly, abolitionist sentiment generally followed the same path: from individuals to public opinion, from public opinion to the governing bodies. In England (as later in Pennsylvania), the movement was launched by the reaction of key religious groups. The Quakers, for instance, banned slavery among their members as early as 1755 in England and 1770 in New England, before turning to proselytism in the 1770s. The movement then spread to the non-conformist churches, such as the Methodists and the Baptists. The Catholic Church was somewhat slower to react, and in countries like France and Spain, it was usually revolutionaries who led the way to abolition. In the second step, abolitionist leaders and societies turned toward public opinion and agitated to convert the population by means of publications and public meetings. In England, this phase started early, in the 1770s. Abolitionist philosophy encountered the public via local press, pamphlets, and Sunday sermons at local churches. Branches of the abolitionist societies emerged all over the country in the 1780s, organizing meetings in all the main English towns. When the 1823 society for gradual abolition was created, it immediately undertook to convert public opinion to its principles. One year later, there were 220 local branches throughout the country. Similarly, when it decided to fight for immediate abolition of slavery, the society created an agency committee— composed of six appointed lecturers and a reserve of honorary lecturers— in the aim of agitating public opinion. Within one year, the number of abolitionist societies grew from 200 to 1,300. The process was comparable in the United States and Spain, although in Spain it occurred much later.[5]

In all the European nations, abolitionist pressure turned from the populace to its governing bodies, often in the form of petitions. In England, a hundred petitions reached the Parliament in 1787 and 1788, including those sent by the London Corporation (governing body of the City of London, London's principal trading and financial center), by the Universities of Oxford and Cambridge, and by clergymen asking for the abolition of the slave trade. In 1824, 750 other petitions were sent, calling for the gradual abolition of slavery. In Spain, numerous petitions were sent to the *Cortes* [the Spanish parliament in Cadiz] between 1864 and 1872, with hundreds of them pouring from all of Spain's towns and villages 1872. In France, the assembly received seven thousand signatures for the abolition of slavery in 1844 and eleven thousand more in 1847. Typically, popular appeals found favorable reception in the various assemblies, where a few members started taking up the fight. In France, such representatives as Jean François

Lacroix and Georges Jacques Danton defended the abolitionist themes in the Convention in 1824. In 1838, Representative Hippolyte Passy presented a bill to the assembly, asking for the abolition of the slave status for children. In England, in the last decade of the eighteenth century, the abolitionists easily found ready sympathy for their cause in the member of Parliament for Yorkshire, William Wilberforce. In 1797, the first bill demanding the abolition of the slave trade failed in the House of Lords because it never obtained the government's support.[6] In 1806, however, the new prime minister, Charles James Fox, was ready to bring the support of his government to the abolition of the slave trade. As time went by, supporting political forces increased as older representatives such as Wilberforce and Thomas Clarkson were joined by a whole new generation of politicians.[7] In Spain, the situation was very similar, ending in the conversion of the king himself. Indeed, in 1872, King Amadeo I even declared in the *Cortes* that he would readily lose his crown in the defense of such a cause as the abolition of slavery ["Si ha de perder mi corona sea en buen hora por la abolición de la esclavitud"] (quoted in Philip, 57).

Political adhesion to the cause was slow to spread, all the countries displaying, at one time or another, failed attempts at obtaining passage of a bill by their parliaments. This was the case in England for each of the various steps of abolition. For the abolition of the trade, for instance, the first motion condemning slavery, presented in the House of Commons in 1776 by two members of Parliament, David Hartley and George Saville, was voted down by a large majority. Wilberforce did not manage to get abolition of the trade passed either in 1789 or in 1792 when it was passed by the Commons but rejected by the Lords (by a majority of 163 to 88). A motion of the Commons also failed in 1806. In Spain, for instance, a first proposal by Guridi Alcocer to abolish the slave trade and slavery was rejected in 1810, as was that of Felix Varela and Jose Arguelles in 1812, together with several others, which experienced the same fate in later periods.

Finally, another common feature among all abolitionist movements is that they were included within larger reform movements. In the United States as in Europe, abolitionism was linked with other demands for a greater degree of equality, and was, for instance, coupled with early feminist causes, as illustrated by the fact that most of the signatures on the Spanish petitions were those of women. Some strong abolitionist voices in the United States came from women fighting for women's causes, such as the Grimke sisters. French abolitionist leaders such as Schoelcher also fought for abolition of the death penalty and the granting of equal rights to women.

Quite naturally, in all these countries, a counter-movement appeared when the threat of abolition became serious. The response generally emanated from planters, whether in the Caribbean or in the American South. Despite differences in the volume of responses, the media used by pro-slavery ideologists were similar in all areas: pamphlets, essays, and even sometimes works of fiction were dedicated to the defense of the threatened institution.

The debate thus followed similar patterns and ultimately, during the course of parallel although not necessarily simultaneous evolution, led to the abandonment of the practice of this specific system of labor. Where the framework for opposition was concerned, however, there were great differences between the United States and the colonial societies of the West Indies, linked with the political status of the territories and with the social, economic, and political contexts of the debate. In the Caribbean (except, at times, in Cuba and Puerto Rico, where opposition to slavery was a means for colonists to rid their island of Spanish domination), abolitionism was an essentially external opposition, often relatively dispassionate and limited in scope. In the United States, the debate over the question of slavery took on the form of internal strife, both heated and all-inclusive, which became even bitterer as the political context evolved. It is thus vital, in the context of the present work, to examine these increasing differences, starting with the colonial societies and then moving to the very specific American context, as we make yet another step forward in the definition of Southern distinctiveness.

Abolitionism and the West Indies

The distinction in the way Caribbean societies expressed opposition to slavery can be traced to their persistent colonial status. The ruling class of white colonists was united around the question of slavery, whereas the opposition was manifested almost entirely outside in the far away metropolitan countries. Very little inner opposition existed, with the exception of that of the slaves themselves. When abolitionist opposition increased in the mother countries, slave rebellions started multiplying. In the French Caribbean, a large-scale movement arose in October 1822 in Martinique at the town of Le Carbet. It was rapidly repressed with extreme severity. In

Jamaica, on Christmas day of 1831, some 50,000 of the 300,000 slaves of the colony rebelled, under the lead of Samuel Sharpe, a Baptist slave. Here again, repression was both immediate and violent. As for the Spanish colonies, they managed to prevent the successful outcome of several large-scale rebellions: in San Juan, Puerto Rico, in 1812; in Ponce, Puerto Rico, in 1848; and in Cuba in 1812, at Matanzas and Havana (in the western part of the island) in 1842, and the famous 1843 Conspiración de la Escalera, all repressed with bloodshed. The main common point is that these rebellions were often triggered by rumors of abolition legislated by the metropolitan mother countries. This was the case in the 1831 Jamaica Christmas rebellion, the 1812 San Juan revolt, and the 1812 rebellion in Cuba led by José Antonio Aponte, who used a decision supposedly made by the Cortes as a pretext to start the insurrection. (In fact, the parliamentary body had rejected a motion calling for the abolition of slavery.)

On the basis of such apparent causes and effects, historians have long contended that European abolitionist movements had led the slaves to rebel, which is partly true, of course. However, a new reading of events tends to demonstrate that the movement was not one-sided and that slave unrest also played a great part in the abolition process by fuelling abolitionist movements in the metropolitan countries.[8] For Craton, the existence of slave rebellions and the horrid repression that necessarily followed are the best proof that the system could only hold together by generating violent racial strife. For him, this violence was decisive in convincing public opinion that the institution had to disappear; political resolution from the parliaments occurred only when a sufficient proportion of the population had rallied the abolitionist cause and when slavery became widely considered "morally evil, economically inefficient and politically unwise" to the point that parliamentarians had no other solution than to follow what public opinion commanded (Craton, 265). What occurred in the colonies often had real significance for the abolitionist movement. The narration of the rebellions and of their repression was decisive, as was the fate of missionaries expelled from the islands for leading slaves to rebellion. Their banishment from the colonies had an important impact on public opinion. Reverend William Shrewsbury, for instance, when he was expelled from Barbados, took an active role in the abolitionist campaigns at home. The churches and societies widely publicized his expulsion and activism, and the missionary became a symbol for the fight against the institution. William Knibb, who was expelled from Jamaica after being accused of fuelling the 1831 Christmas rebellion, also became an ardent defender of the abolitionist cause in England. Wilberforce even asked Parliament to investigate a similar case, that of John Smith, which had taken place in Guyana. Although the motion proposed to Parliament was not adopted, an open debate permitted progression of abolitionist principles. It was then that the English abolitionists started requesting immediate abolition.

Except for the slaves themselves, the other rare forces that internally advocated abolition and tried to convert the colonies from inside were the missionaries, especially those of the reformist churches. They came to the British colonies in small numbers at first, but even though their influx increased in the nineteenth century, they were almost systematically prevented from acting. The missionaries were active not only in the English but also in the Spanish colonies, where Spanish colonial authorities often complained about agitation brought to the islands by English and American abolitionists. Denominations like the Methodists and the Anabaptists sent emissaries to Cuba in the late 1830s with the mission of clandestinely distributing documents—mainly Bibles and anti-slavery literature—to encourage the slaves to rebel. Several documents of the period attest to this increasing movement: Governor General Tacón, for instance, wrote to the Spanish queen in 1837, complaining of the role of the missionaries; declaring that the expulsion measures proposed by the government were insufficient; and asking for severe sanctions.[9] The same year, Cuban authorities intercepted an abolitionist leaflet entitled "El Abolicionista," which emanated from the English Abolitionist Society and described at length its organization, its financial power, and its determination to proselytize. The last part of the document clearly explains how abolitionists intended to gain ground in the colonies by sending emissaries, creating abolitionist societies there, and diffusing propaganda to prove that the principles of humanity, religion, and justice commanded a fight against the institution. This led to the expulsion of some emissaries and to a reinforcement of the control of foreign arrivals in the colony.

English officials in non-English colonies sometimes helped these emissaries. British diplomats are said to have led abolitionist campaigns in the Spanish islands, for instance. They were active in the Mixed Commission, founded to obtain the implementation of the treaty for abolition of the slave trade in the Spanish colonies and signed in 1817 between the two countries. The English consul in Cuba, David Thurnbull, was accused of covertly triggering the 1842 slave rebellion in Havana and Matanzas. These attempts, however, were to no avail in the colonies themselves, since there was usually consensus between local authorities, slave owners, and the white population in general. As for the free people of color, they were mostly involved in their own fight for equal rights and prerogatives and did not often agitate in favor of the slaves.

The debate was thus external to the islands and included much less direct confrontation. Naturally, the planters had their representatives in Europe. In France, the Massiac Club, a coalition of planters and merchants, defended their interests. In England, some absentees managed to get seats in Parliament, and the West Indian lobby was relatively active. The merchants and traders who directly or indirectly had interests in the West Indies often helped them in their counter-attack. The debate, however, largely remained a long distance one, the attacks against the system coming mostly from Europe and the voices raised in defense of the institution remaining mostly within the colonial system itself—with two notable exceptions: the Spanish colonies of Puerto Rico and Cuba.

Indeed these two colonies were the only ones that experienced the emergence of an internal abolitionist trend. In Puerto Rico, a secessionist movement started at Lares in 1868, and a similar revolutionary trend was born in Cuba in October of the same year. The colonists wanted independence for their respective colonies and decided to enroll the slaves in their fight. They imagined a general but gradual emancipation law with compensation granted to the masters. Manuel de Céspedes, the Cuban revolutionary leader, first proclaimed general amnesty for the maroons in December 1868. He also proposed to grant freedom (with compensation) to all slaves who were presented by their masters or went independently to the Cuban revolutionary authorities.[10] In the central region of Cuba, in Camagüey, the revolutionary assembly adopted a resolution in February 1869, declaring that slavery was an institution brought to Cuba by Spanish dominion and thus had to disappear with it.[11] These were the only cases of internal abolitionism among the Caribbean colonies and they were motivated more by opposition to colonial power than by a real philosophical argument, although abolition in the rest of the Caribbean and in the United States probably partially served as an incentive. The Cuban revolutionaries took up the idea and used abolition as a lure for black support.

The abolitionist movements of the Caribbean colonies thus remained largely metropolitan and were often influenced by the political climate. In France, for example, a revolutionary climate, despite the Restoration, favored changes. In England, a new manufacturing and business bourgeoisie, attempting to take the lead from the landed aristocracy, brought about the passage of reforms. They found favorable ferment in public opinion, which was afraid of losing the Caribbean colonies as they had lost the North American ones. The vigor of European abolitionist movements was also sometimes checked by the political context. When England and France went to war in 1793, English abolitionists slowed down their fight, partly for fear of being associated with French revolutionaries and also because they started siding with the French planters, in an attempt to remove the colonies (in particular St. Domingue) from French dominion.

The primarily external nature of Caribbean abolition was also marked by the fact that the disappearance of slavery in the West Indies was generally announced by a series of reforms passed a few years before abolition, whatever the colonial power. In 1824, for instance, England voted reforms concerning crown colonies like Trinidad. These reforms contained measures limiting whipping and banning corporal punishment for women. When absolutely necessary, the whipping had to be inflicted within twenty-four hours after the offense and had to be limited to twenty-five lashes. Similarly, imposed Sunday work was forbidden, marriages were encouraged, families were protected against separation in sales, slaves could own and bestow property, and manumission measures were eased. A protector was also appointed to prevent the mistreatment of slaves. Despite a sometimes strong planter opposition, the measures were generally implemented, as in Barbados, for instance, simply because they provided legal confirmation for custom and current practice.

Similarly, when slavery was reestablished in the French colonies by Napoleon (and maintained under the Restoration, between 1814 and 1830), it was with the advice to treat the slaves with humanity. To avoid having to fight on several fronts, the government tended to be relatively liberal with free people of color—who protested more often and more actively against the discriminatory measures they had to face—by granting them total political and civil equality in 1833. The July Monarchy also launched a real reformation policy. In January 1840, the government required masters to submit to the control of the king's general attorneys and their substitutes. In July 1845, the two houses of the French Parliament voted the Mackau law (after the name of its drafter), which specified that time had to be left for non-obligatory work and that a salary had to be given to the slaves who agreed to work overtime. Moreover, a slave could now own and bestow chattel goods. As in England, legislation often simply made common practice official, under external pressure. This was favored by the adhesion to the abolitionist movement of the Catholic Church, which officially condemned both the slave trade and slavery itself in 1839.

In short, all those who wanted reforms and change fought together under the banner of abolitionism.

In Spain, a similar reform trend appeared, although somewhat later, with passage of the Royal Order of 2 August 1861 that granted emancipation to any slave leaving the colonies for the Peninsula, for the northern United States, or for any territory where all men were free. In 1865, the government appointed a commission of inquiry, La Junta Informativa de Ultramar, composed of nineteen West Indian representatives and twenty Spanish representatives, to reflect on the cases of Cuba and Puerto Rico. Another commission was created in 1869 to discuss the sole case of Puerto Rico, Cuba being by then in a state of insurrection. Of course, the ultimate step was taken with the Moret law of 1870, and the liberal Pronunciamento of Republican Spain later pronounced itself in favor of reforming the system of slavery.[12]

At this point, then, several specific features of Caribbean abolitionism are apparent: the persistent colonial status of the islands led to a relatively clear geographical division of the debate, and the larger reformist movements gave rise to a gradual process that permitted a slow evolution towards abolitionism. The result was relative moderation in the arguments on both sides, as well as in the number of publications, which, although large (especially since over a century separated the first English from the last Spanish manifestations), remained limited compared to the case of the United States.

In the Caribbean colonies, too, the first abolitionist blows were based on matters of principle. In France, for instance, the movement started in the eighteenth century with an abstract condemnation of the principle by philosophers: Voltaire, Rousseau, Montesquieu, and Diderot rejected the principle of slavery without devising any plan for its disappearance or any solution for its replacement. Then, from 1758 onwards, the physiocrats, such as Mirabeau in *L'ami des hommes*, criticized slavery as an anachronism and started devising moderate plans for its gradual abolition. Condorcet and Turgot, for instance, in the revolutionary movement, imagined the suppression of the slave trade and the emancipation of mulattos at age thirty-five and of blacks at age forty. The first abolition of 1794 silenced the abolitionists who, at first, failed to react to the re-enslavement of blacks during Napoleon's Empire.[13] When the monarchy was restored, the abolitionist movement took on a liberal and moderate orientation through the writings of figures such as Abbé Grégoire, Madame de Staël, and Benjamin Constant. Abbé de Pradt's defense of abolition was part of this largely dispassionate trend. In short, the arguments used by the abolitionists were limited in scope and in fervor. Even a leading figure such as Brissot (the founder, in 1789, of the abolitionist society *L'Ami des Noirs*) justified abolition by the rather prosaic necessity of curbing potential slave unrest. They showed that slavery was no longer adapted to the colonial context, ran counter to the revolutionary ideals of freedom and equality, and did not follow the moral precepts of religion. Very often, a large part of the argument was also economic. In 1837, for instance, Simonde de Sismondi published *Etude sur l'Economie Politique*, a purely social and economic study showing that slavery was not profitable and that the institution made the slave societies unstable. The solution he proposed consisted of the suppression of the institution and the introduction of sharecropping.

The English abolitionists developed similar arguments, although they decisively highlighted the religious argument. (Opposition to slavery had come from the reformist churches.) Some thinkers, like James Stephen in *The Slavery of the British West India Colonies Delineated*, used legal and statistical evidence along with the argument of experience to counter the institution. In 1823, in his *Appeal to the Religion, Justice, and Humanity of the Inhabitants of the British Empire: In Behalf of Negro Slaves in the West Indies*, Wilberforce also contended that slavery was immoral and degrading. Overall, however, criticism remained limited to the principle of slavery and was generally moderate, although British opponents of slavery were somewhat more passionate than the French (who might have lost some fervor after the first abolition law of 1794).

Spanish abolitionists marshaled the same types of arguments, although with still more moderation than the English and the French. They essentially denounced the system of labor organization and showed that it was no longer adapted to the society and economy. Most of the time, the main abolitionists—such as Gabriel Rodríguez, Orella y Rincón, or uncontested leader, Rafael María de Labra—tried in their publications to criticize the masters' selfishness, while reassuring the master class at the same time. Their opposition to the institution was never virulent, and although they criticized the practice and wanted its abolition, they never heaped opprobrium on masters. This extreme moderation may be due to several factors. First, it may be explained by the very ancient slavery tradition of the country, including on the peninsula itself. This was never the case in either England or France, which turned to slavery much later than the Spaniards and adopted the institution only in their colonies. Moreover, as indicated by the study of the codes and their implementation, the Spanish institution was globally made more humane by the development of personal relationships between masters and slaves and by the possibilities for the latter to get out of the system, which made servitude less definitive. Finally, the presence, in the colonies themselves of abolitionist trends among separatists made opposition to metropolitan anti-slavery movements less uncompromising. This does not mean that the debates were never heated, since every time abolition was suggested in the Cortes, the debates that followed brought strong resistance from the defenders of the institution.[14]

European abolitionist literature also remained confined to the question of slavery and never expanded to other topics, unlike North American literature of the same theme. The most limited volume of abolitionist literature was certainly found in Spain, where the abolitionist movement appeared much later (in the mid-1860s) and lasted only about twenty years.[15] In England and France, publications were more numerous because of the relatively more active opposition to the institution. In England, publications started early, around 1770, reached a peak between 1788 and 1792, almost ceased for some twenty years, and then resumed in the 1820s, but for less than twenty years. The works published were mostly documents emanating from the churches and treatises written by the key abolitionist leaders.[16] An anti-slavery periodical, *The Anti-Slavery Monthly Reporter*, was created to transmit the main abolitionist principles to public opinion. Travel narratives also played an important part in the diffusion of abolitionist themes, all the more so since the genre was widely appreciated in nineteenth-century Europe.[17]

The same general conclusions can be made with regard to France. As in England, the movement for abolition had its periodicals (such as Cyrille Bissette's *Revue des colonies*) and covered almost the same period, starting in the eighteenth century and experiencing a period of quiet after the 1794 abolition and during the Napoleonic era. The movement resumed in the 1830s—marked by such publications as Agenor de Gaspain's *Esclavage et traite* in 1838—and lasted somewhat longer than in England, where abolitionist pressures had started about fifteen years earlier.[18] The volume of publications was relatively important to the movement, but, as in the English case, was mainly limited to technical documents bearing exclusively on the topic of slavery.[19] A few rare fiction works dealt with the topic, but they were minor works and had no real impact on public opinion.[20]

The most comprehensive and probably the most decisive participation in the debate came from Victor Schoelcher. His first publication in 1833 promoted the same kind of gradual abolition advocated in England, while the second publication, seven years later, critically examined the racial prejudices on which slavery in the colonies was based.[21] He then decided to visit extensively the West Indian colonies of Martinique and Guadeloupe, as well as Jamaica, Antigua, and Dominica. He returned from his journey with the absolute conviction that slavery had to be abolished; that the English model was not good; and that abolition should be total and immediate. He even envisioned the possibility of abolition through insurrection, but the Haitian model made him abandon a violent solution. His next two publications were thus clear in expressing determination to obtain immediate abolition of the institution and perfectly justify his thesis.[22] Schoelcher's books were probably the first non-abstract criticisms of slavery to be published; based on observation, comparison, and reflection, they occasionally resemble journalism. For the first time (with the exception of Bissette who had been so lonely in his cause that he never expressed his opinion very forcefully), when public opinion in France contended that slavery had to be abolished gradually; when Hippolyte Passy imagined the possibility of freeing only as yet unborn slaves; when Alexandre Destult de Tracy and Agenor de Gasparin imagined a period of ten years over which to obtain abolition, someone dared to demand immediate abolition. Schoelcher defended his thesis with a highly developed pragmatism as opposed to the abstract principles of morality, philosophy, and religion that had been used by the other European ideologists. This was the last blow against the institution and was followed by abolition in the French colonies.

Despite the uncompromising nature of his argument, Schoelcher's *Des Colonies françaises, abolition immediate de l'esclavage* resembles a travel narrative more than an abolitionist manifesto. The author constantly justifies his thesis by emphasizing the necessity of holding onto the colonies, and most of the time, he apparently remains objective. Despite denouncing the evils of slavery, he mitigates his comments by showing that the liberal practices of the French colonies ease the daily lives of the slaves. He goes as far as describing the general well-being of the slaves and the frequently affectionate relationships between masters and slaves. Interestingly, Schoelcher apologizes for being prejudiced and sometimes ignorant of realities in his previous books and keeps renewing his gratitude to the colonists for welcoming him, despite his strong abolitionist position. In his dedication, he thanks them for their friendship, assures them he speaks without hatred, and even describes his relationships with them as links of brotherhood.[23] For anyone familiar with the heated writings of American abolitionists, this temperate work has a definitely unusual ring. To sum up, opposition to Caribbean slavery was quite distant from the colonies themselves and relatively toned down and dispassionate. Although there were, at times, fierce local polemics (as in Jamaica over laws imposed from London), the debate remained largely confined to the metropolitan legislative bodies. Abolitionist arguments bore on the principles of the institution, they lacked any deep philosophical dimension and the debate never reached proportions that tore countries apart.

Pro-Slavery Thought and the Caribbean

Pro-slavery responses exhibited similar features, the power of the counter-attack fitting that of the attack. In the very early days of the abolitionist movement, public opinion in the metropolitan countries had been widely ignorant of colonial facts and had not seen anything wrong in the institution of slavery, especially since most Europeans had never witnessed any of its manifestations. They had accepted it, because it had always existed and because it had never seemed unjust to them.[24] It was not until the abolitionist attacks multiplied that they started accepting arguments in opposition to the institution and sided with them, primarily because they had no direct interest in the survival of the system.

In Spain, abolitionism was very weak and started late, mostly under external, essentially English, pressure. Although there were early abolition plans, they had met no real consensus, either in the higher spheres of political life or in public opinion. Most politicians and much of the public remained long convinced that slavery was natural. Because Spanish abolitionism started very late, at a time when slavery had already been abolished everywhere else, including the United States, there was little opposition to the movement, especially since this ideological current was confirmed by abolitionist tendencies displayed by separatists in the islands themselves. There were no political pro-slavery lobbies, no significant manifestations of pro-slavery thought, and no organized pro-slavery literature beyond individual reactions. As opposed to a broad and cohesive pro-slavery movement that agitated public opinion, the defense of slavery was generally confined to individual arguments in the Cortes where the institution was justified on economic and social grounds. The defense largely relied on the idea that any society needed servants and that if slavery was abolished, it would be reborn in another form and with another name.[25] Some politicians also defended the institution in the name of protecting private property.[26] Even the most radical defenders of slavery had non-philosophical arguments. Gutiérrez Salazar, for instance, thought its preservation necessary to protect production and property; José Antonio Saco contended that abolition should not be enacted because it was impossible to compensate the owners immediately, because the colonies were not prepared for it, and because such radical measures could provoke a resistance that might eventually be detrimental to the colonies.

In France and England, the pro-slavery response was similar, although somewhat more organized, probably due to the existence of political and economic lobbies. As the Caribbean planters tended to be absentees, a number of them lived in Europe and agitated to protect their West Indian possessions. In France, they gathered in the Massiac Club; in England, they attained visibility after a parliamentary reform. Some constituencies were created in sparsely populated areas, essentially composed of large estates whose owners did not seize the occasion to enter Parliament. Since franchise was subject to landowning requirements, there were no other voters than these large landowners, who thus chose their own representatives in Parliament and sometimes sold their seats to West Indian owners. The latter, united in the West Indian Society, spoke their minds in Parliament, thus curbing abolitionist attacks and checking abolitionist projects.[27] In both France and England, they were assisted in their resistance by the mercantile interests, which had built their wealth on West Indian commerce. To give a single example, in England, the Society of West India Merchants had been founded in 1780 and replaced in 1780 by the Society of the West India Planters and Merchants. Its membership was composed of British sugar merchants (in such port towns as London, Bristol, Liverpool, Glasgow, and Dublin), absentee planters, and colonial agents appointed by the respective legislatures to represent the various colonies in England.[28] In Spain also, after the abolitionist attacks of the late 1860s (in the form of petitions to the Cortes), when defenders of slavery launched one of their comparable though infrequent counter-attacks, most of the petitions reaching the Cortes emanated from the coastal cities that did business in or with the colonies. In the European countries, some individuals who were not directly involved with the institution also supported the pro-slavery contingent. This was, for example, the case in England of Admiral Nelson, whose wife, Frances Herbert Nibbet, had been born in Nevis. Admiral Rodney, who had won decisive English victories in the Caribbean and whose name was given to a bay in St. Lucia, also maintained a pro-slavery stance.

After the reformist movements of the 1820s, which the pro-slavers had readily joined because they were not sufficiently influential to curb them and because they had thought that reforming the system might save it, the English pro-slavery lobbies tried to use their influence in Parliament to discredit the abolitionists. They sent pamphlets to the other members of Parliament, sometimes containing personal attacks against the leaders of the abolitionist movement. Reverend James Ramsay, for instance, was attacked not on ideological grounds, but for the allegedly depraved life he had led in the colonies during his nineteen-year stay in Nevis.

The pro-slavery argument was also partly ideological, but being a response to the abolitionist argument, it was generally as limited as the latter had been. For its defenders, slavery was beneficial, because it saved the lives of Africans who otherwise would have been put to death in their countries. It protected them by offering them food, clothing, a roof, care during illness and by removing their fear of old age.[29] Slavery also ostensibly benefited mankind by liberating Africans from brutality, ignorance, and paganism. It was completely justified by the scriptures, being, according to these ideologists, contrary neither to morality nor to the precepts of religion. It was justified, too, by the fact that a serving class had to exist in any society, and, according to slavery's defenders, blacks had been born to fulfill that subservient role. Such justifications, however, were limited by the fact that the pro-slavery lobby was defending an interest and certainly not pursuing a cause. Their argument never reached a philosophical or ethical dimension and thus had a very limited scope. As for direct attacks against abolitionists, they were rare. Although European defenders of slavery sometimes accused their opponents of lying or distorting the truth, they explained abolitionist leanings by their excessive sentimentality and lack of insight into colonial reality.[30]

European opposition to abolitionism thus remained unobtrusive and dispassionate. Except for the European pro-planter lobbies, the core of the opposition emanated from the colonies themselves and was principally local, due to the difficulty of communication between the mother countries and the American colonies.[31] There, opposition to abolition was motivated by the economic necessity of the system and by the fear that the slave population, whose numerical importance largely overpowered the white minority, might react to abolition with violence. They thus clung to the principle for economic reasons and on grounds of safety. They also tended to be more critical of the abolitionists than their metropolitan counterparts and sometimes fought their accusations by rejecting any responsibility for the system. American colonials had not invented the system, they argued, and neither were they responsible for directly transporting Africans to the American continent. Overall, they reproached European abolitionists with getting involved in matters that should have remained internal to the colonies, sometimes pointing out hypocrisies that seemed to belie the abolitionist stance. British planters wanted to know why abolitionists would fight for the well-being of slaves whose work day, they contended, was at most nine hours, when metropolitan workers, including children, could be forced by English industrialist employers to work for up to twelve hours.

The Jamaican planters imagined secession from England, and even possible annexation to the Union, counting on the help of the United States. They founded the Colonial Church Union, which fought for the defense of slavery with verbal propaganda and sometimes violence: the union destroyed sixteen churches to prevent missionaries from spreading their abolitionist theories and exciting the slaves to rebellion. The movement finally receded when governor Lord Mulgrave forced the officials belonging to the union to resign from their positions, before declaring the Colonial Church Union altogether illegal in January 1833. The favorite means of expression of these advocates of slavery was the colonial press, often limited to gazettes on colony life, but containing critical reviews of abolitionist writings in Europe.

The pro-slavery argument hardly went further than economic justification and reflections on the impossibility of abolishing slavery for prosperity and safety reasons. The argument was, like the abolitionist one, relatively mild and dispassionate and remained confined to the institution of slavery itself. This is completely in line with the motives for the foundation of the Caribbean colonies; the West Indian planters had definite mercantilist pursuits and were businessmen rather than mythmakers with dreams of building shining cities on a hill. They seldom had a resident mind, so to speak, and were not attempting to erect a glorious society for their descendants as the North American colonists were. Thus, they rarely attempted any general aggrandizement of their societies.

Because of the events in St. Domingue, the French were somewhat more active in opposition to abolitionist themes. The slave rebellion of the 1790s that ultimately led in 1804 to the creation of the first black republic on the American continent, Haiti, had caused the violent deaths of many white inhabitants and the forced flight of the rest of the white, and often mulatto, population. These events lay heavily even on the minds of abolitionists; Schoelcher, for example, had abandoned insurrection as a route to dismantling the institution after considering the Haitian mêlée. The refugees added their voices to those of European travelers who visited the lost colony and described the horror of the aftermath.[32] Travel narratives, such as the very famous account of Jean-Baptiste Labat, a Dominican priest who had spent many years in the West Indies, especially Martinique, had a long tradition of displaying clear pro-slavery views. The refugees, however, focused on describing at length the horrors of the slaves' bloody acts and began a nostalgic glorification of their life before the loss of the colony. A two volume work on the colony and its disastrous loss, published anonymously in 1795 and 1796, was ultimately attributed to a former coffee planter of St. Domingue. Sometimes in the form of direct address to the abolitionists, the books describe life in the former colony as a kind of Golden Age and show the institution of slavery as an ideal system, perfectly adapted to the colony. The idealization is not total: the planter admits to instances of slave abuse and mistreatment, but he portrays such cases as anomalies, far from the norm.[33] The majority of refugees wrote numerous pamphlets tinged with pain, indignations, and desire for revenge.[34] They did not usually try to turn their society into a mythic place, but rather tried to advocate attempts at getting the island back. The events of St. Domingue also fueled a metropolitan production of works displaying racist views, although this trend never went beyond mere reaction to the facts themselves.[35]

Often written after the abolition of slavery, the French islands *did* produce a few literary works that should be mentioned at this point. One of the most famous, still reprinted today in Martinique, is *Les Bambous* by François Marbot, a pastiche of Jean de Lafontaine's animal fables, written in Creole with the aim of displaying definite pro-slavery views.[36] The rest of the literary output has fallen into oblivion and has not even crossed the ocean. It thus took no part in the debate over the question of slavery; its only originality lies in a tendency to glorify the system, the society, and its inhabitants, thereby slightly widening the scope of the defense.[37] Difficult to assess is to what degree these writers had a definite ideological purpose. Some of them may simply have found inspiration in what surrounded them, in what had always been their life and universe, and in what they intimately believed was universal truth, without any wish for propaganda.

In short, both the abolitionist movement and its pro-slavery reaction, in the European metropolitan countries and in the West Indies, were relatively moderate in their rhetoric and arguments. The ocean separating the colonies from their mother countries, the relative ignorance of Europeans with regard to a system most of them had never observed in action, the reciprocal ignorance on the part of most of the colonists of the power of the abolitionist movement in Europe—all this led to a low degree of opposition. Moreover, while the abolitionists defended an abstraction, the European West Indian colonists were no idealists. Their defense of the system was based on a pragmatic wish to protect their financial interests and their daily customs. The scope of their reaction was rarely philosophical and did not encompass the defense of a whole civilization. This limited the profusion of their responses and any mythologizing tendencies therein. Here we can locate the beginning of that decisive divergence between the colonial societies of the Caribbean and the American South, which, culminating in events surrounding abolition and its aftermath, cleared the way for a conspicuous Southern myth-making tendency and the cultural distinctiveness it informs.

The Nineteenth-Century North American Fracture

From the start, the situation was different in the United States. The debate over the existence of slavery occurred within an independent nation, which no longer had any direct European attachment. The former French and Spanish colonies of the South had been progressively incorporated within the national fabric, and the American territory was independent from any European power. This means that the abolitionist debate was purely an internal one in which the two ideological sides were closely interrelated, although they progressively concentrated on either side of the Mason-Dixon line.

When the nation was born, slavery existed in all thirteen colonies. However, slavery started receding from the northern states quite early, and the 1787 North-West Ordinance introduced the first institutional geographical limit to its expansion. The Missouri Compromise reinforced this border, marked by the Ohio River and historically the first restriction set on slavery. As for the original northern states, they erased slavery from their institutions one after the other. This process expanded across about three decades between 1777 and 1804. Vermont initiated the process in 1777 with a law progressively abolishing slavery; children born of slaves were free, although they had to work for their mothers' masters until age twenty-one in compensation. Pennsylvania followed in 1780 by voting a similar law of gradual abolition, the age of definitive freedom being twenty-eight. Behind these frontrunners came Massachusetts in 1783,

Rhode Island and Connecticut in 1784, New York in 1799, and finally New Jersey in 1804. From then on, slavery became the "Peculiar Institution" of the South.

The Mason-Dixon line was therefore first a geographical separation on either side of which slavery either spread or receded. Then it came to be seen as an ideological limit, since opposing views concerning slavery gradually concentrated on each side of it. Anti-slavery sentiment was present in the South until the 1830s. In 1827, Quaker reformer Benjamin Lundy counted 130 societies opposing the institution, 103 of them being located south of the Mason-Dixon line; anti-slavery publications could still be found in the South at the time.[38] Concomitantly, a few individual voices went on defending slavery in the North.[39] The 1830s marked the end of that relative uniformity, and from then on, the defense of slavery became exclusively Southern, while abolitionism became a Northern value. The Mason-Dixon line was no ocean, though, and could be crossed easily, which means that observation was possible, that confrontation was possible, and that publications could travel easily from one side to the other. Although opposed thought trends were geographically polarized, the debate was still internal and, more importantly, materialized through open confrontation. Whereas in the European nations, the voices defending the West Indian interests in Parliament always remained a clear minority, both sides were represented almost equally in the American legislative body. If the Southern and Northern representatives were not exactly equal in numbers, the number of senators representing North and South was balanced. Orators on both sides could respond to each other, thereby fuelling debate, reinforcing both arguments, and making opposition more and more uncompromising.

The other peculiarity of the North American debate was that it encompassed much more than mere opposition of principle on the question of the institution alone. The two camps evolved divergent social models. Political oppositions, provoked by the necessity to maintain a balance of powers in Congress, led to the first debates between North and South. The South was intent on preserving its latitude to block unfavorable legislation in the Senate, if not to initiate favorable laws. It was thus essential for Southerners to preserve an equal number of slave states. This struggle continued to fuel debate at the time of the Missouri Compromise, as well as in 1850 and during the Kansas-Nebraska conflict of 1854. Political conflict was intensified by the development of the States' Rights theory after the nullification

crisis of the early 1830s—a reinforced avatar of the anti-federalist sentiment of the late eighteenth century.

The North-South opposition was also clearly a struggle for influence
between two economic doctrines as the nullification crisis proved. An
agrarian society and a rapidly industrializing region had diverging interests, and tariffs were always a reason for opposition between them. Social
and cultural doctrines also began to diverge as time went by. North-South
conflict was therefore hardly limited to the institution of slavery, and debate could not be confined to an abstract question of principles, because the
stakes were too high. The North's interests hinged upon questions of political strategy and the expansion of its fast industrializing civilization
based on free work. For the South, the stakes were even greater as its political interests progressively transformed into a matter of survival. The
breadth and vigor of the slavery debate thus attained a higher scale than
that of Europe, and the arguments on both sides took on greater amplitude.

While few participated in the debate in the European colonies, many did
in the United States, both in the North and in the South. In Europe, the
debate was at first limited to attacks by abolitionist leaders and churches,
which spread during a second stage to public opinion before reaching the
political sphere where it was discussed in the various parliaments. In the
United States, the process was indisputably reversed: the debate started in
Congress and then spread, via the abolitionists, throughout the entire
population—so widely, in fact, that no one could remain silent. Anti-slavery and anti-abolition arguments were first defined and spelled out during the debate over the admission of Missouri into the Union. Then, and
only then, did abolitionist societies multiply and gather funds that they
used to publish an astounding amount of anti-slavery literature that they
distributed all over the country. In 1835, the Philadelphia-based American
Anti-Slavery Society published thousands of leaflets, among them, *Slave's
Friend, Human Rights, Anti-Slavery Records,* and *The Emancipator.* All of
these were so widely circulated that twenty-five thousand copies of *Slave's
Friend* alone reached the South. Antagonism pervaded the entire political
sphere, and party divisions progressively followed the Mason-Dixon line.
In 1839, for instance, Alabama planter, James Birney, who had been a
member of the Colonization Society, founded the Kentucky Anti-Slavery
Society, after emancipating all his slaves. He had to leave the South—
where such opinions were no longer tolerated—to found the Liberty Party.
In 1848, a convention met under the leadership of some well-known aboli-

tionists and in the presence of some very famous fugitive slaves. These men, including Henry Highland Garnet, Samuel Ward, and Frederick Douglass, founded the Free Soil Party, whose candidate in the presidential election was Martin Van Buren. Similarly, the 1860 presidential campaign showed that not a single politician could remain silent. They all had to take sides in the debate, even if the situation created breaches within the parties themselves, as was the case for the Democratic Party, which renounced any chance for success by splitting up and presenting two candidates, whose only divergences had to do with the way to protect slavery.

The abundance of ideological publications on each side had no limits. Everyone plunged into the struggle: besides the political speeches, quantities of sermons, essays and pamphlets were written and circulated throughout the country. Abolitionist newspapers flourished in every Northern city from the 1830s onward. After the 1831 publication of Garrison's *Liberator* in Boston, dozens of periodicals were founded within just a few years. Among the most famous were James Birney's *Philanthropist*, published in Cincinnati in 1836, and later, Frederick Douglass's *North Star*, published in Rochester, New York, in 1847. This was most certainly the most fertile period in American history for polemical writing. Because these writings circulated beyond the Mason-Dixon line, no one could remain ignorant of what the other side thought and said. Thus, no one could remain indifferent, a circumstance that produced a multitude of direct responses.

The arguments on both sides became very detailed, highly developed, and diversified. The abolitionists, although they based their arguments on principles very close to those of the European ideologues, made very precise and direct attacks. Slavery was criticized on religious and humanitarian grounds, but the specificity of the principles of American democracy, as stated in the founding documents of the nation, made the opposition to the institution still stronger. A nation that proclaimed as its indisputable principles freedom and equality could not accept such servitude. References to the Declaration of Independence and to the Constitution are innumerable, whatever the source considered.[40] Attacks on the slave owners and all those who defended the institution were also much more direct than in Europe. The living conditions of the slaves were narrated in detail and the horrors of the system described at length. Theodore Weld's *American Slavery as It Is*, published in 1839, compiles all the cruelest stories and most hideous testimonies of ill treatment suffered by slaves. In his famous *Appeal in Four Articles*, David Walker constantly describes the masters as "tyrants," "natural enemies," murderers of wives and mothers and even labels them "weak, good-for-nothing" (2, 11, 62).

The tone of the attacks was much more uncompromising than it had ever been in any European country. Walker called for a violent revolution of the slaves to free themselves, and his appeal sometimes verges on an appeal to murder. Addressing the slaves, he explains: "believe this, that it is no more harm for you to kill a man, who is trying to kill you, than it is for you to take a drink of water when you are thirsty" (Walker, 26). When addressing whites, he clearly threatens them: "Remember, Americans . . . that some of you, on the continent of America, will yet curse the day that you ever were born . . . You want slaves, and want us for your slaves!!! My colour will yet root some of you out of the very face of the earth!!!" (Walker, 72). Interestingly, Garrison himself, while finding Walker's appeal too violent and, therefore, detrimental to the abolitionist cause, directly and violently threatened the defenders of the institution himself.[41] The tone of these attacks has clearly nothing to do with Schoelcher's professed friendship for the slave owners of the French colonies.

Another peculiarity of the North American abolitionists is that their action was not limited to intellectual and ideological opposition. They actively participated in the liberation of slaves, first by refusing to implement the constitutional obligation to return runaway slaves to their masters. From 1837 to 1848, the authorities of the free states did not return a single slave. Some states went even further: Massachusetts and Vermont forbade their employees to contribute to the restitution of fugitive slaves on the basis of the jurisprudence of a Supreme Court decision of 1842, according to which states did not have to comply with the law. This was only passive reaction, but there were also very active manifestations of anti-slavery conviction such as the Underground Railroad, organized by free blacks and aided by abolitionists, mainly Quakers. Under the leadership of Robert Purvis, this network permitted the escape of thousands of slaves from 1838 to the eve of the Civil War. The Underground Railroad initiative was naturally favored by the internality of the abolitionist struggle. After all, the Mason-Dixon line was much easier to cross than the Atlantic Ocean. At the same time, though, the initiative denotes more determination than among European abolitionism and a practical mind.

Finally, the last peculiarity of the North American abolitionists is that their arguments were not confined to ideologues and activists. The abolitionist banner was also shouldered by members of the literary world, producing such contributions as Henry David Thoreau's famous—though abstract and theoretical—*Resistance to Civil Government* (1848). The North versus South debate also gave birth to a new American genre: the American slave narrative. Slave narratives number in the hundreds. Emancipated or fugitive slaves, most often prompted by abolitionist leaders, started telling about their lives in bondage. This was not revolutionary, since the genre had been born in England in the eighteenth century with the well-known *Life of Olaudah Equiano or Gustavus Vassa the African Written by Himself*, published in London in 1789. But under the pressure of the abolitionist movement, the genre gathered huge momentum in the 1840s and 1850s, most often with abolitionist financing. The northern public, increasingly converted to the abolitionist cause, avidly read these accounts as expressions of truth, which thus reinforced their anti-slavery sentiments.[42] Some literature went further than this: blatantly propagandistic novels were published, but their reputation was transitory. They were genuine abolitionist manifestoes, which, despite their small literary value, enjoyed true, although ephemeral, success. Among these were the popular *Clotel* (1853) by fugitive slave William Wells Brown and *Blake; or, the Huts of America* (1859) by Martin R. Delany, the story of the organization of a slave rebellion. The success of these novels was short-lived, and history mostly forgot them.

There is, of course, one famous exception to this rapid fall into oblivion: Harriet Beecher Stowe's *Uncle Tom's Cabin*, first published as a serial in *The National Era*, from June 1851 to March 1852, before being published in book form in Boston in 1852. The author also published a second novel, *Dred*, in 1856. The story of a slave rebellion's leader, this book was not as successful as Stowe's first. Twenty-first-century readers might find it hard to imagine how thoroughly *Uncle Tom's Cabin* could rile a nineteenth-century Southern reading public. In fact, the novel fueled incredible reaction in the South. Unmistakably clear in her aims, Stowe set out to criticize the status of human beings as property on religious grounds: the book's original title had been *The Man That Was a Thing*. The novel explicitly illustrates the idea that slavery is a sin opposed to God's Law that leads to physical, moral, and spiritual disaster. Stowe used her novel to criticize both Northerners and Southerners and concludes the novel by admonishing: "Both North and South have been guilty before God; and the Christian church has a heavy account to answer"(629). Despite this even-handedness on Stowe's part, Southerners felt both incriminated and threatened—because of the wide use abolitionists made of the book for their purposes and because of its immediate and tremendous success in the North. By June 1852, about ten thousand copies were being sold per week—an enormous number considering the inefficiency of distribution channels at the time. By October, 300,000 copies had been sold. Within five years, half a million copies had been sold in the United States and twice as many in Great Britain. The success of the book was not even checked by the war. *Uncle Tom's Cabin* is truly *the* bestseller of the nineteenth century.[43] This success can be explained not simply by the atmosphere prevailing in the country at the time or the book's usefulness to abolitionists, but by the literary quality the novel displays and the fact that it was a real projection, in a dramatized form, of the most current arguments of slavery's opponents. It invited readers to identify with the characters, appealed to human emotions, made the abstraction of abolitionism concrete and widely accessible, and provoked a desperately violent reaction in the South.

Thus, due to peculiar conditions in America—especially the internal character of the abolitionist struggle, the several causes of opposition, and the importance of the political power at stake—abolitionist attacks here had a vigor never attained in any European country. The abolitionist debate was characterized by a profusion of reactions, by an argument that was both diversified and precise, by a series of accusations that were no longer abstract criticisms of a mere principle, and by a tone that was uncompromising and could even become threatening.

The result was, of course, an equivalent force in the response from the defenders of slavery. Overall, the same characteristics can be applied to pro-slavery arguments as to abolitionist attacks. Like abolitionist claims, pro-slavery arguments first took form in Congress during the Missouri debate, and these responses to abolitionism were innumerable, diversified—both in argument and in medium—and uncompromising. The flow of pro-slavery responses to abolitionist attacks was also continuous; thousands of sermons, articles, pamphlets, leaflets, and essays appeared between 1830 and 1860. Southerners mobilized against the danger that threatened not only the Peculiar Institution, but the whole of Southern civilization. As George F. Holmes expressly said in 1856, "The question of Negro slavery is implicated with all the great social problems of the current age" (95). The vociferous nature of pro-slavery expression accounts for the large volume of publications that received the unconditional support of the Southern presses: from the *American Quarterly Review* to the

Columbia South Carolinian; and from still more famous periodicals founded later, *De Bow's Review* from 1846 and the *Southern Quarterly Review* from 1849 on.

Another exceptional feature of American pro-slavery argument is its diversity. Compared with the European pro-slavery ideologists, who essentially presented the economic benefits of the institution, Southerners developed a multifaceted defense. They first argued that, historically, all the greatest civilizations on earth had relied on slavery.[44] Another widely used argument derived from scriptural justification of the institution, which relied on the letter rather than on the spirit of the Bible. By quoting all the biblical passages concerned with servitude, Southerners justified slavery as an institution endorsed by God's word.[45] Similarly, whether overt or implicit, the constitutional argument informed a third pro-slavery argument; this argument sought to silence the abolitionists by presenting the nullification argument, or States' Rights theory. According to Southerners, abolition passed by Congress would be unconstitutional and subject to nullification by individual states.[46]

In response to the abolitionist argument that slavery violated American democratic ideals of freedom and equality as expressed in the Declaration of Independence, defenders marshaled the following rationale. Man, they argued, was born into a state of subjection, as evidenced by his dependency upon others throughout childhood and adolescence. According to slavery's defenders, no civil or political right had ever been extended to dependents, even in the most advanced forms of democracy, and the hierarchical organization of every society, they asserted, depended upon this arrangement. Because slaves were regarded as grown children and perpetual dependents, no political or civil rights could accrue to them.[47]

Social justification is also to be found in many pro-slavery writings, where slavery is portrayed as the safest organization of labor for workers, guaranteeing food, clothing, shelter, medical care, and protection in childhood and old age. This defense very often contained elements of comparison with the manufacturing North or with England.[48] The social argument was generally associated with economic interests, either attempting to prove that African workers were the only ones adapted to work in hot southern climates, or that, due to their natural laziness, they could be effective only in bondage. Some ideologues also endeavored to show that production had developed steadily under slavery, using Haiti, which lay in ruins since abolition, as a counter-example.[49] For these theorists, slavery was altogether indispensable on the grounds that all prosperous societies require the labor of a human substratum on which to establish wealth.[50] Defenders also systematically portrayed slavery as a means to preserve social peace and to protect the country from generalized racial war.[51]

American defenders of slavery also built an elaborate racial argument for the institution, undertaking to prove the inferiority of the black race and to use this alleged inferiority to justify enslavement. Slavery, they contended, offered an opportunity to remove Africans from a mire of barbarism and paganism, an opportunity that coincided with their destiny to be subject to a superior race. These propagandists heavily relied on the works of the Comte de Buffon and of Robert Thomas Malthus, as well as on the pseudo-scientific disciplines of phrenology and comparative racial anatomy.[52]

The response of pro-slavery Southerners to adamant abolitionist attacks was also uncompromising to the point that, while they had first tried to demonstrate that slavery was a "necessary evil," they ended up, in the last two decades of the antebellum period, arguing that it was a "positive good."[53] The attacks multiplied. The tone hardened. Southerners joined forces to exert more weight.[54] They developed a Southern brand of nationalism—the "fire-eaters" advocating secession—and took their arguments to the furthest extremes. George Fitzhugh, for example, after demonstrating that slavery was the best possible system, the most harmonious association of work and capital, had no other choice but to conclude that it should be expanded to all workers, whatever their racial origins.[55] Not only did pro-slavery arguments reach dimensions never even imagined in the European colonies, but the writings also displayed an aggressiveness peculiar to the North American context. As early as 1854, Fitzhugh, in an article published in the *Richmond Examiner*, warned his adversaries: "We have stood in the defensive long enough. We can throw fire-brands as well as the abolitionists; and the poor in the free states are much more ready for insurrection than the slaves in the South" (qtd. in Wish, ed., 6). James Hammond echoes this threat in his "Mud-Sill Speech."

Finally, Southern ideologues tended to expand their views to other fields, conscious as they were of a peculiarly regional perception, not just in social and economic matters, but also in cultural ones. Fitzhugh, for instance, claimed the existence of a mode of "Southern Thought" and advocated its development and expansion through education, culture in general, the writing of manuals, and the creation of a totally independent Southern literature. This effort was confirmed by the South's entire literary community under the lead of William Gilmore Simms and thanks to the Southern literary presses: the *Southern Quarterly Review*, directed by Simms himself, and the *Southern Literary Messenger*.

In this wish to support a native literature, the South was a precursor. Southerners, right from the beginning of their struggle against the North, felt it necessary to play a part in the development of an American literature. A form of literary sectionalism, so to speak, thus developed. To highlight their difference from the rest of the nation, they chose to use their environment and their civilization as the frame of their literary production. This trend began with the 1824 publication of George Tucker's *The Valley of Shenandoah*, the first novel to use the South and slavery as a background. Although not a Southerner by birth (he was born in the Bermudas), Tucker came to the South in 1795 at age twenty and spent the remaining fifty years of his life there. His novel is the first to paint a precise and detailed picture of the South, and though he primarily emphasizes its virtues, he does not altogether ignore its darker aspects.

In the 1830s and 1840s, a nascent Southern literature sought to defend the region that was already threatened. The next generation of writers aimed at creating what may be thought of as a typically Southern literature and at participating in the abolitionist debate. William Alexander Caruthers, John Pendleton Kennedy, William Gilmore Simms, and Nathaniel Beverley Tucker stand out as ambassadors of this new trend.[56] Historical and plantation novels—a genre launched with the 1832 publication of Kennedy's *Swallow Barn*—came to celebrate the South, its institutions, its civilization, and its inhabitants.

The publication of *Uncle Tom's Cabin* fueled the energy of Southern writers, all the more so since the Southern nationalism that was pervading the section persuaded writers that they had to elaborate a Southern literature that would be exceptional. Simms's *Woodcraft* was a direct answer to Stowe's novel, with the famous scene in which a slave, cleverly named Tom, refuses the emancipation offered by his master. As for Kennedy, he wrote a new version of *Swallow Barn* from which any potentially negative connotation had been erased and replaced by a celebratory epic of slavery and of the South as a whole. Even poets such as William J. Grayson participated in the celebration.[57] In short, this literature was a celebration of the Southern society at large, as opposed to the ideological writings, which solely defended slavery as an institution. A more detailed study of this type of literature will be made in the last chapter, but it may already be concluded that Southern difference was obvious in the literary field, compared with the slave societies of the West Indies. The pro-slavery response in general was more detailed, more diversified, more uncompromising, and not limited to the defense of the Peculiar Institution.

The study of the ideological trends that built up in the diverse slave societies of the American continent shows developing rifts between the Caribbean and the American South. On the one hand, the disappearance of slavery in the colonies was a slow and relatively painless process that extended over one century, from the first English attempts at abolition to the disappearance of the institution in Spanish colonies. This process generally followed several progressive stages throughout which the opposition was between metropolitan abolitionist pressure groups (goaded by slave unrest) and colonial defenders of slavery (mildly defending slavery compared with the United States). The debate was limited to abstract justifications on both sides, largely toned down by distance and the absence of contact between the contenders. The slavery debate thus remained dispassionate and was largely based upon social and economic realities.

In the United States, on the other hand, antagonism developed between two distinct and diametrically opposed civilizations that were nonetheless sections of the same nation, struggling for power. The confrontation was always more or less direct, first between congressmen, then between ideologues, without any substantial geographical barrier or distance. The attacks made by one side fueled the responses of the other, while, in turn, the vigor of these responses increased the bitterness of the subsequent attacks. The arguments on both sides were highly developed, strongly expressed, and encompassed much more than the preservation or eradication of a mere institution. The arguments issued from every mouth, in the North as well as in the South, even fiction writers, engendering a very specific literature.

The nineteenth century and the ideological debates on slavery thus confirm an increasing divergence between the North American and West Indian slave societies and emphasize the development of Southern difference. This was but a first step. Specific Southern features were further strengthened by the actual enforcement and aftermath of abolition.

Abolition and Its Aftermath

As the preceding chapter indicates, Southern difference quite obviously developed during the ideological debate over the question of slavery. It was further reinforced by the implementation of emancipation itself. All the societies under study, except for the South, experienced a comparatively peaceful abolition and accepted its absolute character. By contrast, it took the South almost a century to come to terms with the change brought about by abolition.

Abolition in the Caribbean

Abolition in the West Indies was a slow process that was finally accepted without much violence. Even though there were reactions motivated by economic and social factors, it took place relatively bloodlessly throughout the Caribbean, without incurring total war.

A single counter-example must be mentioned, that of French St. Domingue, later renamed Haiti. This colony differed from the rest of the Caribbean model in the extreme violence that surrounded abolition. Nonetheless, it cannot be assimilated to the Southern model, because reaction was internal and was fueled almost exclusively by slave unrest at the time of the French Revolution. In the late 1780s, revolutionary ferment spread to all layers of St. Domingue society. It started with the autonomous rebellion of the ruling planter class against revolutionary France as early as 1789. Planters were strongly attracted by the American model through which the colonies had managed to gain total independence from the mother country without losing the institution of slavery. The planters wanted their peculiar colonial status to be taken into account and requested total commercial freedom, as well as self-government. Their unsuccessful reactionary movement gave way to another rebellion, that of the free colored people, who, by 1790, following in the revolutionary wake, were demanding that their rights be protected and guaranteed. Although the 1765 *Code Noir* had ensured all free persons (those born free and those granted freedom) the same rights, the provisions of the code had not been implemented and many subsequent legal decisions had deprived the free colored people of certain rights and privileges. The rebellion, led by Vincent Ogé, was repressed in February 1791.

These antagonisms (colonists versus metropolitan government, whites versus free colored people) probably fueled the ultimate rebellion, the most violent and historically successful one: the slaves' fight for freedom. Slave unrest did not exist solely in St. Domingue, but, there, it was probably exacerbated by the peculiar conditions of the island: the huge numerical superiority of the slaves, the significant economic power granted to the free colored people, and, of course, the numerous oppositions just mentioned. The first uprising, led by Boukman in August 1791, was only partially repressed. As a result, it ultimately spread throughout the entire island in 1793. To try to deal with this bloody rebellion, which caused many deaths in all three racial groups of the population, the civil commissary of the Northern province decided to abolish slavery in August 1793. The decision was discussed at the Convention in February 1794 and adopted by the French Revolutionary Assembly. It was justified by the revolutionary ideals of freedom and equality, but also for strategic reasons, both to try to keep control over the colonies and to destabilize the English and Spanish colonies.[1] Abolition was thus officially confirmed and expanded to all the French colonies. After a few years of violent acts and unsettled power, due to a struggle among Sonthonax, Toussaint-Louverture, and Rigaud to rule the colony, and following the flight of thousands of white colonists and free colored people, Toussaint-Louverture gained absolute control of the island.

In the other French colonies (Martinique, Guadeloupe, St. Lucia, and Tobago), the unrest that occurred remained minor, probably because the revolutionary process was not of local origin, but was directed from France, and also because, as early as 1794, the islands had been transferred to English control. Although France regained Guadeloupe later that year, Martinique, Tobago and St. Lucia remained under English control until 1802. When Napoleon came to power, he initially decided to maintain slavery where it had never been suppressed, that is, in the colonies France had recaptured from English domination. Although he had apparently not intended to reestablish slavery in Guadeloupe and St. Domingue at first, rumor that he had done so led to a large-scale slave rebellion under the leadership of Louis Delgrès in Guadeloupe. This movement was repressed and led to the restoration of slavery. The abolition of 1794 was thus geographically limited, probably because it had been launched rashly, had not been prepared for, and because no provision had been made to compensate the planters' losses. An historical "accident," as it were, the 1794 abolition was short-lived.

As previously stated, the only exception to this rule was St. Domingue, for which colony the abolition of 1794 followed upon years of revolutionary unrest and had been launched from inside—certainly not from outside—the colony. The blacks had taken power and had driven most of the white colonists off the island, although Toussaint-Louverture had attempted to maintain at least some of them on the territory in order to benefit from their financial and agricultural expertise. After a failed attempt to recapture the island by Napoleon's Expeditionary Corps, the colony experienced clear radicalization, which, instead of returning it to French control, made its loss definitive. Toussaint-Louverture surrendered in 1802 (he was jailed in France, where he died), but his submission led to the accession of his lieutenant, Dessalines. He was much more radical than Toussaint had been, and, under his leadership, the last remaining whites were either slaughtered or forced to leave the island. In 1804, the first black republic of the Americas was born and took the name of Haiti. While Haiti is remarkable among the rest of the Caribbean colonies in the discussion of abolition, it does not compare with the American South.

Aside from the Haitian mêlée during the first French abolition, the Caribbean generally followed the same model. Abolition was imposed there peacefully by the metropolitan powers; it was mostly gradual; and slave owners often received compensation. England led the way. Abolition occurred in the English Caribbean colonies in 1833, and a system of apprenticeship was instituted, accompanied by the granting of £20 million in compensation to the masters for the loss of property they had incurred. The ex-slaves were to work as apprentices for their former masters for at least another four years. The principle of compensation went unopposed. It would have been dangerous for the government not to offer any compensation, for it would have jeopardized the principle of private property. This measure was favored all over England, although it was initially developed by the pro-planter periodical *The Glasgow Courrier* and supported by the *Quarterly Review* and all other colonial publications, such as the *Jamaican*

Courant. The acceptance of the principle was sustained by the idea that slavery was a kind of collective sin for which the entire nation had to atone. Abolition was undeniably a national movement, involving the whole population and all the more readily accepted by the government, because the West Indian lobby was still very powerful. In 1823, thirty-nine members of Parliament could be identified with a West Indian interest: eleven merchants, including John Gladstone and Joseph Marrya, and twenty-eight absentee planters. When serious discussion of abolition began, the colonial secretary, Edward Stanley, confidentially negotiated with the West Indian lobby before submitting any proposal to Parliament, so as to avoid a political and economic crisis. The lobby accepted the idea of abolition, but demanded, first, the continuation of protective tariffs on colonial products; second, the establishment of a system devised to ensure masters that ex-slaves would remain on their estates; and finally, of course, generous financial compensation.

The West Indian lobby thus never opposed the principle and never resisted the project that resulted from national consensus, but instead set conditions. The slave owners' wishes were largely provided for in Stanley's abolition project: children under six would be set free immediately; the other slaves would be emancipated, but subject to a twelve-year apprenticeship that would supposedly give them time to become accustomed to the exercise of freedom. Unconditional freedom was thus not to be granted until 1846. Finally, according to the terms of the project, the owners would receive a global compensation of £15 million. The abolitionists opposed the principle of apprenticeship, and the planter lobby thought that £15 million was not sufficient. A compromise was then reached: the duration of apprenticeship was reduced to six years for rural workers (with forty-five weekly hours of compulsory work for their masters) and four years for non-rural workers. The amount of the compensation was increased to £20 million on request of members of the West Indian lobby, who had threatened to make the transition from slavery to freedom difficult if they did not receive more than the amount initially proposed.

Quite importantly, even the colonists did not reject abolition, given assurances that they would be sufficiently compensated and keep their labor force. Moreover, the principle of compensation was never debated by the metropolitan powers, only the amount. Abolition was thus voted on 29 August 1833—all the more easily since everyone had become aware that the system did not work properly. There were too many slaves; they cost too much; and they were not sufficiently productive. The planters were too heavily indebted and had little hope of seeing their situation improve, since development of the sugar beet and establishment of sugar cane production centers elsewhere, especially in India, were making West Indian sugar less vital to the English economy.

The abolition law was accepted by all the colonies and implemented as voted, except in Antigua, which suppressed the intermediary period of apprenticeship, unnecessary in that very small slave community. Elsewhere, apprenticeship was officially maintained, although rejected by the apprentices themselves. Its duration was eventually shortened, however, and it ended in 1838. Apprenticeship was considered a useful transition between slavery and freedom, assuring the masters that their laborers would remain on the plantations and supposedly enabling slaves to accustom themselves to freedom.

The French system displayed many features in common with the English system. When abolition was passed in 1848, it was not violently opposed, but again, the slave owners demanded compensation. Apparently, there were two main differences from the English system, although the two systems were closer than they may appear at first sight. Officially, there was no system of apprenticeship: abolition was immediate, and the emancipated slaves instantaneously became French citizens and were granted political equality. The second difference was that compensation was voted as a separate measure. A compensation of six million francs was granted, although through an independent law. Universal male suffrage was instituted, but between 1848 and 1854, the French government suppressed the elected local assemblies. A governor, with the help of a privy council, administered the colonies. As for the municipal elections, they were subjected to a poll-tax requisite. Finally, although no apprenticeship was instituted, French authorities developed a system of partnership or "association" between the owners and the workers that was similar to English apprenticeship. The owners provided the land and the buildings and retained all their property rights; the workers provided only the manpower. Production was shared according to various principles: the "tiers brut" or "rough third" principle, with two-thirds of the profit granted to the owner and one-third to the workers; the "quart brut" or "rough quarter" principle with three-quarters of the profit going to the owner and one quarter to the workers; or the "revenu net," or an equal division of profits between owner and workers once expenses had been deducted from production. The "revenu net" share was disbursed to a workers' collective through which it was to be distributed equitably among the individual laborers. This method avoided direct remuneration and ensured that the emancipated slaves would remain on the properties.

The Danish and Dutch West Indies followed in the wake of French emancipation. The Dutch half of St. Martin immediately followed the French half, as did the Danish islands of St. Thomas, St. Croix, and St. John in 1848. The rest of the Dutch colonial territories (Surinam) experienced abolition in 1855: the emancipation was immediate and compensated, but required the freed slaves to work for a master (theirs or another) for one year in order to reimburse the government for the compensation. As for the Danish colonies, they had already followed the European pattern: with the initiation of a reformist movement in 1838; the granting of the possibility for slaves to purchase their own freedom in 1840; and the abolition of slavery for children under twelve in 1847. In fact, although the Danish slave population was proportionally significant, this emancipation may be considered a minor case in the history of abolition, since the colonies were very sparsely peopled (St. John, for instance, having a slave population of 1,943 out of a total population of 2,475).

Finally, Spain followed the example of the other European powers, although somewhat later and in a slow and gradual process. There was relative consensus on the necessity of abolition, but as in the case of England, disagreement on methods. Whereas abolitionists wanted immediate, unconditional emancipation, the government—under pressure from England, America, and the inhabitants of the colonies—was more moderate. The process of abolition started with a proposal from overseas minister Sigismundo Moret to the Cortes in 1870. He suggested immediate emancipation of children born to slave mothers after the adoption of the law and purchase by the state and subsequent liberation of those born after 1868. These freed slaves would remain under the patronage of their mothers' masters until age twenty-two. Slaves over sixty would be emancipated without compensation, while the others would be manumitted progressively with compensation. The abolitionists' opposition was the strongest. They wanted immediate abolition and adamantly rejected the clause freeing slaves over sixty, because it made clear that crass economic constraints determined the provisions of the law. It was not until 1873, however, that slavery was abolished in Puerto Rico forever ["para siempre"], with the obligation for the slaves to sign a three-year contract with their masters.

Masters were compensated and could receive an additional 25 percent if no contract was signed. In 1876, all the slaves were granted unconditional freedom as well as civil rights.

Cuba, at the time, was in a state of insurrection. As early as 1870, freedom was granted to slaves who had served the Spanish government (for instance, those whose rebel masters had fought against Spain but who had not joined their masters in the opposition). They were offered the opportunity to sign working contracts with public companies (public works and railroads, for example). Slavery, however, was finally abolished somewhat later in 1880. In this case, as in the other previously analyzed European cases, there was no complete refusal of the principle, only disagreements on the method. A debate occurred in the Cortes, and, after several amendments to the original project, a law similar to the Puerto Rican one and to the English law of fifty years earlier was passed: the emancipated slaves became "patrocinados" [apprentices] and received a monthly salary. In this colony, apprenticeship was supposed to last between five and eight years, with slaves classified into four groups in order to stagger the emancipations. For four additional years, though, they would have to prove that they could "acreditar la contracíon de su trabajos" [provide a work contract]. In fact, the patronage system ended in 1886, but the obligation to have a working contract remained.

A last word has to be said concerning the Caribbean. Among the territories that had been Spanish at one time, the eastern side of Hispaniola, Santo Domingo, experienced a somewhat different fate. The Basel Treaty of 1795 had ceded it to France, which managed to keep it only until 1809, when a Junta seized it. It was returned to Spain by the Treaty of Paris of 1814 and experienced an ephemeral period of independence in 1821. It was apparently not yet ready for this phase however, and was almost immediately deprived of autonomy by a Haitian military intervention. The liberation from the Haitian yoke and subsequent independence occurred in 1844, with the proclamation of the Dominican Republic, which re-annexed itself to Spain in 1861, at the instigation of General Pedro Santana, for four years. Two days after this proclamation, on 27 February, the new republic abolished slavery by a resolution of the Junta Central Gubernativa, which confirmed its action a few months later, by proclaiming, in the 17 July decree, that slavery was ignominious, and contrary to religion. The decree even stipulated that anyone found involved in any type of human trading would incur the death penalty.[2] In short, the fate of this territory, which went from hand to hand for fifty years, did not prevent generally peaceful abolition, as in the rest of the Caribbean (except for Haiti).

Altogether, emancipation in the West Indies was thus the result of broad consensus; it was never strongly opposed, not even by the planter class. The only oppositions had to do with the methods: abolitionists demanded immediate emancipation, while planters and governments in general proposed a progressive approach. Similarly, there were no discussions on the principle of compensation, only disagreements about the amount. In the end, emancipation occurred relatively peacefully, providing compensation to the planters. Moreover, whether it was called patronage, apprenticeship, or association, a system was implemented to ensure the presence of workers on the plantations. Although changes eventually occurred, the first years of emancipation did not radically alter the picture of the Caribbean colonies. In the American South, on the contrary, in the years that immediately followed the end of the Civil War, emancipation revolutionized the social, political, and economic organization.

Abolition in the United States

Unsurprisingly, the situation in the United States presented no similarity whatsoever with the Caribbean model. As is widely known, emancipation came as the result of a bloody war that tore the country apart for exactly four years. The campaign for the 1860 presidential election had been clear enough on the fact that slavery was a divisive issue, although it was far from being the only one. Lincoln's victory with almost 40 percent of the popular vote, most of it from the North, left no doubt in the South that slavery was endangered, a threat which challenged their whole civilization: its economy based on slavery; its social and racial organization; and above all its political life. Southerners believed that emancipation would lead to racial war. They decided to secede, not merely to protect slavery, but because the thirty years that had preceded the election had proved to them that North and South were opposed on almost all the issues concerning the organization of society.

From the start, President Lincoln refused to cite slavery as the cause of the war. In the early days of the Civil War, he clearly stated that his sole aim, as well as the aim of the Northern states, was to preserve the Union, certainly not to abolish slavery. From the time of his first inaugural speech in 1861 to as late as August 1862, his position remained unchanged: "My paramount object in this struggle *is* to save the Union, and is *not* either to save or destroy slavery" (Lincoln, August 1862). Some historians even contend that, at the beginning of the war, he was ready to propose a thirteenth amendment that would constitutionally protect slavery.[3] In the early years of the war, the government constantly tried to reassure the border slave states, which had remained faithful to the Union, that their organization would not be modified. In those states, runaway slaves, for instance, were systematically returned to their masters. As late as December 1862, Lincoln was still putting forward proposals for a gradual, compensated emancipation, with a scheme for overseas colonization by liberated blacks.

Radical Republicans pressured the president until he turned the war for the restoration of the Union into what appeared to be a crusade against slavery. On 22 September 1862, Lincoln issued the preliminary Emancipation Proclamation. He had been ready with it for a while, but Secretary of State Seward had advised him to wait until the North won a decisive victory. Antietam was that victory. According to the Proclamation, the slaves of the rebels would be freed on 1 January 1863 if the South was still in a state of rebellion at that time. If peace had not been restored, the slaves would be "then, thenceforward, and forever free" (Emancipation Proclamation, 1863). This was a clear sign that even though the first aim of the war had been the restoration of the Union, by then, slavery had become the *casus belli*. Slavery had poisoned the life of the nation for over thirty years, and suppressing the main cause for antagonism seemed a way to terminate the war. Lincoln's justification of this change in policy was clear and seemed to imply that his deepest convictions had not changed: "My enemies pretend I am now carrying on this war for the sole purpose of abolition. So long as I am President, it shall be carried on for the sole purpose of restoration of the Union. But no human power can subdue this rebellion without the use of the emancipation policy, and every other policy calculated to weaken the moral and physical force of the rebellion" (speech justifying the Emancipation Proclamation, 1863). For him, abolition was not an end, but a means, and it was the Southern rebels themselves who had made it a priority. The House of Representatives passed a resolution to support the proclamation, and in the afternoon of New Year's Day, 1863, Lincoln signed it.

This was the political turning point of the war, and the effects were immediate. Blacks started leaving the plantations and helping the Union soldiers, thus weakening the Southern war effort. From then on, escaping

slaves were no longer returned to their masters. The North enrolled emancipated slaves in the Union army.[4] Although the Emancipation Proclamation had not ended slavery throughout the territory, since it was still legal
in the border states, total emancipation was on its way. The last step to
permanently eradicate slavery from the territory of the United States was
made in 1865, with the voting of the Thirteenth Amendment outlawing it
forever.

In the United States, as opposed to the Caribbean societies, abolition
was thus obtained without the assent of the slave owning states and was
the outcome of a bloody war that had caused the deaths of as many Americans as all the other wars fought by the United States to date. Over 600,000
Americans were killed, and some 400,000 wounded. Emancipation, obtained with utmost violence, was immediate and without any compensation. Along with the war, it left the South ruined, its economy destroyed,
its society in a state of utter chaos, its political organization shattered.
There was no transitional phase to help blacks become used to freedom or
to help whites gradually accept the citizenship and civil equality of their
former slaves. It left a crushed South prey to bitter feelings, which was
never the case in the other slave societies. The wearisome length of the
Reconstruction—due to Southerners' refusal to accept abolition by ratify-
ing the Thirteenth and Fourteenth Amendments—is a very clear proof of
how difficult it was for the South to come to terms with abolition. The
post-abolition process further testifies to that Southern distinctiveness.

The Aftermath of Abolition in the West Indies

Previously treated, Haiti will be left out of the following discussion due to
its atypical character. No longer a colonial dependence, Haiti was, by that
time, a black republic, from which all the white settlers had been excluded,
either by death or forced migration. The situation was thus very different
from that of all the other slave societies that remained multiracial. With
this notable exception, the colonies of the various European powers experienced very similar post-abolition processes.

First, since devices had been found to maintain the slaves on the estates,
the plantations were not immediately short of manpower, which prevented
an economic crash. In the English colonies, the details of emancipation
were left to local governments. Although, as a consequence, there were
slight differences from one colony to the next, all of them passed measures
to prevent the freed slaves from leaving the estates they had been working

on until then. They all took harsh measures against vagrancy, tended to raise the taxes to try to discourage small-scale land ownership, set high rates for licenses to traders and dealers, and made efforts to introduce long-term working contracts.

At the same time, the apprentices were helped by a number of reforming bodies, set up to protect their newly acquired freedom. The colonial civil servants, as well as the churches—both Anglican and Catholic in the islands that had long been under French rule (St. Lucia and Grenada, for example)—watched over the conditions of the ex-slaves. Stipendiary magistrates were specially appointed as guardians of public order and protectors of the apprentices. For a while, the economy was not drastically modified; the planters used their compensation to pay their debts, and the freed slaves remained on the land. The situation made their freedom virtual, although they were less secluded than before.

The conditions changed with the end of apprenticeship in 1838, although the aftermath of abolition was slightly different from one colony to the next. Where land was available, the emancipated slaves tended to leave the plantations. Such was the case in Jamaica, for instance, and in Trinidad, where the ex-slaves could purchase land at an average price ranging between £4 and £10 per acre. Trade increased, because the slaves had to take their destiny in hand and could rely only on themselves for any purchase or sale. This situation led to a relative decline of the economy, however. Plantations were virtually ruined after some planters decided to go back to England. According to the Jamaican House of Assembly, which met in 1847, six hundred sugar and coffee estates had been abandoned by that date, thereby providing more land for emancipated slaves to purchase. In 1842, in Jamaica, about two hundred new villages had been established. The economy turned to smallholdings and mixed farming, the freed blacks sometimes working part-time on the plantations to complement their revenue. Some planters were ready to get rid of part of their land, since the freed slaves were ready to purchase it for as much as £20 an acre. In 1838, there were 2,114 freeholders owning less than forty acres. By 1845, there were 19,397 freeholders, owning properties smaller than ten acres.[5]

In the colonies with little available land, the workers tended to stay on the plantations, even after the end of their apprenticeships. This was the case, for instance, of Barbados, where land was scarce and could be sold for as much as £200 an acre.[6] Former slaves sometimes rented land from the planters or settled in areas belonging to the crown. Because living conditions were not good, freed men sometimes left the colony, mainly for

Panama, where they participated in the building of the railroad in 1854 and then of the canal in the 1880s. In Antigua, Barbados, and St. Kitts, the workers had no other choice but to stay on the plantations, and in Dominica, it was by choice that they remained.

In the French colonies, the situation was similar. The system of association was progressively replaced by part-time free holding, complemented by part-time wage work on the plantations. The system generally remained unchanged, although the former slaves experienced partial liberty and turned quite slowly to exerting the long-awaited freedom. A system of coercive work was established, although with short-term contracts—a decree of February 1852 obliging ex-slaves to have a one-year contract or to obtain special exemption from contract holding. Altogether, the reform of the colonial systems was not radical, and the planters did not develop any defensive strategy, because their existence was not directly threatened.

The two European nations also launched large-scale immigration policies to complement the manpower of the colonies and institute competition among workers.[7] England and France instituted new indentured system policies that resembled one another, with contracts lasting between five and ten years according to the colony, and obliging the workers to work for seven hours a day on the plantations and up to ten hours a day in factories against room and board and a small daily wage. After the end of their contracts, they could choose either to stay or to go back home. Conditions varied somewhat: workers were sometimes given a piece of land (as in the French colonies until 1870) and public funds were sometimes used to pay for their trip to the West Indies, with a guaranteed return trip, as in the French colonies. (Sometimes the plantation owners themselves had to pay for the return trip.)

The second half of the nineteenth century was thus marked by governmentally organized migration movements from Europe and Africa, but mainly from Asia.[8] As a result, the economies were sustained and tended to modernize. The sugar industry continued to develop, although central plants now did most of the processing. Agriculture became more diversified, including more subsistence products, and much more varied crops, such as coffee, cocoa, and fruit. Some colonies even turned to other sources of revenue besides agriculture. Trinidad, for instance, started extracting oil after the foundation in 1910 of the Trinidad Oilfields Co. Ltd. Even the sugar industry progressively turned to diversification, with the development of rum production, mainly in the French colonies.

Although they had to adapt to the new situation, colonial economies remained alive, which prevented the colonists from developing any violently defensive position. Moreover, the various European nations found means to prevent bitter political struggle between the planters and their now free slaves. Even where it was granted, universal suffrage was closely limited: to avoid political competition between the populations and to prevent the development of resentment.

In the English colonies, suffrage was at first very narrow. In Jamaica, for instance, emancipation brought only two thousand new voters. By 1865, only ten out of forty-seven members of the assembly were colored people. In Barbados, by 1884, only 1,300 voters had been added among a population of 180,000 inhabitants. In Trinidad, in 1938, only 7 percent of the population could vote.[9] With the notable exceptions of Haiti and Santo Domingo, power remained largely in white hands. The transition was slow, thus preventing any survival reflex from the white population. To avoid security problems, the crown also tended to reinforce its control over the colonies. One after the other, the islands became crown colonies—Jamaica and Montserrat in 1861, Antigua, St. Kitts, and Nevis in 1866—ensured protection and regulation directly by the mother country. The English government strengthened the governors' power by creating legislative councils whose members were first partly, then later entirely, appointed by the home country and whose Crown representatives had the decisive vote.[10] Then followed a period when the assemblies had no elected members at all.[11] The only exception to this rule was Barbados, the oldest colony under English control. However, in 1881, the Crown created an executive committee that restricted the powers of the assembly. This very close control by England of its colonies helped preclude local political struggles by reinforcing white rule and thus ensured an easier transition toward more autonomy.

After this transitional period, England gradually reintroduced elected members within the local assemblies in the late nineteenth century. In Jamaica, for instance, nine members out of eighteen were elected members in 1884; other colonies, such as Dominica, St. Lucia, Grenada, Montserrat, and the Virgin Islands, had to wait until the 1910s to see the reintroduction of locally elected members. Everywhere, the emancipated populations learned freedom and citizenship slowly and progressively. Universal suffrage was introduced in the twentieth century throughout the British colonies, in 1921 for men over twenty-one and women over thirty; eligibility was limited only by property requirements.

France, on the contrary, granted universal male suffrage together with emancipation. However, the governments managed to restrict this franchise for a sufficiently long period to avoid political struggles. The representation of the colonies in the French Assembly and Senate was suppressed under the Second Empire (from 1851 to 1870), and was reestablished only by the Third Republic. Universal male suffrage was really applied only after 1875, with the election of a general council of thirty-six members and of one senator and two representatives to the French Parliament. A similar movement occurred in the Dutch West Indies.

Everywhere in the Caribbean, the twentieth century was marked by the development of autonomy from the European colonial powers. Until the late nineteenth century, the only independent territories had been Haiti and the Dominican Republic. The situation changed in the last decade of the nineteenth century, when the status of the remaining Spanish colonies changed, which is the reason why they have been left out of the previous discussion. They remained dependent on the home country for a very short period after emancipation, and thus no real lesson can be drawn from their experience of abolition. Cuba had long developed separatist trends, which had been accompanied by requests for annexation to the United States. The Havana Club had made such requests as early as the mid-nineteenth century, but the 1870s struggle for independence was the occasion for expressing a renewed desire for annexation to the United States. A new revolutionary uprising occurred in 1895, and, after a period of repression, Spain finally made some concessions. A degree of autonomy was granted, but independence was never promised until the intervention of United States in 1898 and the subsequent Treaty of Paris, through which Spain transferred sovereignty over Cuba to the United States. According to the promise made by the United States, through the famous Teller Amendment, not to take control of the island, independence was granted and confirmed by the 1901 constitution, although the island remained under American military administration until 1902. The Treaty of Paris also transferred Puerto Rico to the United States. Its subsequent fate was original, but generally untroubled by violence.

The Dutch colonies also progressed toward more autonomy in the twentieth century, and Holland granted them a status of co-equal partnership in 1954. England unsuccessfully attempted to federate its islands, a seemingly feasible move in the Leeward Islands, but refused by Barbados for the Windward Islands in 1885. The islands never accepted more in terms of federation than the organization of conferences during which they could discuss and solve their common problems. From 1958 to 1961,

England even established a federal government, which disappeared when Jamaica decided, by referendum, to withdraw from the federation. England then let the colonies become independent, the whole process lasting over twenty years.[12] Only Montserrat, Anguilla, and the British Virgin Islands have remained under English rule. As for the territories that had thus been granted their independence, they were federated under the Commonwealth.

Only the French model slightly departed from the Caribbean rule. The French colonies were never granted independence, but their status largely evolved in the twentieth century, since they became, in 1946, French Overseas Departments, which they have remained until today. This status never granted them the autonomy part of their population would have wished, and still wishes as evinced by the existence of today's autonomist movements, but it gave their inhabitants the same rights, privileges, and duties as any metropolitan French citizen, without any consideration of race or prior condition of servitude.

All in all, the aftermath of abolition in the West Indies can be described as a peaceful, gradual process, which followed a pattern of transitional phases. The first period after emancipation kept the ex-slaves in their former place. They were required to remain on the estates by provisions of apprenticeship, patronage, or association; vagrancy was strictly repressed; and they had to have working contracts. Land was not readily available; thus, in their first experience of freedom, they remained what Michael Craton calls a "wage-slave proletariat" (325). Then, progressively, they were more at liberty to leave the plantations, which is the reason why all the European nations appealed to immigration on a relatively large scale. The system remained profitable, and the situation thus did not fuel any unrest among the planting classes.

Everywhere, emancipated slaves were kept in a lower category. First of all, metropolitan powers made sure that no political competition could pit the planters, who had traditionally retained power, against the new working classes of emancipated slaves. Franchise was systematically restricted, and education was minimal. This prevented the emergence of bitter reactions from the planter class in attempts to protect their possessions. The slaves were now free, but they remained at the bottom of the ladder. It is true that West Indian slaves had traditionally enjoyed more autonomy, so that their freedom was less shocking to the West Indian planters. Moreover, there had always been large classes of free colored people, and whites were thus ready to accept the vision offered by emancipation. The situation was not felt as deeply dangerous, since social and political stratification remained. The economies did not falter either, which prevented the development of resentment among the whites. All this, and probably also the numerical superiority of the population of African origin, explains why no segregation was legally introduced in these West Indian societies. In many instances, a *de facto* segregation existed, but it was never institutionalized. Schools, for instance, had been desegregated in the Caribbean societies as early as the late nineteenth century. Moreover, step by step, the West Indian territories peacefully lost their colonial status, whether by gaining independence, or as in the French case, by obtaining the sometimes-disparaged departmental status. To conclude, culturally, a peculiar creolization process intervened in the post-colonial societies, making the situation totally different from what occurred in the American South.

Aftermath of Abolition in the American South

The post-emancipation period was marked by a very different evolution in the American South. Abolition had been anything but consensual, contrary to the case in Caribbean slave societies. The war that resulted in its implementation—although this single issue had, by no means, triggered the conflict—bled the South white and tore the national fabric into pieces. In all fields, the situation was wholly different than that of the Caribbean colonies. First, there was no transitional phase: the slaves were emancipated immediately and unconditionally. No compensation was granted to the ruined slave owners, and no obligation was made to encourage the freed slaves to remain on the estates. As a result, in massive numbers they left the plantations for Southern cities or for other regions of the United States. Their wish for autonomy was stronger than in the Caribbean. Whereas the Caribbean geography left them confined to an island, the United States gave them space. The political situation also gave them the dream of a territory where other Americans had been free for a long time and where they imagined their freedom would be considered totally normal. They thought they would be offered opportunities. Moreover, their independence had been almost non-existent under slavery—much more reduced in scope than in the Caribbean societies, in fact—and their wish for autonomy was thus proportional to the strictness of their former dependence.

As for the confederates, they were sometimes deprived of their property at the end of the war. Others had lost all their wealth: plantations had been destroyed and had become unproductive and there was no labor force left to help rebuild the economy. The freed slaves refused to stay, the planters had no means to finance any salaried work, there was absolutely no immigration policy, and recent history was no incentive for any spontaneous migration. They managed to develop the sharecropping system, which in fact led to a reproduction of the plantation system. This may be considered as the first return to the ancient order, since the new system increased the hierarchical organization of Southern society, even though the ruling planter class had a lesser net benefit.

Needless to add that the overall economic situation did not help Southerners accept the abolition they had always refused and for the prevention of which they had been ready to give their lives. Elsewhere in the Caribbean basin, the old masters retained considerable economic and social power. Their property loss had been compensated; they were not disgraced, since the sin of slavery was largely shared. They thus had a fair share in the organization of the new social order. In the United States, on the contrary, they were considered traitors and sinners, had not been compensated, and were denied any role in the post-emancipation social organization. As a result, they spent the first post-war years trying to reestablish the old order, an attempt fostered by the mildness of the first Reconstruction, under Lincoln and Johnson. The confederates were even given their property back, on the condition that they take the loyalty oath. The rebel states were rapidly "reconstructed," and a form of local government was rapidly restored. The land was thus once again retained by the planters, and the absurdity of the situation was that the economy had returned to the hands of a population which had fallen into utter disgrace, had gone bankrupt, and had been disenfranchised. They could not expect any help from their former slaves and thus became intent on restoring a kind of *status quo ante bellum.*

The situation led to the passing of the 1865–1866 Black Codes, which globally revived the old order and excluded blacks from the political life of the region. These codes officially claimed to accept emancipation and granted legal status to the emancipated slaves. They could get married, although not to a white person; they could sue and be sued in court; they could testify against white persons, hold property, and be paid wages. The codes, however, made them underclass citizens. They could hire themselves out only by the year and were denied the right to strike or leave their employment. The codes instituted very harsh vagrancy laws and included no provision for the education of freed slaves. They were not allowed to carry weapons and were denied political rights, by inclusion of property prerequisites or literacy tests. They were, so to speak, a new race of slaves, not legal slaves, but *de facto* slaves.[13]

This intermediate step closely resembles the situation in the Caribbean colonies immediately after emancipation. However, while the colonial governments accepted and even reinforced this apparent *status quo*, such a return to the old order was unacceptable to the Northern republicans, and their refusal of the situation led to the second reconstruction. They could pressure the South only in the political field, which they immediately did: they passed the Civil Rights Act of March 1866 and added the Fourteenth and Fifteenth Amendments to the Constitution. The three measures went in exactly the same direction, depriving the former confederates of their franchise, but granting suffrage to the emancipated slaves "without reference to any previous condition of slavery or involuntary servitude" the Civil Rights Act stated or to "race, color, or previous condition of servitude," the Fifteenth Amendment added.

The aim of the radical republicans was to take advantage of the situation to ensure the basis of their power by totally crushing the defeated Southerners. They used the freed slaves in this aim, and, for a while, the South was indeed in the hands of coalition governing bodies, composed of scalawags, carpetbaggers, and ex-slaves. Because the confederates had been deprived of their franchise, white voters were in a situation of inferiority, even in areas where the white population remained the majority. In short, the radical republicans used the situation to build their own power. This political maneuvering was wholly different from that in the West Indian colonies, where European powers simply attempted to suppress political oppositions and thus prevent the development of racial hatred. Northern republicans did all they could to fuel this hatred and deny Southerners one ounce of power. They suppressed property qualifications for voting and office-holding and launched education programs for African Americans. This was all the more unacceptable to Southerners as they had gone so far in their pro-slavery arguments to claim that blacks, proven inferior, could not be granted the same rights as whites, let alone more rights. Whites could not accept civil equality, especially since to the shame of defeat had been added the mortification of the deprivation of their own civil rights.

Several forms of reaction developed as a result of this sense of political disenfranchisement. Southern democrats never abandoned the political struggle and finally reached a *status quo* in 1877, thanks to the so-called "compromise" that followed the presidential election. They took the opportunity offered by the end of military Reconstruction to regain power, at least locally and regionally. Once they had managed to do so, they took every measure they could think of to prevent blacks from voting, indirectly supported in this effort by republican passivity. The Redeemers, sometimes also called the "Bourbons," regained control of political life, and white supremacy was enforced all over the "redeemed" states. The Redeemers' main purpose was to prevent the freed slaves from exerting their newly won political rights. They voted legal measures to exclude them from the political scene, including poll-tax qualification, and the famous "grandfather clause" aimed at discriminating among the lower classes of society by enabling poor whites to vote, while depriving the emancipated slaves of their franchise. They also instituted white primaries, which were not proclaimed unconstitutional until *Nixon v. Herndon* in 1925. This Supreme Court decision did not induce the suppression of the system, which remained in force until *Smith v. Allwright* in 1944. In the late 1910s, civil rights for African Americans had been virtually suppressed, and only 1 to 4 percent of them voted, according to the state. This was the last step in the widely shared confusion between race and political power that characterized the post-abolition South and remained a distinct Southern feature until quite recently.

This was the legal side of the slow recovery by white Southerners of their political supremacy. They were helped by illegal, violent organizations and acts. The most famous of these organizations was of course the Ku Klux Klan, founded on Christmas Eve of 1865 at Pulaski, Tennessee, and which, by 1921, counted 100,000 members. This membership had reached three million by 1923 and even eight million by 1925. The Ku Klux Klan was not the only white supremacist organization operative in the South at that time and was supported by the Knights of the White Camellia and the Red Shirts, among other groups. The organizations exerted all kinds of pressure and violence to exclude emancipated slaves from politics: rigging ballots, physically barring African Americans from the polls, using intimidation, and even resorting to lynching. The post-emancipation period was marked by race riots, such as those of April 1866 at Memphis, where forty blacks were killed, or the New Orleans massacre of July 1866, which also killed about forty blacks. These lawless actions did not spread on a wide scale, but they frightened the black population and discouraged the freed slaves from fighting to have their new rights respected. They also probably reinforced the whites' belief in their superiority and constituted their revenge for the terrible defeat of 1865.

The situation set up an impassable barrier between the races. By the time the Civil War broke out, Southern whites had become so sure of their superiority and of the superiority of the system, that they had never thought their most faithful slaves could desert them. When they did, real bitterness developed between the races, precluding the persistence of paternalistic feelings. This led to the appearance of a new form of racism, since whites could not accept coexisting with their former slaves in total equality. Whereas they had worked, traveled, gone to church, and lived with their slaves, they suddenly could no longer bear the companionship of inferior beings now become their equals. Whereas segregation had been a Northern feature before the war, it spread to the whole South in the late nineteenth century. Segregation was instituted in all spheres of society, in the private sphere, but also, legally, in the public one. Housing, public transport, places of entertainment, hotels, public restrooms, restaurants, parks, hospitals, prisons, churches, and even cemeteries were segregated. Some courts, as in Atlanta, for instance, even had different Bibles on which whites and blacks swore.

Once Reconstruction was officially terminated, Northerners never tried to suppress this trend. The Supreme Court even confirmed all the segregation measures, ruling, in 1883, that the 1875 Civil Rights Act was unconstitutional, and confirming the practice of segregation by the famous 1896 "separate but equal" doctrine of *Plessy v. Fergusson*. This opened a new era of Southern distinctiveness that was scarcely shaken by the 1954 *Brown v. Board of Education of Topeka* decision, and did not end until the mid-1960s after the long Civil Rights crusade.

Although some similarities remained among the former slave societies of the Americas, for instance in the development of sharecropping and in a general trend toward black disenfranchisement, abolition and its aftermath greatly widened the breach that had appeared in the nineteenth century between the South and the colonial slave societies of the Caribbean. The debate that divided opponents and defenders of slavery in the nineteenth-century United States had an unprecedented ring. Nowhere did it become so uncompromising, so absolute. Nowhere did it pervade the whole of society as it did in the South. Nowhere did it become such a global opposition bridging all aspects of society, and nowhere did it become a matter of life and death. Nowhere was emancipation so non-consensual, so strongly contested, almost to the point of rejection. Nowhere was it the result of a bloody four-year war. Nowhere was it followed by such a bitter political, legal, and even physical struggle. The ideological opposition had been so strong that a kind of racial war ensued. While all the other ex-slave societies went from slavery to freedom in relative peace and through transitional stages, the South became frozen in a system that was perhaps even harsher than what had existed before the Civil War, especially in terms of black-white relationships.

Due to the assistance of sympathetic colonial governments, the other societies never experienced a bitter struggle for the establishment of white supremacy, which had, in fact, never ceased. Above all, no other slave society of the Americas saw the emergence of legal, institutional segregation, which remained a distinct Southern feature for almost a century. The "Peculiar Institution" which, early on in the South, had equivalents throughout the Caribbean, ultimately gave way to an institution that was peculiar to the South alone.

Together with political struggle, the South's ideological opposition to its position persisted and developed, and the defense of the Old South, which had begun in the antebellum era, took a new turn after the war. The lost cause sentiment gave this defense a nostalgic ring, and Southern resistance to the establishment of a different order renewed the proclamation of Southern cultural distinctiveness. The legend of the Old South became the Southern myth, probably the most blatant manifestation of Southern difference, which has resisted all assaults and is still alive in the twenty-first century.

6

Mythmaking and Cultural Exception

Whereas the first centuries of colonization displayed phases of historical development common to all the American slave societies, the end of North America's colonial status opened a breach between them that never ceased to widen. From the overpowering opposition between North and South to the aftermath of an abolition both unwanted and unaccepted by the main Southern participants, the slave society of the American South underwent an evolution that made it exceptional. The cultural field, which remains to be examined, imparted to this Southern exceptionality a new dimension, still clearly perceptible to this day.

Literature is the first cultural field where the roots of Southern difference reach back to the nineteenth century. This difference is partially grounded in the amplitude of the arguments between abolitionists and pro-slavery ideologues, as well as in the active intervention of Southern writers in that debate. Its temperate conduct controlled chiefly by metropolitan ideologues, debate in the European Caribbean colonies was confined solely to the question of slavery. In the United States, by contrast, the debate drove antagonisms that far exceeded abstract assessment of an institution. Instead, it pulled every constituent of Southern society into a struggle for survival and pushed the polarized civilizations of North and South to the brink of war.

The West Indian Literary Reality in the Caribbean

Very little Caribbean fiction was written to defend the institution of slavery or the society that developed around it. Written defenses of slavery were limited to abstract treatises, pamphlets, and essays written by ideologues and churchmen. The only exception is Marbot's *Les Bambous*, published in 1846, which remains a classic of French West Indian literature as its numerous, and even contemporary, reprints prove. The writer, born in Martinique in 1817, has only one message to advance: the slaves' condition in the French colonies is good, and they should accept their fate.[1] Apart from this classic, some rather obscure works of fiction can be found in France, and their study reveals that the defense of the system was never crucial to their writers.[2] Such novels are typically set in the Caribbean colonies, which often leads to descriptions of the beauties of the tropical islands. The characters are more often than not the inhabitants of a plantation, both planters and slaves. Although the picture drawn of the French Caribbean societies is generally positive, extremely negative portrayals are not absent from the novels.[3] To take an example, J. Levilloux's *Les créoles, ou vie aux Antilles* describes the difficult relationships between the son of a Creole family from Martinique and the mulatto son of a Jamaican planter, who, most of the time, hides the secret of his birth, because it is the *sine qua non* condition of his acceptance into the Creole society of the time.[4] Only the young Creole, whose mind is pervaded with the ideals of equality spread by the French Revolution, accepts, after a period of rejection, the origin of his school friend whom he meets in metropolitan France. The rest of colonial society, including his mother and sister, is full of prejudice. On the point of marrying his friend's sister, the young mulatto is rejected by the whole community, and the only way out of this inextricable situation, for the writer, is to stage the death of the star-crossed lovers.

Racial prejudice, which characterizes the relationships between Creole planters and their slaves, is also the principal theme of this novel. Although there is often much attachment between the two communities, Levilloux's picture is generally bleak. The novel contains, for instance, the description of a slave auction, which ends with the suicide of several slaves who prefer death to slavery, persuaded, as they are, that death will bring them back to their motherland. The "faithful" nurse of the two Creole children is a poisoner, as are many other slaves in the novel. She ends up poisoning her young protégée, while the Creoles are trying to exterminate a group of maroons. Portraits of the planters are often quite degrading. Although the main Creole character, Briolan, and his family are a cut above the rest of their class, the only real hero, who shows nothing but good will and good character, is the mulatto Estève. The planter class as a whole is endowed with very low feelings and habits. Although a note from the author compares the planter class to the industrialists of metropolitan society—much to the advantage of the former—the characters in the novel are highly prejudiced, selfish, stupid, depraved, indolent, and uncompromising, if not cruel. The planters are also portrayed as hypocrites, always ready to take on black mistresses, despite their professed rejection of miscegenation and the mulatto offspring born of such unions.

Another novel, whose story is framed in the post-abolition period, displays the same type of mixed images. Thérèze Bentzon's *Yette, histoire d'une jeune Créole* tells the story of a doomed Creole girl sent to a metropolitan school.[5] Although slavery has been legally abolished, little has changed in the situation of the emancipated slaves. They are still totally subservient, and one of them is even made to exclaim in Creole patois that she is Miss Yette's "nigger" who will serve her for free.[6] Even if, on one hand, the author insists on the affection between Yette and her young black friends, as well as on the overpowering love that links her to her "Da,"[7] the indolence of the planters and their inability to make decisions is emphasized on the other, making the novel's overall portrait of this society ambivalent.[8] The plantation's work organization is minutely described in the tone of a report,[9] and while the novel stresses the absence of life's luxuries in the West Indies,[10] it also describes Creole hospitality,[11] as well as the care with which the heroine and her mother have always tended their slaves, before and after emancipation.[12] Once again, the picture drawn of the West Indian society is full of contrasts.

There is an obvious continuity between the novels written at the time of the debate over slavery and those of the post-abolition period. Importantly, this continuity has persisted to this day. Twentieth-century French literature that deals with the West Indies displays two tendencies, one being the obvious heir to the nineteenth century literary current just discussed. Several works have been produced on the history of the French West Indies throughout the twentieth century, either by Creole writers or by metropolitan authors who have, at one time or another, become acquainted with the Caribbean islands. This is notably the case of novels written by non-Creole authors Robert Gaillard in the mid-1950s (the *Marie des Isles* tetralogy); by Michel Tauriac in a trilogy entitled *Les années creoles*; and by Creole novelist Marie-Reine de Jaham, who tells the story of a planter family whose property is destroyed by the 1902 eruption of the Martinique volcano, Mount Pelée.

All these novels are written in the form of family sagas and use the history of the West Indies as background. From Gaillard's narration of the early colonial period in the seventeenth century through the story of Marie, the great love of Governor du Parquet, to the other two novelists' panoramas of the whole colonial past of Martinique—including the slavery years, post-abolition developments, and the catastrophe that killed the whole population of the island's capital, St. Pierre, in 1902—all rely on historical accounts to situate their characters and the lives of their Creole families. Descriptions of the beauties of the tropics abound, and the heroes are deprived neither of courage, nor adventurous minds and good feelings. While African slaves may be described as dangerous,[13] slavery appears as a negative institution which gives birth to prejudices impossible to cast aside.[14] Moreover, these novels often emphasize the hardships of life in the colonies, the lack of comforts and luxuries.[15] The horrors of the slave trade; the mistreatment of slaves by cruel masters; the forced separation of slave families; the slaves' attempted suicides: nothing is hidden.[16]

Literature about the West Indies also includes contemporary novels that similarly highlight the present-day contradictions of Caribbean societies, where evil coexists with the wonders of the islands. To this category belong works written by the already-named authors of historical novels, including Tauriac's *La fille de couleur*, as well as de Jaham's *La grande Béké, Le Maître-Savane*, and her latest, *Bwa Bandé*. These novels remain marginal, however, and the main corpus of *fine* literature of the French Antilles is produced by writers of African Caribbean origin whose aim is to undeceive modern readers about the slave era and to critique the inferior status of African Caribbeans in post-abolition Antillean society. Their novels praise what they call Creolity—the culture that has emerged from the slaves' African background.[17] Overall, then, the French West Indies have produced a thematically varied literature that sometimes praises Caribbean societies, sometimes purports to defend slavery, but which—maintaining a kind of ambivalence—always remains at least slightly critical of the system.

Caribbean Hispanic literature largely duplicates French West Indian themes and patterns, although the former devotes much less attention to the institution of slavery. The first centuries of colonization primarily produced narratives of colonial experience, which, although they were partly fictional, can hardly be considered fiction. This is the only period during which the literature actually strives to glorify West Indian societies. When Columbus narrated his American experience, he did so with sufficient enthusiasm to enhance the importance of his discovery and to encourage people to join the adventure. This glorifying tendency, however, is tempered in other works by a more critical one, the best example of which is probably the account by Bartolomé de Las Casas, who, as a defender of the rights of the Indians, first suggested their replacement by African slaves, contending that they had no claim to the land. He then regretted this position and opposed African slavery as well. In the end, his writings became a general critique of the Spanish conquest of the New World.

The nineteenth century Spanish Caribbean colonies produced a literature of remarkable homogeneity from one island to the next.[18] Much poetry celebrating the beauties of the Caribbean and the islands was written, usually in a deeply lyrical and clearly romantic style. This is a patriotic and celebratory poetry. Instead of glorifying the colonies and their specific labor system, these poets celebrate their islands' natural beauties, each one using a rhetoric almost identical to that of his neighbor.[19] From Puerto Rican José Gautier Benítez's *A Puerto Rico* to poems by Dominican José Núñez de Cáceres and Cubans Gertrudis Gómez de Avellaneda and José María Heredia, West Indian Hispanic poetry is comprised of romantic and patriotic odes to the islands.

Caribbean Hispanic fiction writers are generally more concerned by questions of autonomy than by the debate over slavery. Puerto Rican poet Luis Muños Rivera ("el campeón de las libertas insulares" [the champion of insular liberties])[20] and Cuban writers, such as José Antonio Saco, José Martí, and Enrique José Varona relay in their works the possibility of creating a West Indian confederation, a possibility that is further developed in the works of Puerto Ricans Román Baldorioty de Castro and Eugenio María de Hortos.

Nineteenth century Hispanic West Indian literature is dominated by fictional works in the form of novels and tales. The West Indian environment is, of course, common to these, but they remain essentially neutral in their presentation of West Indian societies. The social glorifications associated with literary mythmaking is found neither in Cuba nor Puerto Rico. Cirlo Villaverde's *Cecilia Valdés* rather blandly describes Cuban life in the first third of the eighteenth century. Puerto Rican novelist Manuel Zeno Gandía's tetralogy, *Cronicas de un mundo enfermo*,[21] is a social critique of rural Puerto Rico in the late nineteenth century. While the first novel, *Garduña*, deals mainly with the sugar society and the second one, *La Charca*, with the coffee society, both are portrayed as backward, stagnant, and infested with corruption and immorality. The only polemical aspect of West Indian Spanish literature thus has to do, as in poetry, with patriotism and a wish for autonomy.

Another very fertile type of nineteenth-century Spanish West Indian literature is the tale. Tale writers bear witness to the customs of their islands, but never engage in literary mythmaking. In Puerto Rico, the 1849 publication of *El jíbaro* by Manuel Alonso y Pacheco, won the author the title of father of Puerto Rican Creolity for describing the customs, the characters, the language, and the idioms of the countryside of colonial Puerto Rico.[22] The same vernacular interests can be found in several other works, such as Cayetano Coll y Toste's *Leyendes puertorriqueñas,* or Álvaro de la Iglesia's *Tradiciones cubanas.* Interestingly, all of these writers produced their works in the second half of the nineteenth century, during the period of abolitionist debate in Spain. It is as if the islanders had had no knowledge of the debate or as if they chose to have nothing to add to it. This is, of course, probably due to the relative consensus that existed on the question of abolition in Spain and its colonies, since even Cuban separatists had manifested their wish to terminate the institution during the rebellion for independence.

It is not until the twentieth century that examples of pure glorification can be found, as opposed to the darker notes in the nineteenth-century picture.[23] This glorification, however, does not bear on eras or societies, but on islands—their wealth and their beauty. The twentieth-century literature of the Hispanic West Indies becomes a kind of indistinct celebration of all the inhabitants of the islands, without any consideration of race or color. In the Caribbean islands of Spanish cultural background, as in the rest of the West Indies, the twentieth century ushers literary exploration of the races and of interracial relationships, primarily with the emergence of African Caribbean literature.[24]

A survey of English colonial literature shows a repetition of French and Spanish trends. Works of fiction dealing with the West Indies are relatively rare in the early nineteenth century, although a rich production of travel narratives and diaries by metropolitan authors is notable.[25] Creole works in the British Caribbean are almost inexistent, probably due to two main factors: the non-resident mind of the colonists, and, as in the Spanish case, the absence of a heated national debate on slavery.[26] The Creoles did not feel any need to defend an institution that had, for them, a purely economic importance. As for metropolitan writers, they tended to display more antislavery sentiment than their French and Spanish counterparts, a sentiment that is overt in the travel narratives and diaries just mentioned.

English writers did write some fiction using the West Indies as a backdrop. In this group, Michael Scott's *Tom Cringle's Log* may be noted. First published in 1838, after abolition, this novel, written by an English expatriate living in Jamaica, contains many observations about the customs and life of the island's black population. However, the novel is not aimed at glorifying the colonial societies of the English West Indies. The writer is not Creole, and abolition was, by then, a fact that no one even thought of questioning.

The key development in twentieth-century British Caribbean literature, as in that of the other Caribbean societies, is the emergence of African Caribbean literature, which, as one may easily imagine, shows no admiration for the system that prevailed during the first centuries of English colonial history.[27] These writers deeply resent the yoke under which the African Caribbean population was placed, along with the relationships that developed between the two racial communities. If there is any glorification to be noted, it has to do, quite naturally, with the achievements of Creole African Caribbeans.

Some white Creole literature deserves note, of course. Until the 1930s, there was a tradition of Creole celebration of the beauty and originality of the islands within a colonial framework. While certainly not a celebration of slavery or slave societies, this literature is nonetheless part of a movement defending English colonialism.[28] Within the white Creole tradition, there are a few works which celebrate the old order in fiction and poetry. For instance, in her poem "Nana," Mary Adella Wolcott illustrates the continuing affectionate relationships between the ex-slaves and their former masters, emphasizing a kind of permanence of colonial identity as if time had stopped when slavery was abolished.[29] Mitigating the general impression of such permanence, however, the end of the poem inscribes this portrait of the "Mammy" in the world of fancy. Nevertheless, even where such rare nostalgia for the old order can be found, most early-twentieth-century literature of the British Caribbean, like that of the Spanish colonies, entails patriotic celebration of the colonies. *Jamaica's Coronation Ode* by Thomas MacDermot, also known as Tom Redcam; J. E. Clare McFarlane's *My Country*; and Albinia Hutton's *The Empire's Flag*, for instance, attempt to translate the colonies as distinct national entities.[30]

Finally, in the second half of the twentieth century, a number of women writers born in the Caribbean also write about their islands: Jean Rhys, Eliot Bliss, and Phyllis Shand Allfrey. Jean Rhys's *Wide Sargasso Sea*, published in 1966, is set in Jamaica after emancipation. Far from glorifying the old system, this novel treats the impossibility of communication between the island's various social and cultural groups. Rhys often draws a bleak picture of emancipation's aftermath as when the ex-slaves rejoice at the ruin of Antoinette's family following the abolition of slavery. Similarly, when the marriage of Antoinette's mother with an Englishman brings renewed wealth to the estate, the ex-slaves take their revenge on the old system and burn down the plantation. It seems that the past has set up an impassable barrier between the races, even if the most uncompromising manifestations of racism apparently come from the English expatriates, since, as Antoinette explains, her step-father "has made [her] shy about [her] coloured relatives" (43). The same analysis can be made of Eliot Bliss's *Luminous Isle*. The novel tells the story of a young Creole girl who returns from England, where she has been educated, and who, despite her love for her island and for the black community of her childhood, cannot manage to fit into the backward Jamaican society of the 1920s. Similarly, Phyllis Shand Allfrey's *Orchid House* is a criticism of post-colonial Dominica, where abolition has provoked a deep fracture in the safe old order, and where the white Creole society seems unable to find its place any longer. The three novels are, in fact, somber appraisals of the barrier slavery has historically erected between communities and of the inability of white society to come to terms with the new order. Despite their implication that abolition destroyed peace, safety, and harmony, all three novels offer, in fact, a more or less direct criticism of the paradoxes of the old order. At any rate, no glorification is to be found in Rhys, Bliss, or Allfrey —no mythmaking that would turn the slave era into a kind of Golden Age.

Even while celebrating the islands, West Indian literature has never really aimed at glorifying them, their institutions, their founders, their inhabitants, or their societies in general. Throughout the Caribbean, whatever the nationality of the colony or ex-colony, fiction writers and poets have always remained sensitive to the numerous paradoxes their societies displayed. This has not been the case of the American South, which, from the nineteenth century onward, has been the object of an expanding mythmaking process.

The Antebellum Legend of the South

The roots of the mythic South are to be found in nineteenth-century Southern literature. Until the late 1840s, this literature rather resembled that of the West Indian tradition in the critical notes it contained, but it already showed a larger propensity to social glorification. From the 1820s to the 1840s, Southern novelists started producing a characteristic type of literature whose contexts are exclusively regional. These novels are set in the South, often on plantations, and the characters are usually planters and their families. George Tucker's *The Valley of Shenandoah* is probably the first novel to represent this trend. The plot, which revolves around a nearly ruined family of Virginian aristocrats, is relatively tenuous, but the story serves as a pretense for drawing a very minute picture of Southern society. The gorgeous surroundings of the Shenandoah Valley, the beautiful Tidewater plantations, and the apparently natural hospitality of their inhabitants are described with precision and enthusiasm. Glorification of the Virginian past is omnipresent, and the characters present prototypes for figures that have become staples of the literary South: the aristocratic gentleman, full of loyalty, nobility, and generosity; the Southern lady, with her pride, dignity, and nobility of feeling. The picture drawn of slavery is roundly positive, and the slaves are typically portrayed as happy souls, full of love for their masters. There are, however, negative notes, especially concerning the improvidence of the planters, their tendency toward indebtedness, and their exaggerated prodigality. The peculiar institution receives occasional criticism, as the novel describes the cruelty of overseers and the punishments inflicted on slaves. There is a long passage on a slave auction, although, in contrast to the West Indian French novels mentioned earlier, the cruelty of this practice is somewhat mitigated by the sadness of the masters whose slaves are being sold. In short, slavery is portrayed as a necessary evil, just as it is in the writings of Southern ideologues in the early period of the North-South debate. As one character laments: "we must . . . endeavor to *mitigate* a disease which admits of *no cure*" (Tucker, 69). Tucker thus opens the way for a first generation of Southern novelists whose works clearly attempt to illuminate the positive features of the South, while still refusing to ignore the darker corners of the picture.[31]

Between 1830 and 1850, Southern novelists pursued this defensive trend, although they systematically included slight criticism of the slave regime.[32] In response to abolitionist attacks, Southern fiction writers began producing a literature that emphasized distinctive features of Southern culture and praised Southern civilization. William Gilmore Simms published nine historical novels between 1830 and 1850, insisting on the South's glorious past and on the heroism of its inhabitants. William Alexander Caruthers brought out two novels that were successful among Southern readers, the most famous being *The Cavaliers of Virginia* in 1834. In 1836, Nathaniel Beverley Tucker published *The Partisan Leader*, which can be described as a political fantasy of the Civil War, twenty years in advance and informed by an impressively visionary tendency. The most original contribution to this Southern literary trend is probably John

Pendleton Kennedy's third novel of the period, *Swallow Barn*, generally considered the first plantation novel, the ancestor of a long series of Southern novels.[33] All these works indicate the authors' paramount interest in dramatizing the abstract theories of the ideologues, in staging characters who can discuss, sometimes with opposing views, the issues of the time, while even permitting confrontations between masters and slaves. While in his famous study *Cavalier and Yankee*, William Taylor refers to this literature as "defensive fiction" (197), the novels of this period contain just enough social criticism to give an impression of relative objectivity. *Swallow Barn*, for instance, is written with an attitude of ironical distance that partially mitigates Kennedy's overall praise of the South.

The series of novels written in the 1850s at the climax of the sectional debate—after the publication of the best abolitionist weapon, *Uncle Tom's Cabin*—took on a very different tone.[34] The celebration of the South became uncompromising, and negative features almost totally disappear from descriptions of the section. Novelists clearly took to polemics. Fourteen novels were published in the two years that followed Mrs. Stowe's publication, and their titles suggest that their sole aim is to counterbalance the unflattering picture she had drawn of the South: *Uncle Robin in his Cabin in Virginia and Tom without One in Boston* (Richmond, 1853); *Aunt Phillip's Cabin, or Southern Life as It Is* (Philadelphia, 1852); *The Cabin and the Parlor; or Slaves Without Masters* (Philadelphia, 1852); and *Anti-Fanaticism: A Tale of the South* (Philadelphia, 1853).[35] This output, of low literary quality, has not left its mark on history. Some relatively better publications have survived, even if their place in American literature has remained limited. John Esten Cooke's *Leather Stocking and Silk*, *Virginia Comedians*, and *Ellie*, are examples of this response to Mrs. Stowe's publication. In the last antebellum decade, Simms also published five more novels,[36] including his 1852 masterpiece, *The Sword and the Distaff*, renamed *Woodcraft* in 1854. This novel indeed contains the scene that has remained in the annals as being a direct response to Stowe. It shows Porgy, the planter hero, offering his most faithful slave, interestingly named Tom, his freedom, for all the help he has given him throughout his life. Tom refuses this freedom in a long speech which delivers a clear message. Tom first exclaims: "No! No! maussa. . .I kain't t'ink ob letting you off dis way. Ef *I* doesn't b'long to *you, you* b'longs to *me*! You hab dis nigger long as he lib, and him for keep you" (*Woodcraft*, 509). A few lines below these, he even reinforces his new master-slave dialectics: "I much rudder b'long to good maussa, wha'I lub, dan b my own maussa and quarrel wid mese'f ebbery day. Da's it! You Yerry now? I say de wud for all! *You* b'longs to *me* Tom, jes' as much as me Tom b'long to *you;* and you nebber guine git *you* free paper from me long as you lib" (*Woodcraft*, 509). This redefinition of slavery is quite original and admits of no discussion.

In exploring nineteenth-century tendency to over-glorify the South, its institutions, and its society, it is important to note that, in 1851, Kennedy published a revised version of *Swallow Barn*. A line for line, word for word, comparison shows how the legend of the South was really formed.[37] All the slightly negative notes of the first version, all the ironical distance mentioned, have now disappeared. The places are utterly happy and beautiful;[38] the characters have lost their central faults and display only virtues.[39] The picture drawn of slavery is totally altered too, as is the description of relationships between masters and slaves and of the slaves' living conditions. The chapter entitled "The Quarter" insists, in the second version, on the prejudices of the abolitionists, as if trying to warn them about the risk of misconceptions. The modifications brought to this chapter are of three types: the criticism of the abolitionists has become harsher; the dangers of abolition have been developed; and the image drawn of the planter class reveals much more humanity. All in all, the image of the South and its institutions has changed much to its benefit.

This process of over-glorification reveals much about the birth of the Southern legend. It can be described as a slow process, composed of several stages, following the increasing strength of the political and ideological debate between the two sections. When opposition reached its peak, in the last decade before the Civil War, the legendary South took on its full dimension. The South's glorious past, the chivalrous gentlemen, the pure and virtuous ladies, their heroic actions, the beauties of the region, the blessings of slavery, the privileged relationships between the generous planters and their loving slaves, everything was in place. The faint critical notes sounded in the early period gave way to the loud encomiums of the last antebellum decade.

It is also important to add that, unlike West Indian poetry, Southern poetry was not limited to romantic descriptions of regional beauties or to uniform proclamations of patriotic feeling. Instead, this poetry was as much committed to the political defense of the South as were the novels of the period. William J. Grayson's works, for instance, are definitely polemical. In 1851, he published a series of letters, written in prose, supposedly addressed to the editors of the *Charleston Courier* and signed by a certain Curtius.[40] These letters are a series of brief treatises on the South, its institutions, its political life, and clearly reveal the talent of Grayson as a pamphlet writer. Generally speaking, the letters deal with the superiority of slavery, with the necessity of retaliating against abolitionist attacks, and with the urgencies of secession. The last series of letters stage a dialogue between Curtius and a secessionist in order to foreground the arguments of the fire-eaters. Although Curtius opposes such an extreme measure, it is the first time secessionist proposals are presented in a work of fiction. As for his masterpiece *The Hireling and the Slave*, it is a long neo-classical poem, written in heroic couplets, which develops and illustrates the Southern ideologues' themes, while violently criticizing the main abolitionists of the time: Charles Sumner, Horace Greeley, Garrison, William Seward, and, in a still more violent diatribe, Harriet Beecher-Stowe.[41] Grayson's aim is clear: to counter the abolitionist writers' attacks by comparing slavery to the "hireling" system, much to the advantage of the former, of course. As the involvement of Southern writers in the ideological debate became all-encompassing, the legend of the South approached the threshold of myth.

The Mythic South

Within the American national fabric, mythmaking is not a Southern peculiarity. It may be linked with American belief in the Manifest Destiny of the nation and with the original Puritan mission to create an ideal society that would shine bright and far upon the world. Southern mythmaking, however, was privileged by historical exigency, by antebellum defense of Southern culture, and, of course, by the outcome of the war. Post-war Southern fiction writers were no longer protecting a society to ensure its survival. Instead, they were transcending the reality of its degradation.

In the post-war period, white Southern society continued to justify the old order in literature, while attempting to reestablish it politically. Except for those who thought they finally could use slaves to take their revenge on the planter class, Southerners remained persuaded of the inferiority of African Americans and proclaimed it willingly. The only concession, for some Southerners, was to acknowledge that confederates had been heroic, but wrong. The fatal outcome of the Civil War for the South led to a new trend in Southern thought. Writers were no longer justifying an existing order, they were describing a society that no longer existed, that probably had never existed—at least as they imagined it—at all. The legend of the South became a myth, fueled by nostalgia born of devotion to a lost cause.

Southerners were depicted as paternal slaveholders, gallant, chivalrous, and kindly masters; their slaves were faithful and loving. The catalogue of literary types that had emerged in antebellum literature was expanded and completed. Southerners, because they had believed in their cause, because they had died for it, became larger than life in defeat.

Post-war Southern literature is an excellent measure of the lost movement, and because the fiction of this period is neither political nor polemical, it gains a transcendent dimension. Even during the war, all of the Southern poets, including such famous writers as Henry Timrod and Paul Hamilton Hayne, began to exalt the region in what may be called Confederate epics. The production was rich, as the anthology, *Poems and Songs of the Civil War*, demonstrates, displaying, as the editor, Lois Hill, indicates in her introduction "the full spectrum of the history and emotions of the Civil War."[42] Post-war fiction follows suit, and the transcendent dimension of the South is enlarged by the disappearance of the very society such fiction celebrated.[43] Southern writers of the time indeed had an acute consciousness of the past, and their main aim was to preserve the Old South from oblivion. Joel Chandler Harris, who was only thirteen when the war broke out, dedicated most of his works to this preservation. *Uncle Remus: His Songs and His Sayings*, written in 1880, *Nights with Uncle Remus*, written in 1885, and *On the Plantation*, published in 1892, are all dedicated to idealizing the plantation system, glorifying the old order, and celebrating perfect relationships between masters and slaves, usually from the points-of-view of the slave characters.[44]

Virginian novelist Thomas Nelson Page, who was only ten when the Civil War started, is probably the main post-war mythmaker. For Page, antebellum Southern civilization was a Golden Age. His novels stage planters and emancipated slaves who praise their masters and regret the passing of the ancient order. "Marse Chan" and "Meh Lady," two works published in *The Century Magazine* between 1884 and 1886, revolve around two main notions: the loyalty of slaves and the benevolence of masters. Page went further than any of the antebellum writers in his elaboration of the mythic image of Southern planters as "Cavaliers," celebrating their sense of honor, their practice of courtly love, and their celebration of Southern womanhood. By allowing his ex-slave characters to speak, Page attempted to refute all the false ideas that had been spread about the Old South. He purposefully defended the life that had been led there and the people who had inhabited this charmed, lost world. Replete with nostalgia, Page's novels go further than any others of the period in the celebration of a Southern Golden Age. His tales and novels neither threaten nor attack the North. Such attack would have been irrelevant. The myth of the Old South had been born, and its identity was unassailable now that the region had been severed from reality.

Another notable feature of post-war Southern novels that distinguishes them from those of the antebellum period is their apparent participation in a reunification movement, despite their insistence on the righteousness of the Southern combat. As Page himself proclaimed "I have never willingly written a line which I did not hope might tend to bring a better understanding between the North and the South, and finally lead to a more perfect union" (*Collected Edition*, 55). Coinciding with this reunification effort, it seems that post-war Southern literature exited the ghetto to which antebellum fiction had been consigned. In what might be considered a national impulse toward reconciliation, Southern literature became acceptable and even welcomed throughout the rest of the country. The romantic, post-war portrait of the South was apparently drawn to give the rest of the nation a more positive image of the rebel region that had heretofore been considered a national traitor. It became part of a collective American effort at repairing the national fabric.[45]

The nationwide acceptance of the Southern myth is probably the reason why it prospered and expanded after Reconstruction. The further historically removed the Old South was from the Civil War, the more respectable the myth became. In the twentieth century, a whole branch of contemporary American literature is devoted to a "triumphant" form of the myth. This resurrection began in the 1930s with the publication of Margaret Mitchell's *Gone With the Wind*, and since then, the tradition of the plantation novel has never ceased. Several Southern writers continue to reproduce this myth, in literature of very unequal quality, but aimed at achieving bestseller status. Literally hundreds of novels, which will never be anthologized, have been written about the antebellum South, ceaselessly repeating the elements of the nineteenth century myth: Kathleen E. Woodiwiss's *Come Love a Stranger*, written in 1984; Eugenia Prices's *Savannah* quartet, the last volume of which, *Stranger in Savannah*, was published in 1989; and Pamela Jeckel's *Natchez*, published in 1995, among many others. Some authors have even gained international fame, such as Alexandra Ripley, who was chosen by Margaret Mitchell's heirs to write *Scarlett*, the sequel to *Gone With the Wind*, in 1991. Her novels, which are perfect examples of a myth-machine in action, have all become bestsellers: *Charleston* in 1981; *On Leaving Charleston* in 1984; and *New Orleans*

Legacy in 1987. Ann Rivers Siddons also deserves mention for her partici-pation in the resurrection of Southern mythmaking through such novels as *Homeplace* in 1987 or *Peachtree Road* in 1988, although the version of the Southern myth she presents is rather subdued compared to the novels just quoted. The best proof that the myth has become largely shared by the twentieth-century readership is evinced by the fact that all of these latter day plantation sagas are issued by highly "respectable" publishers, such as Ballantine, Harper, and Macmillan.

Celebrated American novelists have also participated in the diffusion of the Southern myth, although in forms that might be considered idiomatic, idiosyncratic, personal, yet nonetheless verisimilar. William Faulkner is probably the first and greatest author to demonstrate such tendencies. His rejection of, but to a certain extent, subjection to the mythic South is a well-known feature of twentieth century American literature. His revital-ized exploration the Southern myth, more personal than rubber-stamp Old South of popular fiction, has opened the way to an authentic Southern literary tradition. Within this tradition, the South becomes that geography of the mind figured in the works of such iconic figures of the Southern canon as Robert Penn Warren, Erskine Caldwell, Eudora Welty, Richard Wright, Ralph Ellison, Margaret Walker, Flannery O'Connor, Ernest Gaines, and Lillian Smith. This list, though certainly not exhaustive, indi-cates the vitality of a myth whose representatives have earned their repu-tations and places in Southern literary history. All these writers are sub-jects of innumerable studies, which explore their very personal visions of the South, visions born of both empathy for and rejection of the features that make the South so unique.

Less studied and less known, partly because they are more recent, are authors such as John Berendt in his well-known *Midnight in the Garden of Good and Evil*—published in 1994 by Random House and revitalized by Clint Eastwood's eponymous film—and Pat Conroy, best known for the popular *The Prince of Tides* (1986). Pat Conroy's vision of the mythic South is particularly revealing, since he seems to have to have reached a high level of understanding and expressing how the Southern myth func-tions. Both *The Prince of Tides* (1986) and *Beach Music* (1995) portray Southerners who try to escape the South and the lethal aspects of its myth, but who finally remain entangled in it, confirming the South's indisput-able overpowering identity. In *The Prince of Tides*, the myth destroys those who become entrapped in it and estranges the various heroes of the novel: it kills the narrator's brother Luke; it makes his sister, Savannah, insane;

and it provokes in the narrator himself a series of psychological distur-
bances. But no matter what its negative effects may be, it remains present
and everlasting.[46] As for the hero of *Beach Music*, he spends the whole
novel rejecting the South and its myth, which has, according to him, killed
his wife. He tries to preserve his daughter from it by taking her away, both
geographically and metaphorically, before falling again, together with his
daughter, under the spell of the South's beauty and power. In the opening
pages, Conroy's narrator describes the process by which the Southern
myth has entered the collective American consciousness. He describes his
flight: "For me, the South was carry-on baggage I could not shed no matter
how many borders I crossed, but my daughter was still a child and I wanted
her to grow into womanhood as a European, blissfully unaware of that soft
ruinous South that had killed her mother in one of its prettiest rivers"
(*Beach Music*, 6). But no matter how hard one tries to destroy it, the
mythic South always catches up, and the narrator unwillingly becomes the
mythmaker of his daughter's birthplace: "I confess that I became the cen-
sor of my daughter's history. The South that I described to Leah at bedtime
every night existed only in my imagination. It admitted no signs of danger
or nightmare. There was no dark side to the Southern moon that I recalled
to my daughter, and the rivers ran clean and the camellias were always in
bloom. It was a South that existed without sting or thorn or heartache"
(*Beach Music*, 6). This is probably the most concise and elegant description
of the process that led to the birth of the myth after the Civil War, a myth
that has persisted, virtually untouched, for almost 150 years.

While today's scholars debate over the *de facto* disappearance of Southern distinctiveness (either through an Americanization of the South, or
through a Southernization of the United States, or a double movement
encompassing both tendencies), the Southern myth is still alive. The Caribbean societies have never produced anything close to it. As discussed
earlier, there was no development of a literature of legendary West Indian
societies during the slavery period, while Southerners were concentrating
all their literary energies on defending the peculiar features of a civilization that they felt was under siege. The post-slavery literature of the West
Indies, although it sometimes celebrated, and still celebrates, the exotic
nature of the islands, has always remained critical of the Antillean colonial
and post-colonial societies. By contrast, in the South, a tendency to social
glorification pervades the literature of the post-slavery era. The Southern
distinctiveness that emerges in this literature is later reinforced by its geographical expansion throughout the country and across literary mediums,
both canonical and popular.

Expansion and Generalization of the Myth

The fact that the Southern myth is no longer limited to one region accounts for its strength. On the one hand, this myth has reached audiences worldwide; on the other, it has spread to other media. Each of the twentieth-century works discussed here has been translated, circulated, widely read, and even achieved bestsellers status outside the United States. It should also be remembered that *Gone With the Wind* is the second best-selling book in the world after the Bible. Hardly anyone in Europe, for instance, has missed the movie, which, in addition to being one of the classics of American and world cinema, has become, though inadvertently, a cult film.

Still more interesting, European literature has embraced the Southern myth. Several twentieth-century French writers, for example, have produced plantation novels, all set in the American South. The French-American writer, Julien Green, is one of these. His three Southern novels, *Les Pays lointains* (1987), *Les Etoiles du sud* (1989), and *Dixie* (1995), are all written and published in French, although the author is bilingual and of Southern descent, his father's family being connected to General Beauregard. Some of the nostalgia imported from American post-war portrayals of a lost Old South can be gleaned from the back cover of Green's *Dixie*: "Dixie, le chant du Sud, flotte sur ce monde comme un cri d'amour" [Dixie, song of the South, pervades this world like a love cry]. Green summons childhood memories to explain his attraction to the mythic South. He was twelve when his mother told him that the South had lost the war. This is why all of his heroes are the same age he was when he still believed that his South had won. Green's novels participate in the sub-genre of the "triumphant" Southern myth, as do the novels of another French writer, whose literary stature is inferior to Green's, but whose novels have nonetheless been very successful in France: Maurice Denuzière. His saga, reminiscent of nineteenth-century Southern literary production, is composed of three novels: *Louisiane* (1977), *Fausse-rivière* (1979), and *Bagatelle* (1981). All were immediately popular in France.

These examples reveal the persistence and the comprehensive range of the Southern myth. Over a century old, it is still alive and well and has crossed national and continental borders. The notable interest of French writers in this myth can be explained in part by the French historical involvement with Louisiana. Green and Denuzière could thus be called writers of the French colonial experience as well as of the American South.

However, the social glorification found in these novels is unequalled in the literary production that treats the Caribbean territories sharing with Louisiana the same French colonial past. The Southern myth has expanded to cover Louisiana, but has not gone beyond the Gulf of Mexico to those not-so-very distant islands of the other shore of the Caribbean Sea, which shared so many experiences with Louisiana and the rest of the South. This internationalization of the myth is a first indication of its power. Another clear sign of its strength lies in the fact that it has not remained confined to a literary sphere. Denuzière's saga, after being translated into fifteen languages, has become the subject of a very popular television serial.

Indeed, the persistent success of the Southern myth is to be witnessed in other fields of American culture, for instance, in cinema. Many of the novels discussed here have been followed by film versions. This is the case, of course, of the mythic movie *Gone with the Wind*, but also, among many others, of Clint Eastwod's *Midnight in the Garden of Good and Evil*, which, to an attentive eye, quite faithfully reproduces the novel's interpretation of the myth. All of Conroy's novels have been made into movies, although the cinematographic version of *The Prince of Tides* obviously misunderstood or totally disregarded the novel's mythic aspect. Popular culture in general has willingly adopted the mythic South, as innumerable television series dealing with the antebellum period, the Civil War, and the post-war era—*North and South* and *Scarlett*, for example—attest.

Beyond these media vehicles, the persistence of the Southern myth informs an American tourist-industry tradition of rehabilitating the figures, events, and heroes of the Confederation. Throughout the South, signs of this trend can be witnessed, in perfect accordance with the general tendency of Americans to search for their roots. Although this trend is not specific to the South, it is manifested, in this region, through the celebration of a very distinct history, turning people who, a century before, were considered traitors to the national cause, into heroes. This tendency began when the romanticizing of the South became acceptable as part of the late nineteenth-century reconciliation movement. As early as the 1880s, the figurehead of the Confederacy, Jefferson Davis, was canonized as an American hero. Today, tourists can travel through the South following the traces of a man who spent two years in prison for treason during Reconstruction. From Natchez, where stands the house where he married, to Biloxi's Beauvoir, where he spent the last period of his life, tourists hear about the greatness of the man as their visit to Beauvoir opens on a film-panegyric to someone who was, *stricto sensu*, a traitor to the United States.

More than this, the mythic South has attained a semiotic dimension in the widespread though controversial display of the Confederate Battle flag. In the South, this flag has always stood for Southern distinctiveness, but also stands as a reminder of the region's past, and of all those who patriotically died for its cause. Banished during Reconstruction, the flag regained popularity in the 1890s, at a time when celebrating the Confederacy was no longer considered traitorous. The United Daughters of the Confederacy, for instance, was openly founded in 1895. Although there is recurrent opposition to its official presence as evinced in the protest movement that spread across South Carolina in early 2000, it still floats over many Southern edifices from Texas to Tallahassee and is still regarded by many Southerners as the symbol of their singularity. It represents another America, an alternative to mainstream values, a reaction to a central government seen as overpowering, and a rejection of capitalism and industrial society. It may also, at times, be interpreted as a reaction against the ultimate victory of the Civil Rights Movement, against the values of affirmative action, and the dream of the melting pot. The flag has also gained worldwide meaning as a positive symbol of rebellion, of a refusal to become mainstream, of widespread political resistance to an overpowering centralized government. Simultaneously, it has become the symbol of racist sentiment. For both of these reasons, it can be seen waving all over the world, in totally non-American contexts, appropriated by racist political organizations, brandished by British hooligans at soccer games, or lofted as a sign of rebellion, courage, and fortitude, as by the Ferrari *Tifosi* at the Formula 1 Grand Prix in San Marino.

No matter what the context, what the symbolism, or what the manifestation, the Southern myth and its emblems is indeed the most significant proof of Southern distinctiveness. Although the colonial societies of the Americas have long shared common historical conditions, the birth of Southern difference is to be found in the way slavery developed and was organized, as well as in the debate that raged over its existence and maintenance, and finally in the aftermath of this debate. The American Manifest Destiny, conducive to mythmaking, paved the way for a Southern myth that has outlived the Old South by almost a century and a half already and is still much in evidence today.

Conclusion

From their first discovery in the late fifteenth century, to the final abolition of slavery in the nineteenth, the "societies with slaves" then "slave
societies" of the Americas have shared significant common historical experiences. Their European history started with the adventurous voyage of
the same man (Columbus); their early settlement is included within the
same population movement and was fuelled partly by the same economic,
demographic and political causes. Very rapidly, due to similar geographical
and climatic situations, agricultural plantation societies emerged. Because
of an urgent need to bring manpower to these plantation societies, the
various European countries, faced with the same shortage of European settlers, turned to the importation of Africans, whom they enslaved. During
their first three centuries of existence, many of the colonies shifted from
one European power to another, and throughout that period, they were
gradually organized according to very similar, highly hierarchical social
and racial patterns. Slavery was progressively institutionalized and carefully codified in all the colonial possessions. In the late eighteenth century,
movements developed everywhere in opposition to this institution, which
had become a commonly shared colonial "peculiarity." Everywhere,
counter-movements emerged to protect an established order, all of them
ultimately defeated. Throughout the South and the Caribbean, slavery was
finally abolished and society was reorganized in accordance with the new
order and with a totally new context. Such is the first lesson that can be
taught by the comparative study attempted.

This is but a first-degree reading of the comparison. Indeed, very early,
differences began to emerge between the South and the Caribbean colonies. The West Indian possessions were marked by remarkable overall homogeneity, despite their belonging to different nations, with different colonial policies, and different religions and cultures. It might seem, at first,
that the main differences between the South and the Caribbean sprang

from the end of colonial status in the United States. This is far from true. Early settlement had already displayed somewhat different trends: while the Caribbean colonies were mostly dominated by all kinds of adventurers, corsairs, freebooters and buccaneers, the colonies of the North American continent experienced colonizing settlement from the very start. While the West Indian territories were the stakes of power struggles between European colonizing powers, the American South, with the exception of Louisiana, until the very early nineteenth century remained more stable politically.

The mentality of the colonists was also very different in the Caribbean and in the colonies of the northern continent. The West Indian planter class had mercantilist aims and generally regarded the islands as places to make money. As a result, the plantation owners were not necessarily resident and took every opportunity to go back to Europe, leaving the management of their properties to overseers. Although the Spanish islands tended to display less absenteeism, the proportion still remained higher than in the American South. Moreover, in the Caribbean, even resident masters were not necessarily involved in the life of the colony. On the whole, they considered their stay temporary, at least in the early periods of colonization. By contrast, from the start, the colonizers of the American South were not only resident, but they developed a "resident mind." The colonies were not merely places in which people could make a fortune; they were a new space open to a different society, free from the old European order. The Puritans' shining city, as well as the Manifest Destiny of the United States, implied a mythmaking spirit, and the aim of the colonists of the northern continent was to build an ideal society that was to spread throughout the Americas.

This necessarily had strong repercussions on the modeling of their institutions, and more particularly of the "Peculiar Institution" of the South. The presence of resident masters led to a somewhat different codification of slavery, stricter in the South than in the Caribbean societies, but largely counterbalanced, in daily practice, by a strong paternalist trend. The close coexistence between masters and slaves led to the development of peculiar living conditions and peculiar relationships. The slave population, although relatively more deprived of autonomy than its Caribbean counterpart, experienced slightly less arduous living conditions. This population thus increased naturally, with much less frequent importations of new labor, a stability that led to the development of an African American culture. Interestingly, the "resident mind" is apparently not solely linked to an

Anglo-Saxon trend, since it did not spread to the English Caribbean colonies, but did tend to develop in French, then Spanish, Louisiana. Among the explanations for this phenomenon, might be the existence of a "continental mind" as opposed to an insular mentality.

Because of the planters' resident mind, the society that developed in the colonies of the American colonial South was highly organized and had definite specific features. After the Revolutionary War, the ideals of American democracy and civilization spread, closely followed by an emerging Southern model which included those American values, although with slight differences of interpretation. The two sections of the United States started a struggle of titans, each of them trying to obtain the expansion of its own ideal society at the expense of the other's. Between the West Indian colonies and their mother countries, the debate over the question of slavery remained relatively abstract, toned down by distance, and mostly limited to a debate over principles founded on economic, proprietary, and security considerations (a repeat of the Haitian experience was assiduously avoided.) Concomitantly, in the United States, the debate over abolition became a question of life and death. It meant, on each side, not only the life or death of certain ideals, but also the life or death of an entire system. This opposition reached beyond metaphor, when, with the advent of the Civil War, people literally staked their lives on their social ideals and customs.

While abolition in the Caribbean was the result of a slow, mostly peaceful, progressive movement, in the United States, it took a four-year war and over 600,000 deaths; it required both the physical and metaphorical ruin of the South. The aftermath of abolition was necessarily very different. Because of the way abolition had been carefully prepared in the West Indies, the process was progressive, and the colonial powers kept close control over the colonies to make sure that emancipation would not end in a racial war for power. In the South, on the contrary, to the infamy of defeat was added the shock of seeing slaves become equal to masters by the mere passing of an amendment. Instantaneously, slaves could refuse to work for their masters, even under such a system as apprenticeship or sharecropping, and they obtained equal civil rights. African American men could vote, and their vote was equal to any white man's. This was unacceptable to people who had spent over three decades "scientifically" proving the inferiority of the Africans. All this led to a deep turmoil and to the development of a social, economic, and political organization peculiar to the American South: legally sanctioned segregation.

This comparison of the slave societies of the Americas thus appears historically revealing. It also enables a deeper understanding of the birth, development, and persistence into the third millennium of an overall Southern cultural distinctiveness. Indeed, from the eve of the debate over the question of abolition, the South started displaying specific cultural features. Because America's brand of slavery was unique, because its master-slave relationships were singular, because the debate over abolition was internal and because its outcome became a matter of life and death, the arguments on both sides were very harsh, uncompromising, broadly based, and elaborate. The protagonists were not solely ideologues and politicians as in the West Indian case. Fiction writers became involved in the fray, and progressively built a literary, legendary antebellum South. The defeat of the South added a nostalgic dimension to the legend, and the lost cause turned the legend into myth. This mythmaking trend can be traced back to shadowy beginnings at the very foundation of the thirteen colonies, but the Civil War fueled this trend and gave tangible birth to a mythic South, which has endured—enriched by time and by the talent of its writers—to the present.

The South died at Appomatox, but it took another century to complete its metaphorical death. Through a dual movement of standardization—both an integration by the South of American values and the mainstreaming of certain Southern values—the South finally died as a really distinct entity, swallowed by the civilization it had so long and so strongly opposed.[1] What remains distinctively Southern is the constantly celebrated, redefined, and reinterpreted myth of a defeated South reborn, the perseverance of which has ensured the survival of the region as ideal.[2]

Because their past, their motives, and their values were different from the very start and because their societies evolved in a singular direction, the Caribbean colonies never developed this mythmaking tendency. The increasing divergence between the Caribbean islands and the continent led to a specific Southern evolution, which has culminated in the enduring cultural distinctiveness still vivid today.

This comparison of slave societies, from their foundation to the end of the slavery era, thus highlights several centuries of parallel development. It also stresses, almost from the start, diverging historical evolutions. More importantly, it gives real insight into the birth of Southern cultural distinctiveness, which has been often evoked in recent historiography of the slave societies of the Americas, without being really explored and accounted for.

Although the results of the present work legitimize the comparative perspective, much remains to be done on the topic. The framework of this study and its initial hypothesis have indeed often reduced the scope of comparison. The inspiration for it sprang from protracted study of the Southern myth and from the initial observation that Caribbean societies today are very different from the American South, despite initial common background conditions. Although the comparison is as thorough as possible, it may be slightly biased by the initial hypothesis. Moreover, because of this hypothesis, some slight differences between Caribbean societies have been overlooked because they were beyond the main focus of the study.

Many aspects of the slave societies of the Americas remain to be discussed. Indeed, throughout the present study, questions sprang from the observation of differences not yet accounted for, which would justify further comparative work. As an example, the development of Creole languages remains largely unexplored in comparative perspective: why did some of these societies give birth to Creole languages, while others did not? No linguistic reason is apparently sufficient to explain these differences.[3] The reasons are then probably essentially sociological and historical. The comparative field is thus wide open, but one of the aims of this study was to show the interest of such a perspective, by delineating the wealth of information to be gleaned from the examination of common features and differences, and by giving a tentative explanation for the birth of Southern distinctiveness. The study also aimed at showing that it is much more revealing to consider this Southern difference in relation to outside territories than in its traditional opposition to the North within the American national fabric.

It is also possible to imagine a still wider frame of study, including, for instance, the slave societies of Latin America, to check the validity of a thesis, which maintains that Southern difference was partly favored by geographical conditions, a continental distinctiveness, so to speak, that left the islands behind. It would also be interesting to compare the colonies of the Americas to others located elsewhere in the world (for instance, to Bourbon Island, now the French overseas department of La Réunion) to determine if any exception might be linked to the American context. There is much to do in terms of comparative history, including in the limited field of the creation, expansion, and ultimate demise of slave societies.

Notes

Author's Note: All translations are mine unless otherwise noted.

Introduction

1. Several historians are today advocating the comparative perspective, especially in matters of slavery and slave societies. See, for instance, the forum published in the April 2000 issue of the *American Historical Review,* with four articles written by leading historians of slavery, David Brion Davis (452–66), Peter Kolchin (467–71), Rebecca J. Scott (472–79), and Stanley L. Engerman (480–84).

2. This interesting distinction between "societies with slaves" and "slave societies" was made by Frank Tannenbaum in *Slave and Citizen.* His extensive explanation of this difference has become the substratum of most later sociological studies in matters of slavery.

3. For instance, Laura Foner, 419–37.

4. It is the case, for instance, of Kolchin's *American Slavery.* Kolchin's study essentially deals with the American South, but very often refers to the slave societies of the Caribbean in a comparative perspective to highlight Southern distinctiveness.

5. Writers such as Thomas Nelson Page or Joel Chandler Harris in the late nineteenth century, and, more recently, Margaret Mitchell or Alexandra Ripley, perfectly illustrate this vein.

6. This trend has proved tremendously rich in the twentieth century, exemplified by such authors as William Faulkner, Eudora Welty, and Flannery O'Connor, among many others.

7. Among the most famous fiction writers of the antebellum South are William Gilmore Simms, John Pendleton Kennedy, William Alexander Caruthers, and Nathaniel Beverley Tucker. The Southern myth in literature will be developed at length in Chapter 6.

Chapter 1. "Discovery" and Settlement

1. See Vincent Huyghes-Belrose, 83–96.

2. Huyghes-Belrose, 87.

3. Luc François, 121–26.

4. Jean Pouquet, 11. For a comprehensive study of the colonization of the Americas, see John H. Parry, *The Age of Reconnaissance.*

5. Michel Devèze, 71.

6. Letter written by Velasquez to the king, qtd. in Devèze, 56.

7. Jacques Adélaïde-Merlande, *Histoire générale*, 77.

8. See the famous account by Alexandre-Olivier Exquemelin, an indentured servant living with buccaneers in Tortuga and French Hispaniola (St. Domingue) in the seventeenth century. Entitled in its French version *Boucaniers & flibustiers des Antilles, Les colons-marins du XVIIe siècle* and first published in 1688, this narrative has been translated into many languages and remains a precious source of information about the period.

9. See Eric Williams, *From Columbus to Castro*, 98.

10. Adélaïde-Merlande, *Histoire Générale*, 110.

11. By *habitants* is meant colonists or settlers—those who had really settled down on the islands and were involved in agriculture—as opposed to adventurers.

12. The author's name has been transformed several times, according to the language in which the account was published. The French spelling has been adopted here, as the edition cited is the French one.

13. "Comme leur nombre s'est toujours accru, et que la Tortue leur semblait trop petite, la plupart, ayant éprouvé que le genre de vie de l'habitant était plus doux que le métier de chasseur, résolurent de faire des habitations" [As their number constantly increased and as Tortuga seemed too small to them, most of them, having had the feeling that the settler's way of life was more pleasant than the hunter's, decided to build plantations] (Exquemelin, 49).

14. Exquemelin, 49–52.

Chapter 2. Society, Societies

1. Hugh Brogan, 54.

2. For more information see Chauleau, *Dans les îles du vent* and Adélaïde-Merlande, *La Caraïbe et la Guyane*, as well as his already-cited *Histoire générale*. Also consult Devèze and Denis Laurent-Ropa. These bibliographical references are, of course, but a few among many.

3. F. R. Augier et al., *The Making of the West Indies*, 114, present a very interesting interpretation of the reason why this movement was more exacerbated in St. Domingue than in the other French colonies: for them, the explanation lies in the smaller degree of planter absenteeism in the French Lesser Antilles (they speak of a "longer-standing resident planter class"), which thus induced a stronger resistance to the revolutionary movement. Consequently, there was less trouble, and the islands were not lost. They also explain that the rebellion in St. Domingue was all the more important and decisive since it started from the inside and was not provoked by outside Jacobin agitators.

4. For more information on the government of the English West Indian colonies, see, for instance, the chapter dealing with the evolution of Bermuda, Barbados, and Jamaica in Michael Craton, 68–103.

5. Augier et al. give interesting examples of how interventions of the West Indian

interest in Parliament successfully inflected English governmental policy. Upon request of the Barbadian planters and Leeward Island legislatures, for example, Parliament passed the 1733 Molasses Act and the 1764 Sugar Act in order to restrict the trade which was then developing between the North American English colonies and the French and Dutch colonies of the Caribbean. For other examples, see especially 106–9.

6. Figures given by the 1790 census, cited, for instance, in André Kaspi, 53.

7. Kaspi, 63.

8. See, for instance, Thomas N. Ingersoll, 12–13. Gwendolyn M. Hall speaks of "penal colonization" and gives details about such importations in her invaluable contribution to the history of colonial Louisiana, *Africans in Colonial Louisiana*, 5–7.

9. Several instances can be found in the literature on the West Indies. For Louisiana, see Ingersoll, 9, and Gwendolyn Hall, 5–6.

10. For instance, Kaspi, 61.

11. See, for example, the already-cited memoirs of indentured servant Exquemelin, and more precisely, the numerous pages devoted to description of indentured servants' living conditions in the French colonies.

12. Kaspi, 61.

13. Ingersoll, 11, gives the percentage of each category of population arriving in Louisiana between 1718 and 1721. Women and children are not included because no details are given concerning the social classes they belonged to (altogether they represented 19.2 percent of the arrivals). Employees represented 0.5 percent, laborers 3.3 percent, indentured servants 27.6 percent, deportees 14.3 percent, soldiers 11.0 percent, officers and concessionaires of the company 2.8 percent, and African slaves 21.3 percent. For the numbers of colonists (including women and children) imported into the colony, see Gwendolyn Hall, 7.

14. Augier et al, *The Making of the West Indies*, 15.

15. Craton, 21.

16. Ingersoll, 10. Also see chapter 1, "The Chaos of French Rule," Gwendolyn Hall, 2–21.

17. To give among many examples that of Martinique, the population grew from 5,310 in 1660 to 91,922 in the 1750s due both to propaganda deployed to attract migrants and to very favorable conditions offered to artisans, among others. On the eve of the French Revolution, though, the total population was only 85,000 persons (12,000 whites, 5,000 colored people, and 68,000 slaves). See Liliane Chauleau, *Dans les îles du vent*, 73.

18. Brogan, 22.

19. For more details, see, for instance, Kaspi, 53–54.

20. Ramon de la Sagra, *Histoire Economique et Politique de l'Ile de Cuba*, cited in Adélaïde-Merlande, *La Caraïbe et la Guyane*, 15.

21. Chauleau, *Dans les îles du vent*, 213.

22. There were 28,000 slaves in the French islands and 120,000 in the British

ones: Moreau de Jonnès, *Recherches statistiques sur l'esclavage colonial,* (Paris 1848), qtd. in Devèze, 189.

23. Adélaïde-Merlande, *Histoire Générale,* 94.

24. See F. R. Augier and S. C. Gordon, 22.

25. In 1700, there were 500 free colored people for 9,000 slaves in French St. Domingue; 239 for 4,780 in Guadeloupe; 507 for 14,566 in Martinique. See Emile Hayot, 55.

26. Augier et al., 111.

27. See Foner, for example.

28. Bandry, 39.

29. Devèze, 180.

30. The example of the Codringtons in Barbados is useful here. Born into a noble family of Gloucestershire, Christopher Codrington the elder (1640–1698) built one of the wealthiest estates on the island and, beginning at an early age, occupied various important political functions. He was councilor at twenty-six, deputy governor at twenty-nine, and was later governor general of the Leeward Islands. The Codringtons remained famous local figures for many generations. See Craton, 59–60.

31. Bruce Collins dedicates a whole chapter to "mobility," 83–97.

32. For more details, see Craton, 60–61. Many examples of upward mobility can be observed among the various colonies. In Barbados, for instance, the example of James Drax (1602–1675), an obscure adventurer, is significant. He represents the perfect self-made man of colonial times. He ended up a large planter, erected the first windmill in the colony, built a huge plantation house, married the daughter of the first Earl of Carlisle, and married his own daughter into the Codrington family. Similar examples can be found in the French Caribbean possessions. Take the case of a certain planter named Roy, mentioned in the very famous account by Jean-Baptiste Labat, a Dominican missionary sent to the West Indies in the late seventeenth century. Roy was first an indentured servant who, after trading tobacco, became a freebooter and finally had enough money to start a sugar plantation. When Labat came to the island, Roy had six sugar plantations and over eight hundred slaves (Labat, 64).

33. Craton, 101.

34. Cattle ranch would be the closest translation.

35. See Labat's description of the Fonds Saint-Jacques plantation belonging to the Dominicans, 48–49.

36. See, among others, Augier et al., 80.

37. See, for instance, Eugene Genovese, *The Political Economy of Slavery.*

38. For more details on architecture in the South and in the Caribbean, see David Buisseret, Mills Lane, and Peter Vlach.

39. This term has attained a symbolic dimension by becoming the title of a novel written by a contemporary Martinique author, Joseph Zobel.

40. Jan Morris, Introduction to *Caribbean Style,* S. Slesin et al.

41. The eighteenth and nineteenth centuries produced a huge number of travel

narratives, a literary genre then in fashion. European travelers narrated their experiences in the New World for European readership. A few examples typical of this literature should be mentioned: Alexandre-Stanislas de Wimpffen's *Voyage à Saint-Domingue*; Claude-Cézar Robin's *Voyages dans l'intérieur de la Louisiane*; Etienne-Michel Massé's *L'île de Cuba*; and Basil Hall's *Travels in North America* along with an account of the same trip by his wife, Mrs. Hall's *The Aristocratic Journey*.

42. Moreau de Saint-Méry, who wrote detailed accounts of the societies of the French and Spanish parts of Hispaniola, writes that there was little society ("peu de société") in Santo Domingo (*Description topographique ... de la partie espagnole de l'isle de Saint-Domingue*, vol. 1, 145).

43. See travel narratives for primary sources, but also the very detailed study of Southern society made by Collins. In his chapter entitled "Rituals" (142–59), he insists on the rituals of Southern society, among which water seasons at Sarasota or White Sulphur Springs in Virginia, the summer season at the seaside, as well as horse races at Natchez in December, New Orleans in April, Memphis in May, and Charleston throughout the year figure prominently.

44. Craton, 53.

45. Or, as Richard Dunn very concisely puts it in his introduction to *Sugar and Slave:* "The Englishmen who settled were not mythmakers in the heroic vein of Captain John Smith. . . . They did not attempt calypso-style Holy Experiments, nor did they build palm-fringed Cities on a Hill" (xv).

Chapter 3. Comparative Systems of Slavery

1. For instance, see the already-mentioned article by Foner or Kolchin's book, as well as chapters in Craton, for instance chapter 10, "The Rope and the Cutlass: Slave Resistance in Plantation America."

2. Kolchin is but one of the most recent examples of a long tradition of studying American slavery. Ira Berlin's latest publication, *Many Thousands Gone*, should also be cited. The bibliography indicates many more references both on the South and on the Caribbean.

3. See Ingersoll and Gwendolyn Hall on Louisiana.

4. Announced by Frank Tannenbaum in 1947, this distinction has been widely referred to since by sociologists.

5. Hubert Deschamp, *Histoire de la traite des noirs de l'Antiquité à nos jours*, cited in Devèze, 153.

6. Devèze, 160.

7. Devèze, 158.

8. Chauleau, *Dans les îles du vent*, 122–23.

9. Craton gives the figure of 400,000 (135, 149). Other figures indicate 523,000. See, for instance, James A. Rawley, 428. Figures vary from one author to the next, but the proportions remain about the same. It is difficult to be totally accurate, due to a lack of overall archival figures on the subject.

10. For more details, see Moreau de St-Méry's *Description[s] topographique[s]*,

both his work on the Spanish section of St. Domingue (1797) and its antecedent volume on the French part of the island (1796).

11. In Spanish, the term *bozals* designates slaves born in Africa, as opposed to the "Creole" slaves born in the colonies. The French word for African-born slaves is similar: *bossales.*

12. For more information, see the numerous works written about the transatlantic slave trade: for instance Philip Curtin, Herbert S. Klein, and Rawley.

13. See Carlos Esteban Deive (vol. 2, 559).

14. Klein, 41.

15. Celsa Albert Batista, 23.

16. Deive quotes two contract letters indicating that one fourth should be women (vol. 2, 560). Batista gives the global figure of one third in Santo Domingo and indicates that from the sixteenth to the eighteenth century, the balance largely inclined to the males; her final figures are 20,756 women for 41,512 men (24).

17. Batista speaks of the role of female slaves as a "mechanismo de contención" or "preservation mechanism," but also as a "máquina de reproductura de esclavos," literally, a machine for the reproduction of slaves (25, 27).

18. Berlin, *Many Thousands Gone,* 83. For detailed figures of the male/female ratio on slave-trade voyages to French and Spanish Louisiana, see Gwendolyn Hall, 172 and 286.

19. Berlin, *Many Thousands Gone,* 112.

20. Berlin, *Many Thousands Gone,* 83. Also see Gwendolyn Hall, 84.

21. Collins, 51.

22. Devèze, 284.

23. See Williams, *Capitalism and Slavery.* See also Jean-Paul Barbiche, 122.

24. The figures sometimes vary, but the proportion ranges from 750,000 in 1790 to 4,441,830 in 1860, even though the transatlantic trade was abolished in 1808. It is difficult to assess the proportion of illegally imported slaves, but it seems relatively insignificant compared with the overall increase of the slave population. The 1860 figure is proof of an extraordinary natural growth.

25. According to the definition generally found in the literature—although some scholars describe the evolution of the term somewhat differently (see for instance Gwendolyn Hall 157)—the word "Creole," deriving from the Portuguese *Crioulo* or the Spanish *Criollo,* first referred to white people born in the colonies. It was progressively expanded to all natives of the colonies. It even came to be used to refer to anything culturally native of, or specific to, the colonies.

26. See, for instance Klein, 51.

27. Craton, 135; Batista, 79. The latter describes the northern societies as more varied, with more women, children, and older people.

28. Klein, 51.

29. "Tiene un metabolismo más accelarado y una maduración más temprana," meaning that they had an accelerated metabolism and a more precocious sexual maturity (59).

30. In the chapter entitled "Hobbesian or Panglossian," Craton studies the slave population of the Rolle family (203–32).

31. Collins, 51.

32. In the Lower South, there were 2,943,200 whites to 2,423,500 slaves and 37,000 free colored persons (Berlin 74). Kaspi indicates that the ratio of whites to blacks was one to two in South Carolina and Mississippi; two to five in Louisiana, Alabama, Florida, and Georgia; and that the proportion of blacks was 13 percent in Maryland, 10 percent in Missouri, and 1.5 percent in Delaware (142).

33. See Berlin, 85, for statistics on Puerto Rico. For Santo Domingo, Adélaïde-Merlande indicates that slaves formed 10.8 percent of the population in 1777 (7,592) and 10.9 percent in 1787 (11,260) (*Histoire Générale*, 127). Blacks are found to be a majority only when free colored people are counted with slaves, for instance in the figures given in Batista, 71.

34. For the free colored population, Adélaïde-Merlande gives a figure of 30,000 in 1735 or 19.7 percent (*Histoire Générale*, 127).

35. If free colored people are not counted, the slave population of Santo Domingo represented about thirty-five percent of the total (Batista 72). According to Adélaïde-Merlande, the slave population of St. Domingue accounted for only 27.4 percent of the total (47,331 slaves) in the late eighteenth century (*Histoire Générale*, 127).

36. Batista, 78.

37. See Douglas Hall, 68.

38. Adélaïde-Merlande, *Histoire Générale*, 120.

39. Adélaïde-Merlande, *Histoire Générale*, 120.

40. See, for instance, Lucien Abénon.

41. Letter from the Governor of Virginia, cited in Berlin, 125.

42. Adélaïde-Merlande, *Histoire Générale*, 134.

43. Collins, 57.

44. For more information on this, see Jane Landers.

45. Berlin, 444 (note 51).

46. Berlin, 444 (note 53).

47. Gwendolyn Hall gives several examples of this in her book. For a better understanding of racial fluidity in colonial Louisiana, see her chapter 8, "The Pointe Coupee Post," 237–74. Also on this topic, see Hanger, 25–26.

48. This was further increased by the tradition of *plaçage*, that is, the custom for white married men to have a second family in town, often a colored mistress and mulatto children. For more information on Spanish Louisiana, see Gilbert Din.

49. Ley 1, qtd. in Batista, 87. Although the *Leyes Suntuarias* were primarily aimed at curbing the importation of luxury goods, some of the measures they included regulated the rights and duties of the free colored class.

50. Laurent-Ropa, 151.

51. Discriminatory laws were passed in the Northern states, including disfranchising and segregating laws.

52. To give one among many examples, in all the English Caribbean societies, slaves were not only legal chattel (as elsewhere), but were also legal real estate, a distinction exercised by the owner class to evade certain laws in matters of inheritance. The only exception to this rule was Barbados, where a 1668 addendum stipulated that slaves could be considered as "chattel" in debt matters. This is clear proof that, even where local provisions were different, they changed neither the spirit of the legislation nor the social order and had only peripheral consequences for the treatment of slaves.

53. Again, see Craton, 97. In Barbados, for instance, in 1661, only two measures represented some kind of attempt at protecting the slaves: their clothes had to be renewed once a year and anyone who killed a slave would be fined. The so-called humanity of the last measure is mitigated first by the fact that it was a mere fine against life and second by the fact that the fine was higher if the victim was someone else's slave. Obviously, a slave's monetary value to the owner was more important than the slave's life.

54. Introductory paragraph of the 1712 South Carolina Slave Code.

55. The French code states that slaves are "sujets à vente, saisie, partage entre héritiers" [subject to sale, seizure, and division among heirs].

56. See *Codigo Negro*, Capítulo 9, ley 1: "arte in profesión alguna mecánica" [art of some mechanical profession]. Translated as section and law, I retain the terms capítulo and ley with reference to the *Codigo Negro* throughout my study.

57. See *Codigo Negro*, Capítulo 20, ley 1: "en remuneración de sus buenos servicios" [in payment of his good services]; "Buena conducta y fidelidad" [good conduct and faithfulness].

58. See *Codigo Negro*, Capítulo 20, ley 1: "mismos que la libertad natural confiere a los ingenuos dándole las mismas prerogatives, derechos y preeminiencias" [give the same prerogatives, rights, and pre-eminences that natural freedom confers on innocents].

59. Six articles bear on this theme. For instance, article 22 states: "seront tenus les maîtres à faire fournir par chacune semaine à leurs esclaves âgés de dix ans et au-dessus, pour leur nourriture, deux pots et demi, mesure de Paris, de farine de magnoc, ou trois cassavas, pesant chacune deux livres et demi au moins, ou choses équivalentes avec deux livres de bœuf salé ou trois livres de poisson, ou autres choses à proportion, et aux enfants depuis qu'ils sont sevrés, jusqu'à l'âge de dix ans, la moitié des vivres ci-dessus" [Masters will have to provide each week to their slaves aged ten and above, for their food, two pots and a half (Paris measurement) of manioc flour, or three cassavas weighing at least two and a half pounds each, or equivalent produce with two pounds of salted beef or three pounds of fish, or other things in proportion, and to children from the day they are weaned to age ten, half the food above]. The precision here is extreme. The type and weight of food products for weekly rationing are specifically enumerated. Moreover, the type and weight of substitute food products is enumerated as well.

60. In a very interesting, though as yet unpublished, symposium presentation, "The Transformation of Slavery in the United States, 1800–1863" (University of Paris VII, 15–17 June 2000), Ira Berlin described the evolution of slavery in the American South during these crucial decades.

61. See Deive, vol. 2, 495.

62. See, among others, accounts by Henry de Saussure, Jean-Baptiste Labat, de Wimpffen, and Massé. Michèle Guicharneau-Tollis has counted no less than forty travel narratives written by Europeans between 1800 and 1880 about the island of Cuba alone.

63. While it would not be practicable to list them all here, an idea of the frequency of Caribbean slave revolts can be indicated by the examples of Guadeloupe in 1639 and 1656, of Jamaica, which experienced five major rebellions between 1734 and 1769, of Antigua in 1736, Montserrat in 1776, and Nevis in 1761, among many others.

64. See David Lowenthal, 43.

65. One famous example is the Le Jeune trial that occurred in St. Domingue in 1788. Accused of killing six of his slaves, Le Jeune was acquitted by the Superior Council of Port-au-Prince for want of evidence and witnesses.

66. Labat, 227–31.

67. Laurent-Ropa, 138.

68. As Craton explains, "Usage and custom were always more important, and generally more lenient, than enacted slave laws, and that when 'ameliorative' laws were introduced under metropolitan pressure from the 1780s they were mostly dead letters, simply enacted what had long been customary, or endorsed changes—such as the wholesale adoption and adaptation of Christianity by the slaves—that were occurring independently" (151–52).

69. See Craton, 64–67. In an essay titled "The Planters' World in the British West Indies," for instance, Craton shows that this tradition is linked with the "ideal of a quasi-feudal aristocracy" and the tradition of a close-knit "patriarchal family household." He adds: "From the sovereign downward, the titled nobility were grand patriarchs with virtually no private family life, heads of great households consisting of servants of different ranks living in intimate proximity with each other" (64).

70. Kolchin, 23.

71. *Many Thousands Gone*, 118.

72. *American Slavery*, 151.

73. See, for instance, chapter 5, "French New Orleans," and chapter 6, "Creole Slaves," in Gwendolyn Hall.

74. Acosta Rodriguez, *La Poblacion de la Louisiana española (1763–1803)*, qtd. in Berlin, *Many Thousands Gone*, 439; also see Gwendolyn Hall, 287.

75. See Ingersoll, 119.

76. See Kolchin, for instance.

77. For more information on this, see Kolchin, 44–59.

Chapter 4. Ideology, Ideologies

1. See Inaugural Editorial by William Lloyd Garrison, *The Liberator* 1, no. 1, (January 1, 1831). There he writes: "In Parkstreet Church, on the Fourth of July, 1829, in an address on slavery, I unreflectingly assented to the popular but pernicious doctrine of *gradual* abolition. I seize this opportunity to make a full and unequivocal recantation, and thus publicly to ask pardon of my God, of my country, and of my brethren the poor slaves, for having uttered a sentiment so full of timidity, injustice and absurdity."

2. See, for instance, Victor Schoelcher's *De l'esclavage des Noirs et de la législation coloniale*, Paris, 1833.

3. See Victor Schoelcher's *Des colonies françaises. Abolition immédiate de l'esclavage*, Paris, 1842, and *Des colonies étrangères et Haïti. Résultats de l'émancipation anglaise. Coup d'œil sur l'état de la question de l'affranchissement*, Paris, 1843.

4. See Garrison on the United States Constitution and the Declaration of Independence ("Inaugural Editorial," *The Liberator*, 1 January 1831).

5. Garrison wrote that he had toured the country "for the purpose of exciting the minds of the people by a series of discourses on the subject of slavery" ("Inaugural Editorial," *The Liberator*, 1 January 1831).

6. William Pitt, the prime minister, had felt it impossible to intervene in the debate because of the divided opinions of his ministers.

7. Thomas Fowell Buxton, James Stephen Canning, and Zachary Macaulay, for instance.

8. New historiography has produced fresh readings and interpretations of the unrest-abolitionism interaction that are often at variance with traditional ones. For instance, Lawrence C. Jenkins, in his as yet unpublished paper, "Slave Resistance and the Abolition of French Colonial Slavery 1830–1848" (delivered at the Annual Conference of the French Colonial Historical Association, Charleston, May 2000) argues that the slaves played a very minor part in their emancipation (except, of course, in Haiti) while older interpretations contended that abolitionism had been largely fueled by slave unrest.

9. Letter from Governor General Tacón to the queen, 31 August 1837, qtd. in Philip, 57.

10. See Carlos Manuel Céspedes (1868): "Cuba libre es incompatible con Cuba esclavista y la abolición de las instituciones españolas debe comprender y comprende por necesidad y por razón de más alta justicia la de esclavitud como la más inicua de todas" [Free Cuba is incompatible with slavery and the abolition of the Spanish institutions must include, and includes from necessity and from the highest justice, that of slavery as the most iniquitous of them].

11. See Asamblea de Representantes del Centro (1869): "La institución de la esclavitud traída a Cuba por la dominación española, debe extinguirse con ella" [The

institution of slavery was brought to Cuba by the Spanish domination; it must be extinguished with it].

12. The Moret law will be discussed further in chapter 5, for it may be considered the first concrete step toward actual abolition.

13. The chronology of the two French abolitions will be detailed in chapter 5.

14. See Concepcíon Navarro Azcue: "La crítica fue tan agrio como en otras ocasiones" [The criticism was as bitter as on other occasions] (22).

15. Again, see Azcue, 22.

16. For the most famous of these, see John Wesley's *Thoughts on Slavery* (1774) and James Ramsay's *Essay on the Treatment and Conversion of African Slaves* (1784); for the later period, see Stephen's *Slavery ... delineated* (1824 and 1830) and Wilberforce's *Appeal* (1823). An idea of the sheer number of abolitionist publications may be indicated by the following names: Granville Sharp, Anthony Benzet, Joseph Ady, John Newton, Thomas Clarkson, Henry Brougham, Zachary Macaulay, or James Cropper.

17. See, for instance, Frances Anne Kemble; also consult Basil Hall's *Travels in North America* as well as a narrative of the same trip written by Hall's wife, *The Aristocratic Journey.*

18. De Gaspain, for instance, thought that abolition could be obtained through some kind of system close to the Spanish *coartación* and computed that if the slaves had two days a week to purchase the remaining five, they could become free in thirteen and a half years.

19. See Antoine Gisler.

20. Novels like *Ourika* by Mme de Duras, for example, cited in Régis Antoine, 231.

21. See Victor Schoelcher, *De l'esclavage des Noirs, et de la législation coloniale* (1833) and *Abolition de l'esclavage. Examen critique du préjugé contre la couleur des Africains* (1840).

22. Schoelcher, *Des Colonies françaises, abolition immédiate de l'esclavage* (1842) and *Des Colonies étrangères et Haïti: Résultats de l'émancipation anglaise. Coup d'œil sur l'état de la question d'affranchissement* (1843).

23. Schoelcher, *Des Colonies françaises,* dedication, xxxi–xxxiii.

24. Consider Boswell, who thought that slavery was an eternal and divinely sanctioned statute that had always been implemented by man. From his perspective, its abolition would not only deprive a large class of English subjects of their property but would be cruel to the African himself, as it saved him from massacre or from a worse servitude in his own country (cited in Devèze, 372).

25. "Los esclavos viven y vivirán por todos los siglos bajo otra forma y por otros nombres. La ley del trabajo impuesta por Dios al formar al hombre es la ley inquebrantable de la servidumbre" [The slaves live and will always live under other names and other systems. The law of work imposed by God to model man is the unshakable law of servitude], Manuel Castellanos y Mojarrieta, *Projecto de manumission de esclavos en las Antillas españolas,* Madrid, 1871.

26. "Si alguna institución merece venerable respeto es la propriedad; no es possible atacarla sin que se conmuevan los cimientos de la sociedad" [If one institution deserves venerable respect, it is property; it is impossible to attack it without removing the cements of society], Juan Hernández Arvizu, *Proyecto de ley sobre la abolición de la esclavitud en la isla de Puerto Rico*, Madrid, 1869.

27. A detailed description of the West Indian lobby can be found in Kathleen Mary Butler, 7–24.

28. Butler, 8.

29. See Abbé Rigord, *Observations sur quelques opinions relatives à l'esclavage* (1845): "L'esclavage, tel qu'il existe, est entouré des égards, des soins que réclame le malheur. Les esclaves sont vêtus, logés, nourris, soignés dans leurs maladies, ils n'ont pas le souci du lendemain, ils voient sans effroi les rides de la vieillesse sillonner leur front" [Slavery as it exists is surrounded with the consideration and care required by misfortune. Slaves are clad, housed, fed, cared for in disease, and are not worried by tomorrow; they see without dread the wrinkles of old age on their forehead] (qtd. in Gisler, 203).

30. See *Histoire des Désastres de Saint-Domingue*: "Hommes sensibles, amis sincères de l'humanité dont l'âme compatissante a été souvent émue par des récits vrais ou exagérés" [Sensitive men, sincere friends of humanity, whose compassionate souls have often been moved by stories, true or exaggerated] (vol. 1, 72).

31. There were some pro-planter organs in the mother country, the *Glasgow Courrier*, for example, but they remained relatively rare.

32. See, for instance, Pamphile de Lacroix.

33. *Histoire des Désastres de Saint-Domingue* (Paris, 1795).

34. Abbé Grégoire counted 330 proslavery publications concerning St. Domingue published in France before 1800, in contrast with the seven hundred abolitionist works written, as he says, in the name of justice (See *De la noblesse de la peau*, 40).

35. See, for instance, Julien-Joseph Virey, *Histoire naturelle*.

36. First published in Fort Royal, Martinique, in 1846 and many times reprinted, Marbot's *Les Bambous* is such a classic that an edition may be found, for instance, at Middleton Library, Louisiana State University, Baton Rouge. It is also regularly reprinted in the French West Indies.

37. Several examples come to mind here: Prevost de Traversay, *Les amours de Zémédare et Carina* (1806); Maynard de Qheilhe, *Outremer* (1835); and (maybe the best because it maintains a clear poetic vision) Poirier de Saint-Aurèle, *La parole de Jéhova*, a poem written to the glory of slavery, in which the institution is shown as an absolute necessity to remain faithful to God's word. A novel by Frédéric Soulié also deserves mention: *Le bananier*, first published in the magazine *Le Voleur* in 1841, then in *La semaine littéraire* in 1843, and in book form in 1858. It is full of negrophobic remarks and is a real plea for slavery. In the end, the hero realizes that he has been the henchman of an English abolitionist and, repentant, is finally cured of his early abolitionist enthusiasm.

38. Consider, for instance, *The Abolition Intelligencer* in Kentucky. For more details, see Nathalie Dessens, "Le Sud des Etats-Unis de 1830 à 1860."

39. James Fenimore Cooper, for instance, displayed pro-slavery feelings as late as 1838 in *The American Democrat*.

40. Consider, for example, one of the classics of abolitionist argument in William Lloyd Garrison's already-cited editorial to the first issue of *The Liberator*, 1 January 1831.

41. Consider Garrison's famous tirade "Let southern oppressors tremble—let their secret abettors tremble—let their northern apologists tremble—let all the enemies of the persecuted blacks tremble ("Inaugural Editorial," *The Liberator*, 1 January 1831).

42. Frederick Douglass's *Narrative of the Life of Frederick Douglass*, published in 1845, was reprinted seven times between 1845 and 1849.

43. As the story goes, in 1862, when Abraham Lincoln was introduced to Stowe, he called her "the little lady that made this big war," a remark which nicely encapsulates the uproar her participation in the slavery debate aroused (qtd. by Jay Hubbell, 386).

44. See, for instance, Thomas Roderick Dew (1832), "Abolition of Negro Slavery," in Drew Gilpin Faust, ed., *The Ideology of Slavery*, 66.

45. For the most detailed example of this type of argument, see Thornton Stringfellow, "A Brief Examination of Scripture Testimony on the Institution of Slavery," in Faust, ed., 136–67.

46. Many writings relate this theory in full, but the most detailed account can be found in John C. Calhoun's anonymously published *South Carolina Exposition and Protest* (1828).

47. See, for instance, William Harper's "Memoir on Slavery" in Faust, ed., 83–85.

48. Again, see Harper in Faust, ed., 94 or Calhoun's "Positive Good" speech of 1837.

49. For instance, Dew (1832), in Faust, ed., 53.

50. Consider James Hammond's "Mud-Sill Speech" in McKitrick ed., 121–25; also see Hammond's comments in Faust, ed., 197.

51. In Calhoun's letter to Parkenham (1844); see also James Hammond's letters to Thomas Clarkson, published in 1845 in the *Columbia South Carolinian* (in Faust, ed., 179).

52. See, for example, Samuel George Morton, *Crania Americana* (1839) and *Crania Aegyptiana* (1844); also consider "Two Lectures on the Natural History of Caucasian and Negro Races" (Mobile, 1844) by one of the most famous racial theorists, Josiah Clark Nott, in Faust, ed., 206–38.

53. See Calhoun's "Positive Good" speech of 1837.

54. See *The Pro-Slavery Argument* (1852) and *Cotton is King* (1860), compilations of articles written by the most prominent figures in defense of slavery.

55. In *Sociology for the South* (1854), George Fitzhugh advocates the expansion of slavery to free blacks (see Harvey Wish ed., 92.); he renews this argument in

Cannibals All. The same argument can be found in Henry Hughes's 1854 "Treatise on Sociology" in Faust, ed., 239–71.

56. This type of literature will be examined in detail in the last chapter of this book.

57. See *The Hireling and the Slave.*

Chapter 5. Abolition and Its Aftermath

1. This argument was defended by Georges Jacques Danton, among others.

2. The decree announced by the Junta Central Gubernativa de la Republica Dominicana on 17 July 1844, reads: "ignominioso, contrario a la libertad natural y a los principios de la religion, prohibe terminantemente el tráfico des esclavos, calificando este proceso de vergonzoso a inhumano y contenando a la pena de muerte a quien ejerciera dicha actividad" [ignominious, contrary to natural freedom and to the principles of religion, forbids forever the slave trade, qualifying this process as shameful and inhuman and exposing to the death penalty anyone engaging in this activity].

3. See Peter Camejo, 25.

4. According to the War Department records, at the end of the war, there were 166 black regiments, with 178,975 enlisted men (although this figure seems too low), which represented about one-eighth of the Union forces. A total of 29,511 blacks were enlisted in the Navy, representing roughly one-fourth of the Navy forces. Altogether, fourteen Congressional Medals of Honor were granted to these regiments. Added to those fighting forces, some 300,000 to 400,000 blacks participated in the war effort without belonging to the army (Camejo, 27).

5. Butler, 114.

6. Butler, 119.

7. In the report presenting the decree of 13 February 1852, Theodore Ducos, Minister of the Colonies, justified the immigration policy by the necessity to restore competition and to rehabilitate agriculture in the eyes of the working populations of the colonies. He used the words: "stimulant pour les travailleurs émancipés" [stimulating for the emancipated workers]. He further defined his aim as follows: "établir une certaine concurrence de la main-d'œuvre agricole, et contribuer à la réhabilitation, aux yeux des populations affranchies, du travail de la terre" [to establish a certain competition among the agricultural labor force and contribute to rehabilitating, in the eyes of the freed population, the cultivation of the land].

8. Between 1835 and 1882, 36,000 Portuguese reached the West Indian colonies as indentured servants, and between 1830 and 1870, almost two million indentured servants reached the English, French, Dutch, and Spanish colonies of the Caribbean from India.

9. Figures given in Jean-Paul Barbiche, 140.

10. In Antigua, in 1868, twelve of the twenty-four members of the Assembly were elected; in Nevis, five out of ten; in St. Kitts, ten out of twenty.

11. This was the case of Nevis from 1877 on, of St. Kitts, from 1878 on, and of Antigua after 1898. In Dominica, where half the members had first been elected from 1898 on, the crown appointed the whole of the legislative council. In Grenada, in 1875, there was also a council of appointed and elected members, from which elected members disappeared in 1877. In St. Vincent as in Tobago, this change occurred in 1877.

12. Jamaica, Trinidad, and Tobago, became independent in 1962, Barbados in 1966, Grenada in 1974, Dominica in 1978, St. Lucia and St. Vincent in 1979, Antigua in 1981, and St. Kitts and Nevis in 1983.

13. To give but one example, the Louisiana code specified: "Bad work shall not be allowed. Failing to obey reasonable orders, neglect of duty, and leaving home without permission will be deemed disobedience; impudence, swearing, or indecent language to or in the presence of the employer, his family, or agent, or quarrelling and fighting with one another shall be deemed disobedience" (Article 57).

Chapter 6. Mythmaking and Cultural Exception

1. To give but one example, the fable entitled "Le loup et le chien" ["The Wolf and the Dog"], ends on a moral which advises the slaves to accept their fate rather than become maroons (Marbot, 28).

2. These novels have been recently reprinted in Martinique in a series of volumes entitled *Romans Antillais du XIXe siècle*.

3. In the introduction to *Romans Antillais*, Volume II, Auguste Joyau indicates that the picture seems close to the reality of the times: "exposer les mœurs de l'époque avec un réalisme, brutal peut-être, mais assez proche sans doute de la réalité" [to reveal the mores of the time with a realism that may be blunt but is no doubt relatively close to reality] (10).

4. Levilloux, in *Romans Antillais*, 12–279.

5. Bentzon, in *Romans Antillais*, 279–409.

6. Bentzon, in *Romans Antillais*, 382.

7. "Da" is the French West Indian equivalent of "mammy."

8. For instance, Yette's father alludes to the discouragement of his own father after the abolition of slavery and to the total neglect of the plantation that followed (294). A long paragraph on indolence also explains the weakness of her parents' attitude to Yette (293–94). Indolence and laziness are mentioned several times (see 369, for instance).

9. Bentzon, in *Romans Antillais*, 285.

10. Bentzon, in *Romans Antillais*, 279.

11. Bentzon, in *Romans Antillais*, 303.

12. Bentzon, in *Romans Antillais*, 286.

13. Gaillard, 128.

14. See Gaillard on dissolute mores after the introduction of slavery, 99.

15. Gaillard, 126–27.

16. Gaillard, 202–3. See descriptions of slave auctions in Gaillard, 214, and De Jaham, *L'Or des Iles*, 257–58. On maroon slaves and punishments for marooning, see De Jaham, *L'Or des Iles*, 312–13.

17. Among the most famous, see Maryse Condé, Joseph Zobel, Raphaël Confiant, and Patrick Chamoiseau.

18. For excerpts from most of the works cited, see *Literatura del Caribe.*

19. While José Gautier Benítez ends his *A Puerto Rico* by "¡Patria!, jardín de la mar, la perla de las Antillas" [Homeland! Garden of the sea, the pearl of the Antilles] (27–28), Gertrudis Gómez de Avellaneda writes about his island, Cuba, in *Al Partir*: "¡Perla del Mar! ¡Estrella de Occidente! ¡Hermosa Cuba! Tu brillante cielo" [Pearl of the sea! Star of the West! Beautiful Cuba! Your bright sky] (35). Both poems are in *Literatura del Caribe.*

20. *Literatura del Caribe*, 28.

21. The tetralogy is composed of *Garduña* (1890), *La Charca* (1894), *El Negocio* (1922), and *Redentores* (1825).

22. See "Padre del criollismo puertorriqueño," *Literatura del Caribe*, 103.

23. See, for instance, the long poem entitled *Las Antillas*, written by Puerto Rican poet Lluis Lloréns Torres in *Literatura del Caribe*, 138–42.

24. See, for instance, *Pueblo negro* and *Danza negra* by Puerto Rican poet Lluis Palés Matos in *Literatura del Caribe*, 143 and 144. See also Dominican poet Manuel del Cabral, *Negro sin sonrisa* and *Tropico pecapedrero*, in *Literatura del Caribe*, 176 and 177.

25. See chapter 4, note 19.

26. Kenneth Ramchand, for instance, in *An Introduction to the Study of West Indian Literature*, favors the first explanation.

27. See, for instance, Derek Walcott or Merle Hodge.

28. See Alison Donnell and Sarah Lawson Welsh, eds., *The Routledge Reader.*

29. "Whilst all else changed around her / She kept the same old place / Till like some faithful guide-post / Became the kindly face; / For to 'Ole Massa's fam'ly' / Her life was rooted past / In fancy we can see her— / The Nana of the past!" (Mary Adella Wolcott, "Nana," *Routledge Reader*, 42).

30. *Routledge Reader*, 47, 50, and 53, respectively.

31. For a more detailed study of this novel, see Dessens, *Le Sud de 1830 à 1860*, 57–76.

32. Dessens, *Le Sud de 1830 à 1860*, 133–235.

33. See Kennedy, both the 1832 original and the 1851 revised version.

34. For a detailed study of these novels, see Dessens, *Le Sud de 1830 à 1860*, 338–76.

35. The references to this and the three following novels are given in John McCardell, without precise reference to the original edition.

36. For instance, *Katharine Walton.*

37. For a detailed comparative study of the two versions, see Dessens, *Le Sud de 1830 à 1860*, 306–36.

38. To give a single example, all the images that conveyed an impression of ruin and sadness were replaced by lighter notes. For instance, the oak that offered, in the first version, "habitation and defense to an antique colony of owls" (1832 ed., vol. 1, 19), is now inhabited by "Sundry friendly colonies of squirrels and woodpeckers" (LSUP reprint of 1852 ed., 27).

39. The description of Prudence Meriwether, the planter's sister, contains negative elements: "her person is very good, although I think it unnecessarily erect, and a hypercritical observer might say her air was rather formal" (47). These are removed from the revised version, while other characteristics are also cleverly altered to avoid any negative undertone.

40. Grayson, *Letters of Curtius*. Published in the *Charleston Courrier*, 1851. Printed in book form the same year.

41. Grayson, *The Hireling and the Slave*. For more detail, see Dessens, *Le Sud de 1830 à 1860*, 378–397.

42. Lois Hill, ed., *Poems and Songs of the Civil War*, xiii (the reference here is to the Barnes and Noble edition of 1996).

43. As Jay Hubbell, the first chronicler of Southern literature explains, "Lost causes have a way of acquiring a glamour not so easily attached to that of the victor" (461).

44. The most famous of Joel Chandler Harris's stories may be read in *The Favorite Uncle Remus*.

45. Among others, Daniel Usner, "Between Creole and Yankees: the Discursive Representation of Colonial Louisiana in American History," delivered at *Colonial Louisiana: A Tricentennial Symposium*, Biloxi, Mississippi, 3–6 March 1999. Publication forthcoming, Louisiana State University Press, Baton Rouge.

46. For a detailed study of Conroy's treatment of the Southern myth in *The Prince of Tides*, see Nathalie Hind [Nathalie Dessens], "Le Sud dans *The Prince of Tides*."

Conclusion

1. There are numerous current studies on the standardization of the United States showing the assimilation of the South into the national fabric. See, for example, the polemical, challenging, and often appealing analysis of Peter Applebome.

2. See, for instance Reed, postface to the 1986 edition.

3. The absence of Spanish Creole languages in the Caribbean territories of Hispanic origin (the Dominican Republic, for instance) cannot be attributed to any specificity of the Spanish language, because of the existence in Venezuela of a Spanish Creole language, called *Papamiento*. The explanation must lie in the peculiarity of the Hispanic societies of the Caribbean and thus has socio-ethnological underpinnings.

Selected Bibliography

Primary Sources

Alonso y Pacheco, Manuel. *El Jíbaro*. 1849. Rio Piedras: Ediciones Huracán, 2001.

Allfrey, Phyllis Shand. *The Orchid House*. 1953. Reprint, London: André Deutsch, 1966.

Asamblea de Representantes del Centro. *Archivo Histórico Nacional*. Leg. 4882. Ultramar, Gobierno, 1869.

Ayers, Edward L. and Bradley C. Mittendorf eds. *The Oxford Book of the American South. Testimony, Memory, and Fiction*. Oxford and New York: Oxford University Press, 1997.

Barbados Slave Code. Slavery. Edited by Stanley Engerman, Seymour Dresher, and Robert Pasquette. Oxford: Oxford University Press, 2001.

Berendt, John. *Midnight in the Garden of Good and Evil*. New York: Random House, 1994.

Bliss, Eliot. *Luminous Isle*. 1934. Reprint, London: Virago, 1984.

Brown, William Wells. *Clotel*. New York: Arno Press, 1969.

Calhoun, John C. *Works*. 6 vols. New York: Russell & Russell, 1968.

Caruthers, William Alexander. *The Cavaliers of Virginia or the Recluse of Jamestown. An Historical Romance of the Old Dominion*. New York: Harper & Brothers, 1834. Reprint, Ridgewood, N.J.: Gregg Press, 1968.

Céspedes, Carlos Manuel. *Archivo Histórico Nacional*. Leg. 4882. Ultramar, Gobierno, 1868.

Code Noir ou Recueil d'Edits, Déclarations et arrêts concernant les esclaves nègres de l'Amérique. Paris: Chez les Libraires Associez, 1714. Available on the website of the University of Nantes <http://palissy.humana.univ-nantes.fr>.

Code Noir de Louisiane. Available on <www.geocities.com>.

Code of Alabama. Prepared by John J. Ormand, Arthur P. Bagby, and George Goldthwaite. Montgomery, Ala.: Brittain and Dewolf, 1852.

Conroy, Pat. *The Prince of Tides*. Boston: Houghton Mifflin, 1986.

———. *Beach Music*. New York: Doubleday, 1995.

Cooke, John Esten. *Leather Stocking and Silk, or Hunter John Myers and His Time*. New York: Harper and Brothers, 1852.

————. *The Virginia Comedians.* New York: Harper and Brothers, 1854. Reprint, Ridgewood, N.J.: Gregg Press, 1968.

————. *Ellie.* Richmond: J. W. Randolph, 1855.

Cooper, James Fenimore. *The American Democrat; or, Hints on the Social and Civic Relations of the United States of America.* New York: H. and E. Phinney, 1838. Reprint, New York: Vintage, 1956.

Cotton Is King and Pro-Slavery Argument. Augusta: Pritchard, Abbott and Loomis, 1860.

de Jaham, Marie-Reine. *La grande Béké.* Paris: Robert Laffont, 1989.

————. *Le Maître-Savanne.* Paris: Robert Laffont, 1991.

————. *L'Or des îles.* Paris: Robert Laffont, 1996.

————. *Le Sang du volcan.* Paris: Robert Laffont, 1997.

————. *Les Héritiers du Paradis.* Paris: Robert Laffont, 1998.

————. *Bwa Bandé.* Paris: Robert Lafont, 1999.

de Pradel, Jean-Charles. *Le Chevalier de Pradel: Vie d'un colon français en Louisiane au XVIIIe siècle d'après sa correspondance et celle de sa famille.* A. Baillardel and A. Prioult, eds. Paris: Librairie Orientale et Américaine, 1928.

de Saussure, Henry. *Voyage aux Antilles et au Mexique 1854–1856.* Geneva: Editions Olizane, 1993.

de Wimpffen, Alexandre-Stanislas. *Voyage à Saint-Domingue pendant les années 1788, 1789, 1790 par le baron de Wimpffen.* 1797. Reprint, Paris: Karthala, 1993.

Delany, Martin R. *Blake; or, The Huts of America.* Boston: Beacon Press, 1970.

Denuzière, Maurice. *Louisiane.* Paris: Jean-Claude Lattès, 1977.

————. *Fausse-Rivière.* 2 vols. Paris: Jean-Claude Lattès, 1979.

————. *Bagatelle.* 2 vols. Paris: Jean-Claude Lattès, 1981.

Descourtilz, Michel Etienne. *Histoire des désastres de Saint-Domingue, précédée d'un tableau du régime et des progrès de cette colonie, depuis sa fondation, jusqu'à l'époque de la Révolution française.* Paris: Garnery, 1795.

Donnell, Alison, and Sarah Lawson Welsh, eds. *The Routledge Reader in Caribbean Literature.* London: Routledge, 1996.

Douglass, Frederick. *Narrative of the life of Frederick Douglass, an American Slave / Written by Himself.* New York: Laurel, 1997.

Duras, Claire de. *Ourika.* Reprint (1823 original version together with translation by John Fowles), New York: Modern Language Association, 1995.

Du Tertre, Jean-Baptiste. *Histoire générale des Isles de Saint-Christophe, de la Guadeloupe, de la Martinique et autres dans l'Amérique, où l'on verra l'establissement des colonies françaises dans ces Isles.* Paris: Langlois, 1654.

Equiano, Olaudah. *Life of Olaudah Equiano or Gustavus Vassa the African. Written by Himself.* Mineola, N.Y.: Dover, 1999.

Exquemelin, Alexandre-Olivier. *Boucaniers & flibustiers des Antilles, Les colons-marins du XVIIe siècle.* Fort de France: Désormeaux, 1986.

Faust, Drew Gilpin, ed. *The Ideology of Slavery.* Baton Rouge: Louisiana State University Press, 1981.

Fitzhugh, George. *Cannibals All, or Slaves Without Masters.* Richmond: A. Morris, 1857.

———. "Southern Thought." *De Bow's Review* XXIII (1857): 338–50.

Fleury, Charles. *Relation d'un voyage infortuné fait aux Indes occidentales par le capitaine Fleury avec la description de quelques îles qu'on y rencontre recueillie par l'un de ceux de la compagnie qui fit le voyage.* Paris: Seghers, 1990.

Gaillard, Robert. *Marie des Isles, Marie-Galante, Capitaine Le Fort, L'héritier des Isles.* 1947–1961. Reprint, Paris: Omnibus, 1999.

Gandía, Manuel Zeno. *Garduña.* 1896. San Juan: Ediciones del Instituto de Literatura Puertorriqueña, Universidad de Puerto Rico, 1955.

———. *La Charca.* 1898. Río Pedra: Ediciones Huracán, Colección Clásicos, 1999.

Garrison, William Lloyd. *Liberator.* 35 vols. Boston: W.L. Garrison & I. Knapp, 1831–65.

Gasparin, Agénor de. *Esclavage et traite.* Paris: Joubert, 1938.

Goguet, Antoine, and Marie Goguet. *Lettres d'amour créoles: Des événements de Saint-Domingue à la Restauration.* Paris: Karthala, 1996.

Grayson, William J. *Letters of Curtius.* Charleston: A. E. Miller, 1851.

———. *The Hireling and the Slave.* Charleston: McCarter, 1856. Reprint, Miami: Mnemosyne, 1969.

Green, Julien. *Les Pays lointains.* Paris: Seuil, 1987.

———. *Les Etoiles du sud.* Paris: Seuil, 1989.

———. *Dixie.* Paris: Fayard, 1995.

Grégoire, Abbé (Henri). *De la noblesse de la peau.* Paris: Beaudoin Frères, 1826.

Hall, Basil. *Travels in North America 1827–1828.* London: Simkin & Marshall, 1829.

Hall, Mrs. *The Aristocratic Journey. Being the Outspoken Letters of Mrs. Basil Hall Written during a Fourteen Months' Sojourn in America 1827–1828.* New York: G. P. Putnam's Sons, 1931.

Harris, Joel Chandler. *The Favorite Uncle Remus.* New York: Houghton Mifflin, 1948.

Harwell, Richard B. *The Confederate Reader.* New York: Longmans, Green, and Co., 1957.

Hill, Lois, ed. *Poems and Songs of the Civil War.* New York: Barnes and Noble, 1996.

Jekel, Pamela. *Natchez.* New York: Kensington Publishing, 1995.

Kemble, Frances Anne. *Journal of Residence on a Georgian Plantation in 1838–1839.* Athens: University of Georgia Press, 1984.

Kennedy, John Pendleton. *Swallow Barn.* Philadelphia: Carey and Lea, 1832. Extensively revised version, New York: G. P. Putnam, 1851. Reprint of the 1852 version, Baton Rouge: Louisiana State University Press, 1986.

Labat, Jean-Baptiste. *Voyage aux Isles. Chronique aventureuses des Caraïbes 1693–1705.* 1720. Reprint, Paris: Phébus, 1993.

Lacroix, Pamphile. *Mémoire pour servir à l'histoire de la Révolution de Saint-Domingue.* 1819. Reprint, Paris: Karthala, 1995.

Laussat, Pierre-Clément de. *Memoirs of My Life, to my Son during the Years 1803 and after.* Pau: E. Vignancourt, 1831. Reprint, Baton Rouge: Louisiana State University Press, 1978.

Lincoln, Abraham. *Abraham Lincoln: Speeches and Writings, 1859–1865.* Edited by Don E. Fehrenbacher. New York: The Library of America, 1989.

Literatura del Caribe. Antologia Siglos XIX y XX, Puerto Rico, Cuba, Republica Dominicana. Madrid: Editorial Playor, 1984.

Marbot, François. *Les Bambous, Fables de La Fontaine travesties en patois créole par un vieux Commandeur.* Fort-de-France: Librairie de Frédéric Thomas, 1869. Reprint, Paris: Casterman, 1975.

Massé, Etienne-Michel. *L'île de Cuba et la Havane.* Paris: Lebègue et Aubin, 1825.

Maynard de Qheilhe, Louis de. *Outre-Mer.* Paris: Renduel, 1835.

McKitrick, Eric, ed. *Slavery Defended.* Englewood Cliffs: Prentice Hall, 1963.

Mitchell, Margaret. *Gone with the Wind.* London: Macmillan, 1936.

Moreau de Saint-Méry, Médéric. *Description topographique, physique, civile, politique et historique de la partie française de l'isle de Saint-Domingue.* Philadelphia, 1796. Reprint, Paris: Société de l'Histoire des Colonies Françaises, 1958.

———. *Description topographique, physique, civile, politique et historique de la partie espagnole de l'isle de Saint-Domingue.* 2 vols. Philadelphia, 1797. Reprint, Paris: Société de l'Histoire des Colonies Françaises, 1958.

Morton, Samuel George. *Crania Americana.* Philadelphia: J. Dobson, 1839.

Page, Thomas Nelson. *Collected Edition of the Work of Thomas Nelson Page.* New York: Harper and Brothers, 1905.

Pitot, James. *Observations on the Colony of Louisiana from 1796 to 1802.* Baton Rouge: Louisiana State University Press, 1979.

Poirié de Saint-Aurèle, *Veillées françaises.* Paris: Gosselin, 1826.

———. *Le Flibustier.* Paris: Gosselin, 1827.

———. *Cyprès et Palmistes.* Paris: Gosselin, 1833.

Prévost de Traversay, Jean-Baptiste de Sansac de. *Les Amours de Zémédare et Carina (description de la Martinique en 1766).* Paris: Gicquet et Richard, 1806.

Price, Eugenia. *Stranger in Savannah.* New York: Doubleday, 1989.

The Pro-Slavery Argument as Maintained by the Most Distinguished Writers of the Southern States. Charleston: Walker, Richards and Co., 1852.

Ramsay, James. *An Essay on the Treatment and Conversion of African Slaves in the British Sugar Colonies.* London: J. Phillips, 1784.

Rhys, Jean. *Wide Sargasso Sea.* London: Penguin, 1968.

Ripley, Alexandra. *Charleston.* New York: Warner, 1981.

———. *On Leaving Charleston.* New York: Warner, 1984.

———. *New Orleans Legacy.* New York: Warner, 1988.

———. *Scarlett.* New York: Warner, 1991.

Rivers Siddons, Anne. *Homeplace.* New York: Harper and Row, 1987.

———. *Peachtree Road.* New York: Harper and Row, 1988.

Robin, Claude-Cézar. *Voyages dans l'intérieur de la Louisiane, de la Floride occiden-*

Selected Bibliography

tale et dans les îles de la Martinique et de Saint-Domingue pendant les années 1802, 1803, 1804, 1805, et 1806. Paris: F. Buisson, 1807.

Romans Antillais du XIXe siècle. 3 vols. Morne Rouge, Martinique: Editions des Horizons Caraïbes, 1977.

Schoelcher, Victor. *De l'esclavage des Noirs et de la législation coloniale.* 1833. Reprint, Paris: Hachette, 1972.

———. *Abolition de l'esclavage. Examen critique du préjugé contre la couleur des Africains.* Paris: Pagnerre, 1840.

———. *Des colonies françaises, abolition immédiate de l'esclavage.* 1842. Reprint, Paris: Editions du C.H.T.S., 1998.

———. *Des colonies étrangères et Haïti. Résultats de l'émancipation anglaise. Coup d'œil sur l'état de la question de l'affranchissement.* Paris, 1843.

Scott, Michael. *Tom Cringle's Log.* London: Everyman's Library, 1938.

Simms, William Gilmore. *Katharine Walton.* Philadelphia: A. Hart, 1851.

———. *The Sword and the Distaff.* Charleston: Walker, Richard and Co., 1852. Reprinted under the title *Woodcraft, or Hawks about the Dovecote.* New York: Redfield, 1854. Reprint, Ridgewood, N.J.: Gregg Press, 1968.

———. *The Forayers.* New York: Redfield, 1855.

———. *Eustaw.* New York: Redfield, 1856.

———. *The Cassique of Kiawah.* New York: Redfield, 1859.

Soulié, Frédéric. *Le bananier.* Paris: Michel Lévy et Frères, 1858.

South Carolina Slave Code of 1712. An Act for the Better Order and Government of Negroes and Slaves. Available on the website of the Southwest Missouri State University <http://history.smsu.edu>.

Stephen, James. *The Slavery of the British West India Colonies Delineated, as It Exists Both in Law and Practice, and Compared with the Slavery of Other Countries, Ancient and Modern.* 2 vols. London: J. Butterworth and Son, 1824 and 1830.

Stowe, Harriet Beecher. *Dred: a Tale of the Great Dismal Swamp.* 1856. Edited with introduction and notes by Robert S. Levine. New York: Penguin, 2000.

———. *Uncle Tom's Cabin, or Life Among the Lowly.* 1852. Reprint, New York: Penguin, 1981.

Tauriac, Michel. *La Catastrophe.* Paris: La Table Ronde, 1982.

———. *La fleur de la passion.* Paris: La Table Ronde, 1983.

———. *Sangs mêlés.* Paris: La Table Ronde, 1984.

———. *La fille de couleur.* Paris: Plon, 1998.

Thoreau, Henry David. *Walden and Resistance to Civil Government: Authoritative Texts.* 2nd ed. Edited by William Rossi. New York: W. W. Norton, 1992.

Tucker, George. *The Valley of Shenandoah.* New York: Harper and Brothers, 1824.

Tucker, Nathaniel Beverley. *The Partisan Leader.* Washington, D.C.: Duff Green, 1836. Reprint, Upper Saddle River, N.J.: Gregg Press, 1968.

Valverde, Sánchez. *Ideal del valor de la Isla Espanola, y utilidades, que de ella puede sacar su monarquia.* Madrid: Imprenta de Don Pedro Marin, 1785.

Villaverde, Cirilo. *Cecilia Valdés o la Loma del Angel*. 1882. Madrid: Cátedra, 1992.

Virey, Julien-Joseph. *Histoire naturelle du genre humain*. 1801. Paris: Crochard, 1824.

Walker, David. *Appeal in Four Articles. Together with a Preamble to Coloured Citizens of the World, but in particular, and very expressly, to those of the United States of America*. 1829. Reprint, New York: Hill and Wang, 1965.

Weld, Theodore. *American Slavery as It Is*. New York: Harper and Brothers, 1839.

Wesley, John. *Thoughts on Slavery*. New York: Wesleyan Anti-Slavery Society, 1835.

Wilberforce, William. *An Appeal to the Religion, Justice, and Humanity of the Inhabitants of the British Empire: In Behalf of the Negro Slaves in the West Indies*. London: J. Hatchard and Son, 1823.

Wish, Harvey, ed. *Ante Bellum*. New York: G. P. Putnam's sons, 1960.

Secondary Sources

Abenon, Lucien. *La Guadeloupe de 1671 à 1759, étude politique, économique et sociale*. Paris: L'Harmattan, 1987.

Abenon, Lucien, Jacques Cauna, et Liliane Chauleau. *La Révolution aux Caraïbes*. Paris: Nathan, 1989.

Adélaïde-Merlande, Jacques. *Delgrès. La Guadeloupe en 1802*. Paris: Karthala, 1986.

———. *La Caraïbe et la Guyane au temps de la Révolution et de l'Empire*. Paris: Karthala, 1992.

———. *Histoire générale des Antilles et des Guyanes des Précolombiens à nos jours*. Paris: L'Harmattan, 1994.

Anstey, Roger. *The Atlantic Slave Trade and British Abolition, 1760–1810*. London: Macmillan, 1975.

Antoine, Régis. *Les écrivains français et les Antilles (des premiers Pères Blancs aux Surréalistes Noirs)*. Paris: Maisonneuve et Larose, 1978.

———. *La littérature franco-antillaise. Haïti, Guadeloupe et Martinique*. Paris: Karthala, 1992.

Applebome, Peter. *Dixie Rising: How the South Is Shaping American Values, Politics, and Culture*. New York: Times Books, 1996.

Augier, F. R., S. C. Gordon, D. G. Hall, and M. Reckord. *The Making of the West Indies*. Trinidad and Jamaica: Longman Caribbean, 1960.

Augier, F. R., and S. C. Gordon, *Sources of West Indian History*. London: Longman, 1967.

Azcue, Concepcíon Navarro. *La abolición de la esclavitud negra en la legislación española 1870–1886*. Madrid: Ediciones Cultura Hispanica, Instituto de Cooperacion Iberoamericana, 1987.

Bandry, Michel. *Le Sud*. Nancy: Presses Universitaires de Nancy, 1992.

Barbiche, Jean-Paul. *Les Antilles Britanniques. De l'époque coloniale aux indépendances*. Paris: L'Harmattan, 1989.

Batista, Celsa Albert. *Mujer y esclavitud en Santo Domingo.* Santo Domingo: Ediciones CEDEE, 1993.

Blassingame, John W. *The Slave Community: Plantation Life in the Antebellum South.* New York: Oxford University Press, 1972.

Berlin, Ira. *Slaves without Masters: The Free Negro in the Antebellum South.* New York: Oxford University Press, 1974.

———. *Many Thousands Gone, The First Two Centuries of Slavery in North America.* Cambridge: Belknap Press of Harvard University Press, 1998.

Brasseaux, Carl A., Keith P. Fontenot, and Claude F. Oubre, eds. *Creoles of Color in the Bayou Country.* Jackson: University Press of Mississippi, 1994.

Brathwaite, Edward. *The Development of Creole Society in Jamaica, 1770–1820.* Oxford: Clarendon Press, 1971.

Brogan, Hugh. *The Longman History of the United States of America.* New York: Longman, 1985.

———. *The Penguin History of the United States of America.* New York: Penguin, 1990.

Buisseret, David. *Histoire de l'architecture dans la Caraïbe.* Paris: Editions caribbéennes, 1984.

Burns, Alan. *History of the British West Indies.* Revised edition, London: Georges Allen and Unwin, 1965.

Butler, Kathleen Mary. *The Economics of Emancipation: Jamaica and Barbados 1823–1843.* Chapel Hill: University of North Carolina Press, 1995.

Camejo, Peter. *Racism, Revolution, Reaction, 1861–1877. The Rise and Fall of Radical Reconstruction.* New York: Pathfinder, 1976.

Carrasco, Pedro, and Guillermo Cespedes. *Historia de America Latina 1: America Indigena y la conquista.* Madrid: Alianza Editorial, 1985.

Carrol, P. N., and D. W. Noble. *The Free and the Unfree: A New History of the United States.* New York: Penguin, 1977.

Cash, Wilbur. *The Mind of the South.* New York: Vintage, 1941.

Cauna, Jacques. *Au temps des isles à sucre: Histoire d'une plantation de Saint-Domingue au XVIIIe siècle.* Paris: Karthala, 1987.

Chauleau, Liliane. *La Vie quotidienne aux Antilles Françaises au temps de Victor Schoelcher, XIXe siècle.* Paris: Hachette, 1979.

———. *Dans les îles du vent: La Martinique (XVIIe–XIXe siècle).* Paris: L'Harmattan, 1993.

Cohen, David W., and Jack P. Greene, eds. *Neither Slave Nor Free: The Freedmen of African Descent in the Slave Societies of the Free World.* Baltimore: Johns Hopkins University Press, 1972.

Collins, Bruce. *White Society in the Antebellum South.* New York: Longman, 1985.

Corsani, Jack. *Littérature des Antilles-Guyane françaises.* Fort de France: Désormeaux, 1978.

Craton, Michael. *Empire, Enslavement, and Freedom.* Kingston: Ian Randle Publishers, 1997.

Craton, Michael, James Walvin, and David Wright. *Slavery: Abolition and Emancipation.* London: Longman, 1976.

Crété, Liliane. *La Vie quotidienne en Louisiane, 1815–1830.* Paris: Hachette, 1978.

———. *La traite des nègres sous l'Ancien Régime.* Paris: Perrin, 1989.

Curtin, Philip. *The Atlantic Slave Trade: A Census.* Madison: University of Wisconsin Press, 1969.

Davis, David Brion. "Looking at Slavery from Broader Perspectives." *American Historical Review* 105, no.2 (April 2000): 452–66.

de Vaissière, Pierre. *La Société et la vie créole sous l'Ancien Régime (1629–1789).* Paris: Perrin, 1909.

Debien, Gabriel. *Etudes Antillaises XVIIIe siècle.* Paris: Association Marc Bloch, 1956.

———. *Les Esclaves aux Antilles françaises, XVIIe–XVIIIe.* Basse-Terre et Fort-de-France: Sociétés d'Histoire de la Guadeloupe et de la Martinique, 1974.

Deive, Carlos Esteban. *La esclavitud del negro en Santo Domingo, 1492–1844.* 2 vols. Santo Domingo: Museo del Hombre Dominicano, 1988.

Dessens, Nathalie. "Le Sud de 1830 à 1860: Littérature et idéologie." Ph.D. diss., Université de Toulouse-Le Mirail, France, 1991.

Devèze, Michel. *Antilles, Guyane, la mer des Caraïbes, de 1492 à 1789.* Paris: SEDES, 1977.

Díaz Soler, Luis M. *História de la esclavitud negra en Puerto Rico.* Puerto Rico: Editorial Universitaria, 1974.

Din, Gilbert. *Spaniards, Planters and Slaves: The Spanish Regulation of Slavery in Louisiana 1763–1803.* College Station: Texas A&M University Press, 1999.

Dormon, James H., ed. *Creoles of Color of the Gulf South.* Knoxville: University of Tennessee Press, 1996.

Dunn, Richard. *Sugar and Slave, The Rise of the Planter Class in the English West Indies 1624–1713.* New York: Norton, 1973.

Du Pratz, Antoine-Simon Le Page. *The History of Louisiana, Or of the Western Parts of Virginia and Carolina.* 1774. Reprint, edited by Joseph G. Treggle, Jr., Baton Rouge: Louisiana State University Press, 1975.

Eaton, Clement. *Freedom of Thought in the Old South.* Durham: Duke University Press, 1940.

———. *A History of the Old South.* New York: Macmillan, 1957.

———. *The Growth of Southern Civilization 1770–1860.* New York: Harper, 1961.

———. *The Mind of the Old South.* Baton Rouge: Louisiana State University Press, 1967.

Eccles, William John. *The French in North America, 1500–1783.* East Lansing: Michigan State University Press, 1998.

Elkins, Stanley M. *Slavery: A Problem in American Institutional and Intellectual Life.* Chicago: University of Chicago Press, 1976.

Engerman, Stanley L. "Slavery at Different Times and Places." *American Historical Review* 105, no. 2 (April 2000): 480–84.

Faust, Drew Gilpin, ed. *The Ideology of Slavery: Proslavery Thought in the Antebellum South, 1830–1860*. Baton Rouge: Louisiana State University Press, 1981.

————. "Slavery in the American Experience." *Before Freedom Came: African-American Life in the Antebellum South*. Edited by Edward D.C. Campbell Jr., 1–20. Charlottesville: University Press of Virginia, 1991.

Fogel, Robert W. *Without Consent or Contract: The Rise and Fall of American Slavery*. New York: Norton, 1989.

Fogel, Robert W., and Stanley L. Engerman. *Time on the Cross: The Economics of American Negro Slavery*. 2 vols. Boston: Little, Brown, 1974.

Foner, Laura. "The Free People of Color in Louisiana and St. Domingue: A Comparative Portrait of Two-Caste Slave Societies." *Journal of Social History* 3 (1970): 419–37.

François, Luc. "L'Esprit de la Renaissance." *Les Cahiers du Patrimoine* 13–14 (Octobre 1993): 121–26.

Franklin, John Hope. *The Free Negro in North Carolina, 1790–1860*. Chapel Hill: University of North Carolina Press, 1943.

————. *From Slavery to Freedom: A History of Negro Americans*. New York: Knopf, 1988.

Freehling, William W. *The Road to Disunion: Secessionists at Bay 1776–1854*. New York: Oxford University Press, 1990.

Gauthier, Arlette. *Les Soeurs de solitude: La condition féminine dans l'esclavage aux Antilles du XVIIe siècle*. Paris: Editions Caribéennes, 1985.

Genovese, Eugene. *The Political Economy of Slavery*. New York: Pantheon Books, 1965.

————. *The World the Slaveholders Made*. New York: Pantheon Books, 1969.

————. *Roll, Jordan, Roll*. New York: Vintage, 1974.

Girod, François. *La vie quotidienne de la société créole: Saint-Domingue au XVIIIe siècle*. Paris: Hachette, 1972.

Gisler, Antoine. *L'esclavage aux Antilles françaises (XVIIe-XIXe siècle): Contribution au problème de l'esclavage*. Friburg: Editions Universitaires, 1965. Reprint, Paris: Karthala, 1981.

Gonzalez, Jose Luis. *Literatura y sociedad en Puerto Rico. De los cronistas de Indias a la generacion del 98*. Mexico: Fondo de Cultura Economica, 1976.

Guicharneau-Tollis, Michèle. *Regards sur Cuba au XIXe siècle. Témoignages européens*. Paris: L'Harmattan, 1996.

Hall, Douglas. *Free Jamaica, 1838–1865: An Economic History*. New Haven: Yale University Press, 1969.

Hall, Gwendolyn Midlo. *Africans in Colonial Louisiana: The Development of Afro-Creole Culture in the Eighteenth Century*. Baton Rouge: Louisiana State University Press, 1995.

Hanger, Kimberly. *Bounded Lives, Bounded Places: Free Black Society in Colonial New Orleans, 1769–1803*. Durham: Duke University Press, 1997.

Harris, J. William. *Society and Culture in the Slave South*. New York: Routledge, 1992.

Hayot, Emile. "Les gens de couleur libres du Fort Royal (1679–1823)." *Revue Française d'Histoire d'Outre-Mer* 56 (1969): 50–65.

Highman, Barry W. *Slave Populations of the British Caribbean, 1807–1834*. Baltimore: Johns Hopkins University Press, 1984.

Hind, Nathalie [Nathalie Dessens]. "*The Hireling and the Slave:* La littérature au service de l'idéologie." *Caliban* XXVI (1989): 21–29.

————"Le Sud dans *The Prince of Tides:* Représentation d'un mythe en crise?" *Eclats de voix : Crises en représentation dans la littérature nord-américaine.* Edited by Christine Raguet-Bouvart, 41–47. La Rochelle: Rumeur des Ages, 1995.

Hirsh, Arnold R., and Joseph Logsdon, eds. *Creole New Orleans: Race and Americanization*. Baton Rouge: Louisiana State University Press, 1992.

Holman, Hugh C. *The Roots of Southern Writing: Essays on the Literature of the American South*. Athens: University of Georgia Press, 1972.

Holmes, George F. "Slavery and Freedom." *Southern Quarterly Review* 1, no. 1 (1856): 62–95.

Hubbell, Jay B. *The South in American Literature, 1607–1900*. Durham: Duke University Press, 1954.

Huyghes-Belrose, Vincent. "La situation générale de l'Europe en 1492." *Les Cahiers du Patrimoine* 13–14 (Octobre 1993): 83–96.

Ingersoll, Thomas N. *Mammon and Manon in Early New Orleans: The First Slave Society in the Deep South, 1718–1819*. Knoxville: University of Tennessee Press, 1999.

James, Louis. *Caribbean Literature in English*. London: Longman, 1999.

Jenkins, William S. *Pro-Slavery Thought in the Old South*. Chapel Hill: University of North Carolina Press, 1935.

Johnson, Robert U. *Race Relations in Virginia and Miscegenation in the South, 1776–1860*. Amherst: University of Massachusetts Press, 1970.

Jordan, Winthrop D. *White over Black: American Attitudes Toward the Negro, 1550–1812*. Chapel Hill: University of North Carolina Press, 1968.

Kaspi, André. *Les Américains*. Paris: Seuil, 1986.

Katz, Friedrich, John Womack, Jean Meyer, et al. *History of Latin America*. London: Cambridge University Press, 1990.

Kein, Sybil, ed. *Creole: The History and Legacy of Louisiana's Free People of Color*. Baton Rouge: Louisiana State University Press, 2000.

Klein, Herbert S. *The Middle Passage: Comparative Studies in the Atlantic Slave Trade*. Princeton: Princeton University Press, 1978.

Knight, Franklin W. *The Caribbean: The Genesis of a Fragmented Nationalism*. 2nd ed. New York: Oxford University Press, 1990.

Kolchin, Peter. *American Slavery*. New York and London: Penguin, 1993.

————. "The Big Picture." *American Historical Review* 105, no. 2 (April 2000): 467–71.

Landers, Jane. *Black Society in Spanish Florida.* Urbana: University of Illinois Press, 1999.

Lane, Mills. *Architecture of the Old South.* New York: Abbeville Press, 1993.

Laurent-Ropa, Denis. *Haïti: Une colonie française, 1625–1802.* Paris: L'Harmattan, 1993.

Lazo, Raimundo. *Historia de la literature cubana.* Mexico: Dirección General de Publicaciones, 1974.

Le Riverend, Julio. *Historia Economica de Cuba.* Havana: Instituto Cubano del Libro, 1974.

Levy, Claude. *Emancipation, Sugar, and Federalism: Barbados and the West Indies, 1833–1876.* Gainesville: University Press of Florida, 1980.

Lewis, Gordon K. *Main Currents in Caribbean Thought: The Historical Evolution of Caribbean Society in its Ideological Aspects, 1492–1900.* Baltimore: Johns Hopkins University Press, 1983.

Lowenthal, David. *West Indian Societies.* London: Oxford University Press, 1972.

McCardell, John. *The Idea of a Southern Nation: Southern Nationalists and Southern Nationalism, 1830–1860.* New York: Norton, 1979.

Mills, Gary B. *Cane River's Creoles of Color.* Baton Rouge: Louisiana State University Press, 1977.

Navarro García, Luis. *Hispanoamérica en el siglo XVIII.* Sevilla: Publicaciones de la Universidad de Madrid, 1975.

Oates, Stephen B. *The Approaching Fury: Voices of the Storm, 1820–1861.* New York: Harper Collins, 1997.

Osterweis, Rollin. *Romanticism and Nationalism in the Old South.* Baton Rouge: Louisiana State University Press, 1967.

Paquette, Robert L., and Stanley L. Engerman, eds. *The Lesser Antilles in the Age of European Expansion.* Gainesville: University Press of Florida, 1996.

Parry, John H. *The Age of Reconnaissance. Discovery, Exploration, and Settlement, 1450–1650.* Berkeley: University of California Press, 1982.

Perez, Louis A. *Essays on Cuban History: Historiography and Research.* Gainesville: University Press of Florida, 1995.

Perez Mallaina, Pablo Emilio. *La colonizacion: La huella de España en America.* Madrid: Araya, 1980.

Peters, William. *The Southern Temper.* Garden City: Doubleday, 1959.

Philip, Jacqueline. *L'esclavage à Cuba au XIXè siècle d'après les documents de l'Archivo Histórico Nacional de Madrid.* Paris: L'Harmattan, 1995.

Phillips, Ulrich B. *Plantation and Frontier.* Cleveland: A. H. Clark, 1910.

————. *American Negro Slavery: A Survey of the Supply, Employment and Control of Negro Labor as Determined by the Plantation Regime.* New York: D. Appleton, 1918.

————. *Life and Labor in the Old South.* Boston: Little, Brown, 1929.

————. *The Slave Economy of the Old South: Selected Essays in Economic and Social History.* Edited by Eugene D. Genovese. Baton Rouge: Louisiana State University Press, 1968.

Pluchon, Pierre. *Toussaint Louverture. De l'esclavage au pouvoir.* Paris: Fayard, 1989.

Pouquet, Jean. *Les Antilles françaises.* Paris: Presses Universitaires de France, 1964.

Ramchand, Kenneth. *An Introduction to the Study of West Indian Literature.* Sunburry-on-Thames: Nelson Caribbean, 1976.

Rawley, James A. *The Transatlantic Slave Trade. A History.* New York: Norton, 1981.

Reed, John Shelton. *The Enduring South.* Chapel Hill: University of North Carolina Press, 1986.

Richardson, Bonham C. *Economy and Environment in the Caribbean: Barbados and the Windwards in the Late 1800s.* Gainesville: University Press of Florida, 1997.

Rubin, Louis D. *The Writer in the South.* Athens: University of Georgia Press, 1972.

Sala-Molins, Louis. *Le code noir ou le calvaire de Canaan.* Paris: Presses Universitaires de France, 1987.

————. *L'Afrique aux Amériques. Le code noir espagnol.* Paris: Presses Universitaires de France, 1992.

Scott, Rebecca J. "Small-Scale Dynamics of Large-Scale Processes." *American Historical Review* 105, no. 2 (April 2000): 472–79.

Sherlock, P. M. *West Indian Story.* Trinidad and Jamaica: Longman Caribbean, 1960.

Simkins, Francis Butler. *The Everlasting South.* Baton Rouge: Louisiana State University Press, 1963.

Slesin, S., S. Cliff, J. Berthelot, M. Gaumé, and D. Rozensztroch. *Caribbean Style.* New York: Clarckson N. Potter, 1985.

Stampp, Kenneth M. *The Peculiar Institution: Slavery in the Ante-Bellum South.* New York: Knopf, 1956.

Sullivan-González, Douglass, and Charles Reagan Wilson, eds. *The South and the Caribbean.* Jackson: University of Mississippi Press, 2001.

Tannenbaum, Frank. *Slave and Citizen: The Negro in the Americas.* New York: Knopf, 1947.

Taylor, William. *Cavalier and Yankee: The Old South and American Character.* New York: Doubleday, 1961.

Usner, Daniel. *Indians, Settlers, and Slaves in a Frontier Exchange Economy: The Lower Mississippi Valley before 1803.* Chapel Hill: University of North Carolina Press, 1992.

————. "Between Creole and Yankees: The Discursive Representation of Colonial Louisiana in American History." Paper presented at *Colonial Louisiana: A Tricentennial Symposium,* Biloxi, Mississippi, March 3–6, 1999. Baton Rouge: Louisiana State University Press, in press.

Viatte, Auguste. *Histoire littéraire de l'Amérique française.* Paris: Presses Universitaires de France, 1954.

Vlach, John Michael. "Plantation Landscapes in the Antebellum South." *Before Freedom Came: African-American Life in the Antebellum South.* Edited by D. C. Campbell Jr. Charlottesville: University Press of Virginia, 1991.

Ward, John R. *British West Indian Slavery, 1750–1834: The Process of Amelioration.* Oxford: Clarendon Press, 1988.

Weber, David. *The Spanish Frontier in North America.* New Haven: Yale University Press, 1992.

Williams, Eric. *The Negro in the Caribbean.* New York: Negro Universities Press, 1942.

———. *Capitalism and Slavery.* Chapel Hill: University of North Carolina Press, 1944.

———. *From Columbus to Castro: The History of the Caribbean, 1492–1969.* London: André Deutsch, 1970.

Wilson, Theodore Brantner. *The Black Codes of the South.* Alabama: University of Alabama Press, 1965.

Yacou, Alain, ed. *Créoles de la Caraïbe.* Paris: Karthala, 1996.

Zinn, Howard. *The Southern Mystique.* New York: Knopf, 1961.

Index

Nathalie Dessens is a professor of American history and civilization at the University of Toulouse-Le Mirail, France. For the past fifteen years, she has conducted research on Southern ideology, on the Southern myth in literature, and on the history of the slave societies in the Americas. She has written several articles on each of these topics, which have been published in France.